Women Versed in Myth

Women Versed in Myth

Essays on Modern Poets

Edited by
COLLEEN S. HARRIS *and*
VALERIE ESTELLE FRANKEL

McFarland & Company, Inc., Publishers
Jefferson, North Carolina

ISBN (print) 978-0-7864-7192-8
ISBN (ebook) 978-1-4766-2608-6

LIBRARY OF CONGRESS CATALOGUING DATA ARE AVAILABLE

British Library cataloguing data are available

© 2016 Colleen S. Harris and Valerie Estelle Frankel.
All rights reserved

No part of this book may be reproduced or transmitted in any form or by any means, electronic or mechanical, including photocopying or recording, or by any information storage and retrieval system, without permission in writing from the publisher.

Front cover image of Greek goddess Persephone
© 2016 sSplajn/iStock

Manufactured in the United States of America

McFarland & Company, Inc., Publishers
Box 611, Jefferson, North Carolina 28640
www.mcfarlandpub.com

For my mother Joanne K. Reilly Harris,
who taught me early the power of reading
stories and telling my own.
—Colleen S. Harris

To my Grandma Phyllis Kanter,
a teacher who loved world myth
and would've adored this book.
—Valerie Estelle Frankel

Table of Contents

Introduction	1

Part I: Classical Myth Subverted

Sap Rising: Bodies Figured as Trees in H.D., Atwood and Glück	
Wendy Whelan-Stewart	5
Mythotropism: A Psychology of Writing (to) Myth	
Coco Owen	14
Burying Helen: H.D.'s Anthropoetics	
Lisa D. Simon	25
The Needed Underworld: Modern Reactions to Symbolic Death	
Rachel McCoppin	34
From Persephone's Lips: Three Retellings by Louise Glück	
Valerie Estelle Frankel	43
Reimagining Myth and the Maternal with Ruth Fainlight, Margaret Atwood and Katie Donovan	
Charlotte Beyer	50
"Out of the Ash I Rise": Sylvia Plath and the Rebirth of the Woman Poet	
Kate Williams	59

Part II: Outside the Greek Tradition— From the Near East to the Aztecs

Coatlicue and Chicana Grrl Power	
Sarah R. Wakefield	67

Table of Contents

Conduits and Conjurers: Heroic Characters, Sacred Nature and Social Order in Kelly Norman Ellis, Nikky Finney and Patricia Smith
JANINE HARRISON   73

When Pele Blows: Trask's Repositioning of the Hawaiian Creation Epic
JAMES A. WREN   83

Mythic Reenactment from Sandra Alcosser and Pattiann Rogers
TAMI HAALAND   91

Utilizing and Disrupting Legends in Indian Poetry
PRAMILA VENKATESWARAN   97

The Mything Link: The Feminine Voice in the Shifting Australian National Myth
PHIL FITZSIMMONS   106

Sister of Life, Sister of Death: Fluid Roles in Catherynne M. Valente's *The Descent of Inanna*
VALERIE ESTELLE FRANKEL   114

Part III: Within the Classroom

Female Icons in Popular Culture: A Semiotic Approach to Teaching
ELIZABETH JOHNSTON   121

La Llorona and La Malinche in Re-Vision: Chicana Poets Countering Traditions and Claiming Voice
LEIGH C. JOHNSON   140

Ancient Voices: Bringing the Greeks to Life for Students K–12
KATE HOVEY   148

Taking Pomegranates from Strangers: Contemporary Female Poets on Persephone
SARAH R. WAKEFIELD   160

Part IV: Ancestry, the Personal and Self-Writing Women

Family Lore, Suffragist Ancestors and the Scrapbook of a 19th Century Poetess; or, How to Find a Topic for the Dissertation
LAURA MADELINE WISEMAN   169

Creating Light: Myth-making of Lucille Clifton GLENIS REDMOND	179
Penelope at the Loom: Mythology and the Modern Workplace in the Poetry of 21st Century Women KRISTIN BERKEY-ABBOTT	187
In My Own Image: Crafting Poetry About the Sacred Feminine PAULA J. VAUGHAN	194
Telling a Truth versus Telling the Truth: On Writing from Personal History JENNY SADRE-ORAFAI	203
They're Not Mermaids, Really: Shame and Re-visioning the Mermaid Mythos JENNIFER JEAN	209
Calling the Goddess JANINE CANAN	218
About the Contributors	229
Index	233

Introduction

Mythology is a realm of violent satyrs where powerful men seize nymphs and mortal women and savagely carry them off. Across the world in myths of India, Australia, and the Aztec people, things are often little better. The epic writers, almost uniformly male, help to account for this. Even through modern times, the epic poem is often considered a strictly male form.

Despite this, many modern women have tried their hand at rethinking the brawling heroes and fainting damsels of mythology. Louise Glück and H.D., particularly, addressed the victims of misogynist myth such as Helen, Persephone, Penelope, and Eurydice, exploring their journeys and speaking with their silenced voices. Likewise, Muriel Rukeyser, Ruth Fainlight, Alice Jones, Margaret Atwood, Rita Dove, Denise Levertov, Pamela White Hadas, and Katie Donovan all explore classical myth and attempt to determine what the stories can offer the modern woman. All practice *re-inscription,* retelling the myths with new perspectives or nuances to show Persephone voluntarily choosing a life in hell, or Helen embarking on her own epic journey in Egypt, returning agency to these captured brides.

In this volume critics and professors deeply analyze these poems, celebrating the subversion and creativity each poet found as she reinterpreted the mythology. In "Part I: Classical Myth Subverted," Wendy Whelan-Stewart introduces the collection with mythic women transformed, Daphne-like, into trees, reflecting on their bodies in myth. H.D.'s *Helen in Egypt,* Margaret Atwood's *You Are Happy,* and Louise Glück's *Meadowlands* all present this image, disrupting the heroines' original narratives. What precisely do women get from myth? Poet Coco Owen explores this, through archetypal study as well as the careers of Glück, H.D., and Muriel Rukeyser. Charlotte Beyer considers reimaginings through the European tradition, as Ruth Fainlight recreates the sibyl as a writer and Katie Donovan tackles gender politics for the Irish Queen Medb and violated goddess Macha. Beyer continues through Margaret Atwood's poem "A Red Shirt," a re-envisioning of "The Red Shoes," throughout looking at images of the maternal and their struggle with power.

2   Introduction

Valerie Estelle Frankel's essay "From Persephone's Lips" contrasts the character across three Louise Glück poems, demonstrating her depths and twist on the classic narrative. The author of *The Lessons of Nature in Mythology*, Rachel McCoppin, touchingly reveals the value of death and the underworld as a catalyst for growth across this sort of reinterpreted mythology, bringing in Rita Dove, Alice Jones, Denise Levertov, Pamela White Hadas, and H.D. to illustrate her point. Lisa D. Simon cleverly reveals how H.D.'s Helen, commonly dismissed by scholars as being unrooted in the classics, actually comes from older traditions than Homer, such as the archeology of her day. Kate Williams, meanwhile, movingly explores Sylvia Plath's reinterpretation "Lady Lazarus" and how it reflects her own memorable life.

In "Part II: Outside the Greek Tradition—From the Near East to the Aztecs," we travel across the seas to the New World and other lands. Poet and professor Janine Harrison, examining works of Kelly Norman Ellis, Nikky Finney, and Patricia Smith, explores goddesses of Nigeria and New Orleans alike, stirringly contrasting them with Kwan Yin, Buddhist goddess of mercy. Sarah R. Wakefield, author of *Folklore in British Literature: Naming and Narrating in Women's Fiction, 1750 to 1880*, tackles groundbreaking interpretations of Coatlicue and her sister Aztec goddesses in "Emplumada" by Lorna Dee Cervantes and in Gloria Anzaldúa's *Borderlands/La Frontera*. Poet Haunani-Kay Trask evokes Hawaiian volcano goddess Pele for a new generation, analyzed here by Professor James A. Wren. Across the world, Pramila Venkateswaran, poet laureate of Suffolk County, Long Island (2013–15), and author of many books, describes how Sita, Kannagi, and other classic heroines of India are given voice by a multitude of modern writers. Tami Haaland looks at lyrical reenactment that blends Native American and Christian imagery in the poetry of Sandra Alcosser and Pattiann Rogers. While Phil Fitzsimmons tackles the shifting metaphors of the Australian national myth, Valerie Estelle Frankel looks at Sumerian Inanna, arguably the oldest goddess on record, and specifically analyzes how Catherynne M. Valente's joyous modern epic recreates the character.

In "Part III: Within the Classroom" professors also contributed their experiences with women's poetry and myth in the classroom setting. Leigh C. Johnson writes on teaching La Llorona and La Malinche, with a far different reception as she transfers from West to East Coast. Kate Hovey, metalsmith and author of three award-winning books of poetry for young readers, explores Greek mask-making and performance in the children's classroom. In a darker turn, Persephone's story can be used as a gateway to discuss sexual abuse in college and the nebulous issue of consent, as Sarah R. Wakefield discovered in her university career. Aiding fellow professors everywhere, Pushcart Award nominee Elizabeth Johnston lays out an entire course on women's iconography, bringing in characters from myth like Eve to modern

Pocahontas and Marilyn Monroe to show off how legendary and real women become archetypes.

Finally, in "Part IV: Ancestry, the Personal and Self-Writing Women" many poets wrote for this collection about exploring personal myth in their own lives. These are working writers, as well as creative writing professors with MFAs. All these essays are passionate and lyrical, offering generous snippets of their own gorgeous poetry. Laura Madeline Wiseman describes her search into her own family legends, separating fact from truth and finding inspiration. Meanwhile, Poet-in-Residence Glenis Redmond finds inspiration in Lucille Clifton ("you from Dahomey women") for her own stories. Penelope at her loom and other such images inspire Kristin Berkey-Abbott, who examines the noise, pollution, and drudgery modern women struggle with in the workplace through myth's lens. Jennifer Jean explores mermaids and their reimaginings, offering them a modern twist as she tells of her struggle to write a new myth for herself and today's women. Jenny Sadre-Orafai, author of *Paper, Cotton, Leather,* looks at her own history while comparing herself with Anne Sexton and other great writers of the past. Mythologist Paula J. Vaughan writes about the spectrum of goddesses, as the sacred feminine brought to life for a new audience. Janine Canan, author of twenty books, finishes with a celebration of them all, to whom she's devoted her own beautiful poetry throughout a lengthy career.

While H.D., Atwood, and Glück have made strong marks on this field, many more mythic poets emerge each day. A growing proportion of these are women. Louise Bogan, May Sarton, Mary Leapor, Eavan Boland, Jorie Graham, and Genevieve Taggard have tackled patriarchal victims Persephone, Eurydice, and Medusa and revised their tales. National Book Award winner and U.S. Poet Laureate Mona Van Duyn wrote her own takes on Greek myth, while British Poet Laureate Carol Ann Duffy authored *The World's Wife*— revealing the powerful women behind mythology's men. As they and those like them fill the entire globe with their lines, today's poets write worldwide, offering legends of Yemaya or Kwan Yin, not only Mary or Helen. Ingrid de Kok, Michelle McGrane, and Phillippa Yaa de Villiers, all of South Africa, re-envision the Greek muses for a modern era, transforming them from dainty women meant to inspire only men, while Lebogang Mashile and Sindiwe Magona from the same country examine the staples of gender myth. Shefali Shah Choksi, with myths of India, Jeannine Hall Gailey, with hers of Japan, or Alicia Ostriker, author of *Feminist Revision and the Bible,* are vibrant voices in the field. They're joined by Jamaican-American June Millicent Jordan, Laguna Pueblo writer Paula Gunn Allen, Inuit Denise Duhamel, Indian-British Suniti Namjoshi, Luisah Teish of New Orleans, Navajo Luci Tapahonso, Alta—editor of the *Shameless Hussy Review,* and many many more. All these poets join to create a new mythology for a modern world of women.

PART I:
CLASSICAL MYTH SUBVERTED

Sap Rising
Bodies Figured as Trees in H.D., Atwood and Glück

WENDY WHELAN-STEWART

In H.D.'s *Helen in Egypt* (1961), the eponymous Greek heroine ponders the mystery of her own transformation as she examines a version of herself, seemingly alive in the wooden idol the child Achilles holds. In her vision, young Achilles traces the wood grain of the figurine throbbing with life, "as if sap were rising within her" (292).[1] In Margaret Atwood's *You Are Happy* (1974), Circe, the semi-divine woman who has not yet met Odysseus, confides to the reader her dulling disinterest in men whose ambition has led to their transformations as pig or eagle hybrids. She has, instead, a fresh interest in the worn-down and closed off—those who "would rather be trees" (47). Finally, Louise Glück's Penelope in *Meadowlands* (1996) addresses the ideal listener and husband, but not the real Odysseus, whose wooden emotions similarly mold his wife's heart and body. In "Departure," Odysseus leans over his seated wife to caress Penelope's "body and the wood in exactly the same way" (line 16). What is held in common by these passages are explicit or implicit allusions to Ovidian metamorphosis and the tales of women's bodies turned into trees. The speakers, all women, are not Daphnes, Myrrhas, or Philyras (women who become trees in Ovid's oeuvre), nor are they or their poems situated within an Ovidian context. Surprisingly, these speakers are characters that belong to the world of Homer—a world with an alphabet and literary culture quite distinct from Ovid's own. Yet these lyrical voices of Circe, Helen, and Penelope (respectively) reach beyond the Homeric narrative, attracted by Ovid's repertoire, to muse over the female (or male) body and its relationship to Daphne-like transformations.

Begun after the close of the Second World War and finished just before her death, H.D.'s *Helen in Egypt* represents her most sustained engagement with myth and poetry. The collection is ordered by three sections, which each have six or seven books of approximately seven lyrical poems each. This epic unfolds as post–Iliad Helen comes into contact with a slain Achilles and seeks to unravel the truth of her involvement in the Trojan War. As Helen, no longer in a peopled Greece but alone in an Egyptian temple, probes cultural myth, her memory, and the mysteries of metamorphosis, H.D. restores Helen's reputation to the point of deifying her. Like H.D., Helen is not interested in reading or retelling the traditional epic of bodies continually dilated with vengeance or desecrated in battle. In fact, H.D. quickly replaces that narrative with one of trauma by invoking Troy's toppled gates "in memory of the Body / wounded, stricken," in order to highlight the vulnerability of bodies (7). Other images in this first section, "Pallinode," focus on vulnerable body parts: After readers meet a confused and contemplative Helen, Achilles washes onto the shore by the temple—fresh from battle. Recurring images of his bruised heel and light tread are meant to establish Helen's empathy as she walks "heel and soul" with him (6) and feels the stiffening of his Achilles tendon, famously pierced by Paris' arrow (8). Perhaps the most famous scene of vulnerability is the moment Achilles, siting with Helen at a campfire and struggling to recall his past, sees a dark bird, associates it with the vultures of the momentarily quiet battlefield, and recognizes Helen as the woman responsible for the war. The lines describe Achilles' hand ruthlessly close around Helen's neck, and then the materiality of the moment vaporizes as Helen loses herself in contemplation and eventually wills Achilles away (17). The violence prompts Helen to detach herself from the moment of physical and emotional intensity and to study the act, her feelings, and their significance. This moment of Helen's body under duress alludes to tales of metamorphosis.

    This moment is bracketed by the "night bird," which appears before Helen's strangulation and is afterward in her thoughts (13). The identity of the bird is never fixed: it is said to "hoot" like an owl but to look like a vulture. The bird's lack of a fixed state and its ability to fly beyond danger symbolize Helen herself. Helen intuitively reads the bird as a hieroglyph for the mother, Isis, and according to Geraldine Pinch, ancient Egyptians represented the mother goddess Nekhbet as a vulture. In fact, the words for vulture and mother sounded identical, a concept with which H.D. deftly plays.[2] Isis herself was often thought to take the shape of a carrion bird associated with battlefields—the kite. Isis-as-kite also represented protection, as Isis' great wings, once expanded, could provide shelter or, if beaten, could provide the breath of rebirth. Finally, the good soul after death became half vulture-half human, and it alone could course the skies and land without provocation (121). H.D. elides all of these ideas together, and Helen is also able to temporarily morph into the bird herself and move from associations with Death to Isis (23). It is Helen's fluidity that allows her to figuratively slip from Achilles' grip and command all of these forms at once. Helen is the good soul after death, the mother who is also called Isis and Thetis (Achilles' mother).[3]

Yet one of the most notable forms Helen assumes is the tree.[4] In the second book, "Leuke," she takes on a new name and identity—Helen Dentritis, lover of Paris. Tree imagery proliferates in this section as Helen first recollects girlishly hiding from Paris beneath apple trees and then reunites with him on Leuke, an island that like the temple stands outside of real space and time. In a cabin filled with the aroma of pine, Paris reminds Helen she is called "Dendritis, 'Helena of the Trees'" (141). Seeking to lure Helen from Egypt and her romance with Achilles, Paris likens Helen's growing love for Achilles to a wounding or "waiting for the sap to rise" (141). Paris bids Helen to embody "Helena Dendritis," a tree-woman not violated and punctured, but intact and protected. In fact, Helen begins to understand transformation as a space of mental recovery and an act of stability in fluidity as she seeks a full vision of herself rather than the limited versions Achilles, Paris, and (later) Theseus offer her. Rowena Fowler believes women writers are attracted to the Daphne myth because it "may promote either resistance or healing" as the subject is able "to transcend the boundaries of the human." Moreover, this transcendence is "numbing and even renders an 'estrangement from self that is 'painless and dazzling'" (388). As Helen cobbles together a sense of herself, she is able to momentarily dispense with her material body and the emotional claims of the men around her, becoming a "tree" that throbs to life as she accumulates knowledge of herself.

For the rest of the epic, Helen will appear twice before the reader as a hardened or hardening tree. Leaving Paris, stiffened with cold, she encounters Theseus, who describes her as a statue made from the olive tree, her tunic as stiff as the "carven folds of Pallas" (149). H.D. has made Helen into the palladium, the small form of Athena in the *Iliad* made from the olive tree.[5] At the conclusion of the epic, Helen again becomes "a wooden doll" "carved of red cedar," or an idol of Thetis, the mother-goddess. This carved image is both an idol and a moment of metamorphosis for "the living grain of the tree [pulsates] / as if sap were rising within her" (292). Like the initial vulture symbol, which often also translated as the phoenix and predicts Helen's rebirth as Aphrodite-Isis-Artemis, the tree shows Helen's multiple identities rooted in the same complex being. Through these transformations, Helen begins to understand herself not as mortal adulteress but as an ancient goddess of life, death, and passion, who appears in various manifestations in Egyptian and Greek religions and is intimately bound to Achilles, her consort.

Margaret Atwood's *You Are Happy* contains four sections, though we are concerned with only the first three: the first concerns an unsatisfied woman living with her male partner in the wilderness; the second, "Transformations," contains poems written largely in the voices of humans transformed into animals or animals "othered" by humans; and the third section, "Circe/Mud Poems," retells Odysseus's stay on Aiaia through Circe's point of view.[6] It is worth noting that the dysfunctional couple of the first section anticipates Circe and Odysseus in the third section, and the second section of transformed beings (which include pig-men) also resonates with Circe and Odysseus' story. According to Helane Levine-Keating, one of the overarching themes of the entire collection is a woman's self-victimization in her heterosexual relationship of strict gender-essentialism (153). Multiple female speakers in the various sections reveal their vulnerability, enact a kind of frustrated helplessness, and find comfort in a position of victimhood at the same time that they engage in abusive retaliation. In this narrative, women associate the body-as-tree with emotional and physical security.

For many of the speakers of Atwood's collection, the woman's body is highly vulnerable, and this vulnerability is best expressed in "Transformations," the second section. In "Song of the Hen's Head," a female voice speaks as her head rests on the chopping block and her body flails and runs amuck. The body, troublingly incoherent and unruly according to the hen, performs its life-long frustrations: its "flopping breast" flails as it eludes the "rape" of its "flesh / caves" (lines 14, 18, 21–22). The hen invites her pursuers to take away her lower half, finally relieved to be rid of her troublesome body by this latest, brutal—but clearly painless—transformation (line 26). This is the best that can come from transformation in Atwood's world, as it costs much and affords little. In "Corpse Song," the speaker evokes the Daphne myth only to reveal it as a storybook dream with little grounding in reality. As the corpse speaks to the reader, she warns of an afterlife like a prison in an inferior world and encourages the speaker to enjoy her voice and body now. In asides, though, she begrudges the living their flesh and breath and sarcastically denies any salvation in Ovid's brand of transformation. Bemoaning her body's betrayal, she says, "I did not become a tree / or a constellation" (line 18). Rather than offering the safety and regeneration Fowler associates with the Daphne myth, Atwood provides a hideous alternative: a voice that lives on and seeks a listener as the body decays and is removed from society.

In "Circe / Mud Poems," Circe counteracts the vulnerability of her body with passive attacks on male bodies, which are always attended by power. As Odysseus arrives on her shore, Circe can feel the wash of his dominance soak her island (Levine-Keating 156). Circe associates the ambitious male body with friction and far-reaching, ruthless effects. She describes her island as burnt and the men who encounter it and each other as sparking upon contact (46). She groups Odysseus with other ambitiously transformed bodies: men like Daedalus and Icarus, who aspired to fly or to fly too high, and Odysseus's greedy crew turned into pigs (47). These men's bodies are transformed to augment their aspiration, hunger, and advancement, and their augmentations, in most cases, are predatorial or martial and threatening to others. Circe claims to have been attracted to these bodies in the past, but they have become "common as flies" and so destructive that she has given them up (47). Circe lets on that she does not actively transform these men, but that she allows their natures to mold and consume them.

By the time Odysseus arrives on her shore, she claims to have turned her attention to those "who have escaped from these / mythologies with barely their lives" (47). Men who "would rather be trees" and "think / of themselves as / wrong somehow" are her new safer interests (47). These men are coded as "feminine" in that they are briefly but tellingly equated with Daphne and experience their bodies as "beleaguered towns," whose boundaries and entrances have been as relentlessly assaulted as the female body (Douglas 152). The men's worry that they are "wrong somehow" calls up associations with violated women's bodies and their resulting stigma of pollution.[7] It is unclear whether Circe feels these men are more companionable because they theoretically inhabit the class position of many women and might be more empathetic or are more easily dominated because they are too bruised to assert their authority. She does, however, identify her body, reflected in the destruction and "penetrations" of her island, and her tired entrapment within the narrative of *The Odyssey* with the men who would escape "these / mythologies" (Foster 18).

Though John Foster believes that "Atwood betrays a horror of fixed form" and a love for "re-formation" and metamorphosis in her work, her subjects are denied what she sees as the ease of a Daphne-like escape (17, 6).[8] They achieve none of the healing and numbing benefits H.D.'s Helen finds, nor do they assume a more stable or desirable form. Just as there is no facile, romantic transformation for the corpse of "The Corpse Song" and other female subjects from the world's "wreckage" (a common theme in Atwood, as Foster points out) (18), so too are Circe and the men who "would rather be trees" likely condemned to less satisfying but ever-altering forms.

Louise Glück's engagement with Ovidian metamorphosis and tree imagery has been extensive and essential. In her well-known review of Glück's *The Triumph of Achilles* (1985), Helen Vendler states that Glück's craft is "to give experience the permanent form of myth" (437). Vendler's argument is that there is something of the mundane, human moment isolated, halted, and emblematized in Glück's work that recalls Ovid's process. Vendler's descriptions further evoke the Roman poet as she describes the poems as "sometimes narrative, as in the Greek myths, sometimes archetypal, as in the encounter of Man with Woman" (437). To illustrate her point, she calls up "Mythic Fragment," Glück's retelling of Ovid's Daphne and Apollo as a tale of a daughter's losing a potential paramour and the affections of her father, "the stern god" (438). The bleakness of Glück's world is that she uses transformation to capture and caption "the unchangingness of writhing human experience" (439).

Glück returns in each collection of poetry to this story of unwilling, but necessary contact between man and woman, a meeting accompanied frequently by the image of woman as tree or some other soil-rooted flora. In "Matins," found in *Wild Iris* (1993), a couple is caught in an argument over why spring irritates the clinically depressed. In an act that symbolically disengages her from her male companion and identifies her as preferably solitary, the woman fixes on a birch tree, which thrives in moist winters, as an inviting emblem of solitude. Rather than seeing her skin as bark, the speaker is safely enwombed, her fluids, her heart, and her limbs one with the birch's trunk. She imagines her body resting "within the split trunk," focusing on the space where the tree divides in two (line 10). When she perceives the "sap frothing and rising" from within the tree, she implies that she experiences it, thereby merging her interiority and her "frothing" vitality with the tree's (line 13). The cleft in the tree resonates with her divided interests—one in living with her male partner, and the other in finding greater, but incomplete contentment in solitude. Here again is the same pattern running through H.D. and Atwood's use of the Daphne myth—the desire for relief from assault (here, emotional) and for healing and stability that Rowena Fowler finds in poets' use of the myth. However, Glück depicts this female desire as pathological.

Much of this Daphne imagery carries over into *Meadowlands*, a narrative blending Penelope and Odysseus' dysfunctional marriage with a contemporary couple's unraveling. Penelope herself is associated with the impermeability of trees. In "Penelope's Song," the speaker sends her soul to scout Odysseus' coming by positioning itself at the tip of a tree. As the speaker imagines Odysseus' unmentionable escapades and his predictable domestic demands (he will expect his favorite meal—grilled chicken—waiting for him), she becomes defensive and threateningly appropriates the tree's needles. Upon his approach, she decides to wave the branches in seeming celebration, but then ends her fantasy by focusing on the needles that will inevitably fall and prick his upturned, handsome face. The needles, shaken by the wind or spirit of Penelope, are weaponized and intended to punish the face that has attracted so many goddesses. Penelope's actual body is dismissed from the poem, allowing the tree's body to stand in for it. In "Departure," Penelope speaks as she and Odysseus emotionally manage another of his departures. Penelope observes that Odysseus' hardening heart makes her own body wooden. Odysseus' hands move back and forth from the chair Penelope sits in to her shoulders, and at first, his caresses are light. However, as he continues, she notes that his hands begin to touch her in the same way as they do the wood of the chair, and she connects this act with her husband's emotional distance, the "departure" suggested by the title. By the end of the poem, however, it is Penelope's hardness—a hardness prefigured by the woodenness of her body—that becomes more apparent. With a surge of cruelty, she wishes Odysseus would demonstrate keen pain, not longing, at his departure. In a reversal of the Daphne story, Odysseus' emotional and physical distance initiates Penelope's pathological transformation into a variant of isolated birch tree of "Matins."

The motif of transformation doesn't end with Penelope's poems; rather it becomes more pronounced in the parable poems of the collection. In "Parable of the Trellis," Joanne Feit Diehl reads the tale of the vine's colonizing and eclipsing the trellis as a story of a child's (or Telemachus') use of his mother as a prop to the point of stamping her out. As the poem concludes, the speaker urges the reader to see the beauty and integrity of the trellis, a stand-in for artistic mothers like Penelope, who come into a sense of themselves, finally, later in life (86). From the beginning of the tale, Glück reminds us that all trellises were designed to imitate trees and that the trellis of her poem takes on those qualities of immutability, steadfastness, and patience in the face of appropriation. But as Diehl tells us, this parable is also about the necessary hardening of the mother's heart for the sake of her own preservation, and fittingly, Glück returns to the image of the tree in the final line to describe the mother-artist. Using a brilliant simile, Glück compares the mother, formerly a mere wooden scaffold, to a willow, with its quiet, desolate beauty. The female-body-as-tree is hardened enough to withstand others' uses while maintaining its rich, solitary existence.

In each of these poetry collections, where the body's materiality is fathomed, so is its potential for transformation. Despite the writers' intentions to set their characters in Homeric landscapes and contexts, they provocatively and freely call on Ovid's stories of women like Daphne shifting into trees. Bodies that become problematic in the presence of male company are rendered into trees for the sake of sanity, stability, and integrity. Yet isolation is not without its problems, as society insists that women define themselves as companions to others—mothers, spouses, partners. In response, women writers may view their Daphnes as clinically cold and unadjusted. Regardless, like Daphne, women writers continually turn to and adapt the process of metamorphosis to study the body's changing relationship to intimate male and female encounters as well as to public attitudes.

NOTES

1. By H.D. (Hilda Doolittle), from *Helen in Egypt,* copyright ©1961 by Norman Holmes Pearson. Reprinted by permission of New Directions Publishing Corp.

2. Rachel Blau DuPlessis elegantly details H.D.'s use of word play—her chanting of words linked by their alliteration, assonance, rhyme, and "etymology"—as "agent[s]

of transformation" (349). Her coupling of words enacts a transformative logic that generates developments in her poetic sequences' narratives.

3. For more on H.D.'s syncretism of goddesses and fusion into a prehistoric and pre-patriarchal mother-deity, see Susan Stanford Friedman, "The Professor Was Not Always Right," particularly pages 145–56.

4. Many scholars have seen H.D., the dryad, as Helena of the trees, methodically working through her past lovers, who collate in Paris. Refer to "Hilda in Egypt" by Albert Gelpi.

5. Whoever possesses the palladium can ensure safety for his city.

6. Excerpts from "Song of the Hen's Head," "Corpse Song," and "Circe / Mud Poems" by Margaret Atwood, included by permission of the Author. Originally published in *You Are Happy*, currently available in the following collections: In the United States, *Selected Poems* I, 1965–1975, Published by Houghton Mifflin, ©1976 by Margaret Atwood; In Canada, *Selected Poems*, 1966–1984, published by Oxford University Press, ©Margaret Atwood 1990; In the UK, *Eating Fire*, published by Virago Press, ©Margaret Atwood 1998.

7. For more, see Douglas' discussion of Hindu women's socially proscribed sexual roles and their figurative pollution if they cannot or do no perform those roles (156).

8. Atwood has another story of degenerative transformation retelling the story of the Sybil entitled "The Elysium Lifestyle Mansions" published in *Ovid Metamorphosed*.

WORKS CITED

Atwood, Margaret. "The Elysium Lifestyle Mansions." *Ovid Metamorphosed*. Ed. Philip Terry. London: Vintage, 2001. 206–13. Print.

_____. *You Are Happy*. Oxford: Oxford University Press, 1974. Print.

Diehl, Joanna Feit. *On Louise Glück: Change What You See*. Ann Arbor: University of Michigan Press, 2005. Print.

Douglas, Mary. *Purity and Danger*. New York: Routledge, 1966. Print.

DuPlessis, Rachel Blau. "No Rules of Procedure: The Open Poetics of H.D." *Signets: Reading H.D.* Ed. Susan Stanford Friedman and Rachel Blau DuPlessis. Madison: University of Wisconsin Press, 1990. 336–51. Print.

Foster, John Wilson. "The Poetry of Margaret Atwood." *Canadian Literature*. 74 (1977): 5–20. Print.

Fowler, Rowena. "'This Tart Fable': Daphne and Apollo in Modern Women's Poetry." *Laughing with Medusa: Classical Myth and Feminist Thought*. Eds. Vanda Zajko and Miriam Leonard. Oxford: Oxford University Press, 2008. 381–98. Print.

Friedman, Susan Stanford. *Psyche Reborn: The Emergence of H.D.* Bloomington: Indiana University Press, 1981. Print.

Gelpi, Albert. "H.D.: Hilda in Egypt." *Coming to Light: American Women Poets in the Twentieth Century*. Ed. Diane Wood Middlebrook and Marilyn Yalom. Ann Arbor: University of Michigan, 1985. 74–91. Print.

Glück, Louise. *Meadowlands*. New York: HarperCollins, 1996. Print.

_____. *The Triumph of Achilles*. New York: Ecco, 1985. Print.

_____. *Wild Iris*. New York: Ecco, 1993. Print.

H.D. *Helen in Egypt*. New York: New Directions, 1961.

Levine-Keating, Helane. "Atwood's *You Are Happy*: Power Politics, Gender Roles, and the Transformation of Myth." *Approaches to Teaching Atwood's* The Handmaid's

Tale *and Other Works*. Ed. Sharon R. Wilson, Thomas B. Friedman, and Shannon Hengen. New York: MLA, 1996. 153–60. Print.

Pinch, Geraldine. *Egyptian Mythology: A Guide to the Gods, Goddesses, and Traditions of Ancient Egypt*. Oxford: Oxford University Press, 2002. Print.

Vendler, Helen. "Louise Glück, Stephen Dunn, Brad Leithauser, Rita Dove." *The Music of What Happens: Poems, Poets, Critics*. Cambridge: Harvard University Press, 1988. 437–54. Print.

Mythotropism
A Psychology of Writing (to) Myth

Coco Owen

In 1963, Denise Levertov wrote that she "prayed/to Apollo" to keep "the flame of the poem" alive in her (66). Why, in 1963, would a poet—a woman—petition a Greek god honored nowhere but poetry since the Christian story displaced the classical Greek myths as the West's dominant narrative? What would motivate a woman poet to return to stories from that patriarchal tradition? If these myths arose in an epoch when women were muses not makers—more pawns than power brokers—what, *psychologically*, has inspired women poets to continue using myths as pretext and material in what I call *mythotropism*, or a turn to the trope of myth?

To answer this question, I would like to consider the work of three poets, H.D., Muriel Rukeyser, and Louise Glück, all known for drawing deeply on myth in their work. Each has written of and through myth not only because it signals one's membership in the educated class or can disguise personal material, but for psychological reasons especially resonant for women poets.

The Psychology of Writing to Myth

I want to investigate here the psychological reasons I think are unique to women poets' use of myth: First, since women lacked the automatic "ascribed credibility" accorded to male poets qua male, women have had to fight for what cross-cultural psychologists Sue and Zane call "achieved credibility" (37).[1] Second, the many divinities and female figures of classical mythology provide a challenge to Judeo-Christian beliefs, as well as a wealth of alternate personae (There are goddesses!) and life-scripts (There are priestesses!) unavailable to women in those traditions. Adopting stories from other contexts—like contact with a new culture—has allowed women poets to explore other modes of being through art. Third, the metamorphoses of myth both model and incite critique and/or revision of dominant cultural narratives.[2] Finally, and perhaps the most radical reason for women poets' turn to myth, may be that women poets neither believe nor experience any relevant psychological or linguistic distinction between the material (from *mater*, or mother) of poem and the material of myth.

I will ground this last idea in the work of James Hillman, a depth psychologist in the post–Jungian tradition. Hillman holds that "...in the mythic perspective, words too are persons" (*Re-Visioning Psychology* 34). I will also review some thoughts of poet and critic Barbara Guest on the same topic, using Hillman's archetypal psychology approach to explore the mythic nature of poetry, and vice versa, to explore why this idea may have special appeal for the three women poets I'll consider here.[3] (And from here on I will simply refer to them as poets, without qualification.)

Depth Psychology and Poiesis

Depth psychology is the psychological theory, pioneered by Freud, that arose with Modernism.[4] Depth psychology differs from other branches of academic and research psychology because it posits an unconscious and takes images, language, memories, and dreams as its chief material. Because of its reliance on language, archetype, and image, I find depth psychology—whether following Freud or Jung—to be a relevant heuristic for examining poets' use of myth, just as H.D., Rukeyser, and Glück all imagine poetry as a means of accessing what H.D. called "out of time" experience (*Tribute to Freud* 36), that mystical or underworld realm which came to be seen as the unconscious of depth psychology. In *The Dream and the Underworld*, Hillman observes that "the underworld has gone into the unconscious: even become the unconscious" (65). He maintains that "Depth psychology has been the modern movement within our culture that returns to it a sense of the underworld" (66). Hillman further holds that the "dream has nothing to do with the waking world but is the psyche speaking to itself in its own language" (12).

Following Carl Jung, I would add that it isn't only the dream, but poem and myth that speak psyche's language. Jung was the first modern psychologist to theorize "an intimate relationship between dreams, myths, and art in that all three serve as media through which archetypes become accessible to consciousness" (Guerin et al. 207). Here is depth psychology's explanation for the likeness of poetry and myth—their mutual attraction, if you will. Hillman holds that "the metaphorical discourse of myths" in fact constitutes the psyche's "poetic basis of mind" (*Archetypal Psychology* 3). More than that, Hillman sees the psyche as "an *inscape of personified images*" (*Re-Visioning* 33), so that to write (to) myth is literally to create the psyche through writing and—following Jung's thinking—to engage in *poiesis*, or the making of poetry.

So What Do Women Want with Myth?

Louise Glück has given us an example of the poeticity of these inner "personified images" in a stanza from "A Myth of Devotion" which emblematizes a woman's dilemma vis-à-vis the myths, and perhaps patriarchal cultures in general, when Hades wants to tell Persephone that his love can protect her, but in fact it's only because she's dead that "*nothing can hurt you*" (541) Glück portrays a male speaker who realizes that the woman (i.e., Persephone) becomes invulnerable once she understands that patriarchy makes them *both* powerless. So why have women continued writing in the lingua franca of myth when so many myths (to be blunt) portray a woman's rape or death? To paraphrase Freud—what do women want with myth?[5] If a woman can be a poet—and this has been a very big if until recently—she can expose and rewrite received truths about gender and power dynamics.[6]

Keeping in mind that a poet can exercise metamorphic power through writing, I would like first to consider H.D. and her celebration of myth. Reams have been written about H.D.'s relationship to myth, but I would like to focus here on the "why" of it.[7] One easy answer—and the one most relevant to my psychological discussion here—is that she felt compelled to because of her striking "supranormal" experiences (*Tribute to Freud* 91). In 1933 and again in 1934, H.D. went to consult Freud largely because of these "actual psychic or occult experiences" that no one had been able to explain to her satisfaction (*Tribute to Freud* 39). During her analysis, Freud told H.D. that she had "discovered for yourself what I discovered for the race" (18), drawing an explicit connection between her visionary explorations of imagery and myth through poetry and his method of psychoanalytic inquiry using the productions of the unconscious, such as dreams. But, unlike Freud, when H.D. wrote of visiting mythic realms, she was not talking allegorically, saying in *Sea-Garden* that she as visionary poet had experienced "their inmost rites" (16).

Freud told H.D. he thought she had "an unconscious desire to 'found a new religion'" (*Tribute* 51). H.D. rephrased his observation his way: "Do I wish myself, in the deepest unconscious or subconscious layers of my being, to be the founder of a new religion?" (37). She may not have answered yes, but she believed the mythopoetic realms were a "*real* dream" (91) and she wanted others (including Freud) to see and accept that. In "The Walls Do Not Fall," for example, H.D. averred that the purpose of one's "scribblings" is to "take them with us / beyond death" (*Trilogy* 47). This is the deeper psychology informing H.D.'s mythotropism: a desire to replace stale, received truths with new, self-discovered ones in order to show that even death could be transcended through personal knowledge of metaphysical verities.[8]

Diane di Prima, in published notes for a lecture on H.D., agrees: "What we tend so eagerly to forget is that poiesis, especially visionary poiesis, *is* a religious path, sought and chosen" (di Prima, *Notes* 5). H.D.'s mythotropism was thus motivated by the psychological ambition to write poems that would arise "from the same source as the script or Scripture, the Holy Writ or Word" (*Tribute to Freud* 35). It was important for H.D., as a woman, to claim the same authority of "the *illuminati*" who get their "credentials" (i.e., their "achieved credibility") from their knowledge of the "supranormal" realm, source of the visions she prized (*Tribute to Freud* 91). Perhaps each poet using myth reenacts H.D.'s "unconscious" ambition to found a religion; each ambitious poet attempting the Promethean poetic work, as James Merrill put it, of "choosing the words he [sic] will live by" (Kalstone 82). For a woman, claiming the right to forge and follow one's own principles and values was (and may still be?) revolutionary. Rewriting myth has provided some cover.

(Personal) Myth as (Political) Power

Muriel Rukeyser (1913–1980), a poet more conventionally thought of as an activist rather than a mystic, often used myth in her advocacy of a fuller, more just existence. Many readers of Rukeyser's ever-evolving work have read Rukeyser as valorizing either a sociopolitical view or a lyrical, depending on the decade.[9] Her famous line, "Not Sappho, Sacco," from her first book (*Out of Silence: Selected Poems* 1), has been taken as Rukeyser's rejection of the notion that there could be anything useful in the patriarchal, mythic tradition. However, that line is just one in a lifetime's poetic project, which includes political analysis *and* reliance on dream and myth. Rukeyser herself decried "reductive" descriptions of her work (Daniels 247).

Rukeyser's politically engaged stance did not preclude her efforts to renew myth in a way that would include women's experiences, such as childbirth, as a vital subject for poetry. We could say she wanted female experience to have the "ascribed credibility" that men's concerns enjoyed. Rukeyser's important "Poem as Mask," a gripping poem about her experience in childbirth, has the lines, "No more masks! No more mythologies!" (122). These lines effectively became a feminist mantra[10]; they were not, however, a blanket refusal of myth. Psychologically, Rukeyser asserts the validity of her experience; at the same time, she doesn't completely reject the Orphic myth as a theme, but reworks it. As Lorrie Goldensohn notes, "Her makeover of the

Orpheus legend clearly had two aims: one, to reconnect poetry to its older roots in prophecy and wisdom literature, crippling discourse in favor of image; two, to provide a poetics that would acknowledge the full range of female experience as not incidental to poetry, but essential to it..." (124).

In "Poem as Mask," Rukeyser claims the female body as a site of mythic and political power. She does not reject use of (patriarchal) myths for a woman poet, because the end of the poem does reinvoke the god, though with a difference. She also continued to write about Orpheus throughout her career— as well as goddess figures like Niobe and Changing Woman, along with the poet Sappho.

In her earlier poem titled "Orpheus," Rukeyser critiques the Orpheus myth for its loss of the body and the mother: "Orpheus, / without his origin: the body, mother of self..." (107). Rukeyser claims here a poet's right to correct myth's primal stories. A later line expounds her philosophy of myth: "All myths are within the body..." (107). She uses the female body and myth reciprocally, showing that either one could recompose something whole out of brokenness. By saying that "All myths are within the body" (107), Rukeyser makes what can still read as the radical move of asserting an equivalence between myth as high culture and women's bodily experience: "And every myth netted itself in flesh" (Rukeyser 55).[11]

In her introduction to Rukeyser's selected poems, Katie Daniels says that Rukeyser's "primary issue in life, as well as in art, was always the possibility of transformation: how to move from one state to another..." (xvi) as she advocated for a woman's right to exercise myth's metamorphic capacities in her life and art. This stance is different from H.D.'s mythotropism—where the poet's reliance on myth serves a poetic and personal mission seen as sacred. Although Rukeyser shares H.D.'s interest in the archaic, in a pointed epigram about Plath's death, Rukeyser praises real life achievements over mythic renown: "I'd rather be Muriel/ than be dead and be Ariel" (Rukeyser 154). Still, the psychology of Rukeyser's recourse to myth is grounded in a celebration of women's metamorphic power and potential as well as in a love of justice. As such, Rukeyser can be read as a fitting avatar for the humanistic psychology of the sixties, which focused on this human potential and self-actualization rather than on neurosis and pathology, as the Freudian tradition did.[12]

Louise Glück: One to Whom These Depths Were Offered

I would like now to look at the psychological motivations behind Louise Glück's use of the myth, which is constant throughout her oeuvre. Rather than deploying myth like a prophet, or promoting myth's spiritual and human utility, Glück has worked "to give experience the permanent form of myth" because "the lean shape of myth is the nakedness guaranteeing all stories" (Helen Vendler, "In the Zoo of the New"). Vendler further defines Glück's work as "mythical lyric" or "archetypal poetry," almost as if it were its own genre. We get a vivid feel for this style in "Saturnalia," where Glück writes: "I wake to frost / On marble and a chill..." (53).

As we saw in "A Myth of Devotion," Glück often uses the Persephone "mytheme" to write this "mythic," "archetypal" poetry.[13] In the poem "Pomegranate," Glück has Hades chide Persephone for her anger about her fate, remarking that amid her grief over losing her mother she must recall "that she is one to whom /these depths were not offered" (Glück 82).

At the heart of this psychological triangle is the daughter's violent initiation through a (welcome) separation from the mother. We can imagine a poet or any woman in Persephone's position, living out the problem of how to reconcile the upper and underworlds—the realm of the mother and the realm (not of the Father) but the Lover: the real reward is to get a taste of the Mystery, a rare, initiate's experience of "these depths" (82).

A later poem, "Under Taurus" from *House on Marshland*, ends with the request, "Instruct me in the dark" (Glück 92). This petition announces that the speaker's maturation—the poetic apprenticeship—happens at a remove from everyday life and consciousness. In "Dedication to Hunger," the speaker (referring to her anorexia) conveys how she had "the need to perfect..." standing apart "in that power to expose / the underlying body, like a god" (Glück 126). This poetic vision seconds Hillman's assertion that the imagination is "not merely a human faculty but is an activity of soul to which the human imagination bears witness. It is not we who imagine but we who are imagined" (*Archetypal Psychology* 8).

Glück tells us in an epigraph that Averno was "regarded by the ancient Romans as the entrance to the underworld" (487). That is where she situates her work and takes her reader—to a mythic, "dark," unconscious realm. Glück has returned in particular to the Persephone myth because Glück is on the side of the turn inward, however difficult, to the large implications of one's emotional experience. Glück's turn to myth—the psychological "why" of the work—seems like a reenactment of the "need to perfect" and the quest to "make ... eternal ... like a god" (126) whatever violence to self or mother that this engenders. Glück's approach is therefore more akin to H.D.'s vision of the literal and mythic worlds as parallel dreams than it is to Rukeyser's odes to body *and* myth. However, Glück's work, in turn, is more redolent of and beholden to the Freudian worldview than H.D.'s is—despite H.D.'s analysis with Freud. Glück's work seems intent on fulfilling the Freudian dictum to "make the unconscious conscious"—but to do so in and as *poems*.

Poems as Persons

To elaborate on why these three poets have relied to such an extent on myth for their poems, I'd like to consider some thoughts of Barbara Guest's for illumination. She offers a poet's explanation for the turn to myth and does so in the language of myth; and Guest knows her myths, having written a biography of H.D. called *Herself Defined: The Poet H.D. and Her World*. In an essay in a posthumous collection called *Forces of Imagination*, Guest writes, "Underneath the surface of the poem there is the presence of 'the something else'" (84). In another piece, Guest suggests that "You [the poet] enter the poem like Ulysses embarking on a 'beautiful voyage'" ("The Beautiful Voyage" 80). Note that she is saying that the poet is entering a poem not even written *yet*, meaning, effectively, that the poem somehow exists before the poet writes it. Guest says that "you are not exactly in charge," because "*someone here allows the poem's powers, even as magic entered the sails of Ulysses*" (80). She does not clarify who this "someone" is. She continues, saying: "'the poem wrote itself,' *when the identity of the poem is so fixed the poem is willing to trust itself to the poet*" (81).

This possibility upends my thesis: what if the mythotropic impulse is in our *poems* rather than in our *poets*? What if poems—the poetic—call to themselves their poet? This view in fact also echoes Hillman's archetypal psychology in which the poem itself, like a dream, is about "persons" (*Re-Visioning* 34). The poet is not just randomly choosing mythic motifs to costume instinctual conflicts or gender and power dynamics like drapery. As Marina Tsetaeva said:

> Everything is myth, since there is nothing that is not myth, nothing that is outside of myth, nothing that departs from myth, since myth anticipated and formed everything once and for all [qtd. in Bahun-Radunovic and Rajan 115].

That is an enormous claim, suggesting that myth created reality, not the other way around, as we usually assume. Guest cautions that "*before the poem can 'write itself' ... / the dark identity of the poem must be encountered*" (81). Guest is herself rewriting a myth here: it isn't Cerebrus or Hades the poet encounters, it is Poetry—an entity or "person" of the psyche. Guest shows that poetry is capable of manifesting or iterating itself by arising, as myths do, using the language/medium of a writer like H.D., Rukeyser, or Glück: a poet who is ready to relate her own reality for the highest purposes she can envision.

And what is the "dark identity" of the poem? Guest says it is "the presence of 'the something else'" (84). She adds that "the poem is the unburdening of ghosts of the past who have come to haunt the writer exposed to the labyrinth" (85). That is, a poem manifests to the writer who turns to it, drawn to or *by* inner forces, images, and stories. A psychological orientation to the mythopoetic sends a poet downward, inward, backward, or toward this state in which "every concrete object / has abstract value, is timeless / in the dream parallel" (H.D., *Trilogy* 24). This turning either yields the poem or it is the poem. To poem, psychologically, is to turn from ordinary time and speech to enter the poem-state. Hillman would say that in *poiesis*, as in dreaming, the imaginal psyche composes itself—for as we saw previously, Hillman believes mind is poetic by nature.

Thus access to the poetic and to the images of myth and dream is of real therapeutic and political use for women for this crucial reason: work with inner images serves "*to save the diversity and autonomy of the psyche from domination by any single power*," as Hillman notes (*Re-Visioning* 32). Therefore, psychologically, turning to the myths—mythotropism—allows subversion of oppressive narratives, the creation of new ones, and the assertion of a woman's reality through the invocation and deployment of creative power. Diane di Prima, writing about H.D.'s visionary work, described the creation of psychic autonomy this way:

> ... the work of the poem is the work of transformation—it is too easy to say language is transformative. But it is nonetheless true that by our incantation we make and unmake worlds [31].

This power to "make and unmake worlds" lets women poets reimagine the structures militating against their literal and imaginative freedoms. As Schessler notes about H.D.'s mythotropic work, "palimpsestual desire finds satisfaction in ancient stories, and relies heavily on the writing-over of Greek myth." In the end, such mythtropism has allowed women poets such as H.D., Rukeyser, and Glück and any of us psychological access to poetry's profound, metamorphic power and the assertion of our right to poetic and intellectual self-determination—a beautifully "achieved credibility."

NOTES

1. Psychologists Stanley Sue and Nolan Zane introduced the concepts of "achieved credibility" and "ascribed credibility," or "status," in an influential analysis of mental health therapists' success, or lack thereof, with clients from cultures different than their own. I extrapolate these useful concepts to describe the difficulty women have had being accepted into the literary canon.

2. See Elena Tzelepis and Athena Athanasiou, *Rewriting Difference: Luce Irigaray and "The Greeks,"* Albany: State University of New York Press, 2010, for a whole education on the thought of Luce Irigaray, the French theorist of *l'écriture féminine*.

3. Hillman defined archetypal psychology as a psychology whose "first links are with culture and imagination rather than with medical and empirical psychologies which tend to confine psychology to the positivistic manifestations of the nineteenth-century condition of the soul" (*Archetypal Psychology* 1). Hillman also says, "a fundamental tenet of archetypal psychology [is]: the interchangeability of mythology and psychology. Mythology is a psychology of antiquity. Psychology is a mythology of modernity" (*Dream and Underworld* 23).

4. The classic text on the development and historical antecedents of depth psychology is Henri Ellenberger's *The Discovery of the Unconscious*.
  5. Shoshana Felman's reading of "the dream from which psychoanalysis proceeds" (74) revisits Freud's famous quote (in a letter to Marie Bonaparte): "The great question that has never been answered, and which I have not yet been able to answer, despite my thirty years of research into the feminine soul, is 'What does a woman want?'" (Freud, qtd. in Felman 73).
  6. See Sara Teasdale, telling us how it was: "'A women ought not to write. Somehow it is indelicate and unbecoming. She ought to imitate the female birds, who are silent—or if she sings, no one ought to hear her music until she is dead.'" (qtd. in Daniels xv).
  7. Some major critical and biographical appraisals of H.D.'s life and work are by Robert Duncan, Barbara Guest, and Susan Stanford Friedman.
  8. Stephen Schessler discusses the intensity of H.D.'s drive to recuperate loved ones lost to death in every facet of her life and poetry: "As she blurs the distinction between action, image, and memory, H.D. builds a monument to loss and death that reinstantiates her lost loved ones in the present moment through these poetic memorials" (Schessler).
  9. See Daniels, "Muriel Rukeyser and Her Critics" 247.
  10. Florence Howe chose Rukeyser's phrase, "No more masks," for the title of her groundbreaking anthology of women's poetry originally published in 1973.
  11. Humanistic psychology focuses on people's highest potential and optimal adjustment to life's existential demands. This theory used high-functioning people as models for its theories rather than people suffering from psychopathology. Abraham Maslow's "hierarchy of needs" in *Toward a Psychology of Being* and Carl Rogers' person-centered approach in *On Becoming a Person* are key texts in humanistic psychology.
  12. See Shawna Benston for an analysis of "re-membering" (1) and Rukeyser's Orphic poetics.
  13. Claude Levi-Strauss, anthropologist and early theorist of structuralism, identified "mythemes" as those "units of myth ... whose structural patterns invest the myth with meaning..." (qtd. in *A Handbook of Critical Approaches to Literature* 207). He saw mythemes as tapping "deep reservoirs of feeling and experience ... often invested with divine origins" (270).

WORKS CITED

Benston, Shawna. "Myself, Split Open: Ovid, Rukeyser, and the Traumatic Poetics of Orphic Re-Membering." *New Voices in Classical Reception Studies* Issue 5 (2010). 15 Oct. 2012. Web.
Daniels, Katie. "Introduction." *Out of Silence: Selected Poems*. By Muriel Rukeyser. Evanston, IL: Triquarterly Books, 1992. Print.
_____. "Muriel Rukeyser and Her Literary Critics." *Gendered Modernisms: American Woman Poets and Their Readers*. Ed. Margaret Dickie and Thomas Travisano. Philadelphia: University of Pennsylvania Press, 1996. 247–263. Print.
Davis, Christina. Rev. of *Orpheus and Company: Contemporary Poems on Greek Mythology*, Ed. Deborah DeNicola. *Boston Review*. Oct/Nov 1999. Web. 1 Sept. 2012. http://bostonreview.net/BR24.5/micropoetry.html.
DeNicola, Deborah, ed. *Orpheus and Company: Contemporary Poems on Greek Mythology*. Hanover: University Press of New England, 1999. Print.

di Prima, Diane. *The Mysteries of Vision: Some Notes on H.D.* Series 2, Number 2. Ed. Ana Božičević. New York: City University of New York, 2011. Print.
Duncan, Robert. *The H.D. Book: The Collected Writings of Robert Duncan.* Berkeley and Los Angeles: University of California Press, 2011. Print.
Ellenberger, Henri. *The Discovery of the Unconscious: The History and Evolution of Dynamic Psychiatry.* 1st ed. New York: Basic Books, 1981. Print.
Felman, Shoshana. *What Does a Woman Want?: Reading and Sexual Difference.* Baltimore, MD: The Johns Hopkins University Press, 1993. Print.
Friedman, Susan Stanford. *The Emergence of H.D.: Psyche Reborn.* 2nd. Bloomington: Indiana University Press, 1987. Print.
Glück, Louise. *Poems 1962–2012.* New York: Farrar, Straus and Giroux, 2012. Print.
Goldensohn, Lorrie. "Our Mother Muriel." *How Shall We Tell Each Other of the Poet: The Life and Writing of Muriel Rukeyser.* Anne R. Herzog and Janet E. Kaufman. New York: St. Martin's Press, 1999. 121–134. Print.
Guerin, Wilfred L., et al, eds. *A Handbook of Critical Approaches to Literature.* 6th ed. New York: Oxford University Press, USA, 2010. Print.
Guest, Barbara. "The Beautiful Voyage." *Forces of Imagination: Writing on Writing.* Ed. Kelsey Street Press. Berkeley: Kelsey Street Press, 2003. 78–81. Print.
_____. *Forces of Imagination: Writing on Writing.* Berkeley: Kelsey Street Press, 2003. Print.
_____. *Herself Defined: The Poet H.D. and Her World.* New York: Doubleday, 1984. Print.
_____. "Mysteriously Defining the Mysterious: Byzantine Proposals of Poetry." *Forces of Imagination: Writing on Writing.* Ed. Kelsey St. Press. Berkeley: Kelsey St. Press, 2003. 83–86. Print.
H.D. (Hilda Doolittle). *Sea-Garden.* 1916. Whitefish, MT: Kessinger Publishing, 2004. Print.
_____. *Tribute to Freud.* 2nd ed. New York: New Directions, 2012. Print.
_____. *Trilogy.* New York: New Directions, 1973. Print.
Hillman, James. *Archetypal Psychology: A Brief Account.* Dallas, TX: Spring Publications, 1985. Print.
_____. *The Dream and the Underworld.* 1st Edition. New York: Harper & Row, 1985. Print.
_____. *Re-Visioning Psychology.* 1st Edition. New York: Harper & Row, 1975. Print.
Howe, Florence. *No More Masks: An Anthology of Twentieth-Century American Women Poets.* 2nd Revised. New York: Harper Collins, 1993. Print.
Kalstone, David. "On 'Yánnina': An Interview with David Kalstone." *Collected Prose/James Merrill.* Ed. J.D. McClatchy and Stephen Yenser. New York: Alfred A. Knopf, 2004. 74–84. Print.
Levertov, Denise. "The Prayer." *Poetry* Oct. 1963: 66–67. Dec. 2012. Web. 11 August 2012.
Maslow, Abraham. *Toward a Theory of Being.* 3rd. New York: Wiley, 1998. Print.
Rogers, Carl. *On Becoming a Person: A Therapist's View of Psychotherapy.* 2nd. New York: Houghton Mifflin, 1989. Print.
Rukeyser, Muriel. *Out of Silence: Selected Poems.* Evanston, IL: Triquarterly Books, 1992. Print.
Schessler, Steve. "'Let the Impressions Come': H.D., Illness, and Remembrance of the Traumatic Past." *PSYART: A Hyperlink Journal for the Psychological Study of the Arts.* 15 Dec 2009. Web. 8 Mar 2013.
Sue, Stanley, and Nolan Zane. "The Role of Culture and Cultural Techniques in

Psychotherapy: A Critique and Reformulation." *American Psychologist.* 42.1 (1987): 37–45. Print.

Tsvetaeva, Marina. "The House at Old St. Pimen's." 1933. Trans. Olga Peters Hasty. *Myth and Violence in the Contemporary Female Text: New Cassandras.* Ed. Sanja Bahun-Radunovic and V.G. Julie Rajan. Burlington: Ashgate Publishing Co., 2011. Print.

Tzelepis, Elena, and Athena Athanasiou. *Rewriting Difference: Luce Irigaray and "The Greeks,"* Albany: State University of New York Press, 2010. Print.

Vendler, Helen. "In the Zoo of the New." *New York Review of Books* (1986). Web. 20 Nov. 2012. http://www.nybooks.com/articles/archives/1986/oct/23/in-the-zoo-of-the-

Burying Helen
H.D.'s Anthropoetics

Lisa D. Simon

In her study *Writing Beyond the Ending*, Rachel Blau DuPlessis describes a strategy of women poets who open up and alter well-known narratives to reflect the true diversity of real women's lives. She describes this method as especially powerful when applied to the classical myths of high culture that have, since the start of the written tradition, systematically obscured and diminished the roles of women in culture. With revisionary mythology, modern women poets alter the course of the Classical tradition by affixing new chapters to old scripts. In doing so, they provide a sense of possibility and hope for modern women. Along with DuPlessis, feminist critics Susan Friedman and Alicia Ostriker name the modernist poet H.D. as a foremother of mythic, poetic revision, pointing to her use of ancient figures such as Helen of Troy, Eurydice, Demeter, Cassandra and many others. Yet, Classical references have never been regarded as flawless in H.D.'s *oeuvre*; other critics have found her sources difficult to follow, causing some to call into question her knowledge of the classics, while others dismiss her allusions as merely "dramatic masks" (Martz xiv) of her private life. We see a performance of both in the critical frustration of Thomas Swann, who authored the first study on H.D.'s Classicism in 1960. After consulting the many written sources on the Trojan War Cycle and petitioning the poet herself to confess her sources, he concludes with palpable disappointment: "There is no exact prototype for H.D's characterization of Helen" (54). Swann seems even more irritated when poems speak in ancient personas without naming a character outright. Swann brushes aside five such poems in H.D.'s first volume by saying, "We are not given enough facts to identify Sappho or anyone else in the poem and the blurred outlines ... make it difficult to relate their heroines to H.D.'s more fully realized women" (71). He goes on, "these monologues with their crippling faults of incompleteness and inaccessibility amount to but an insignificant segment in the body of H.D.'s work" (72). One might expect this in 1960, before the feminist revival of H.D.'s work; yet these same poems that Swann calls an "insignificant segment" have remained, perhaps in part as a result of this dismissal, neglected. The poems that the feminist revival chose to elucidate are precisely the ones favored by Swann, those with "more fully realized women" or identifiable mythological characters like Helen or Eurydice, for which they could demonstrate clear revision. Yet literary criticism leaves untouched a good many poems that deal with antiquity and, in the case of Helen of Troy, has produced a body of essays that don't precisely or accurately deal with the felt experience of the poem. It is my contention that the felt aura of H.D.'s work is very much tied to her creative techniques that are connected to her unconventional relationship to antiquity. It is our frequent misunderstanding of that technique—our reluctance to recognize patterns and influences outside our usual academic toolbox—that lead inappropriately back to the same readings of her life as the sort of key to apprehending her poetry.

H.D.'s engagement with antiquity is misunderstood largely because she *exceeds* classical allusions to mythic characters in myriad ways. Many are rooted in the material tradition that she accessed through museums, travel, and the reading of unorthodox texts. For instance, she repeatedly calls in ancient cities and ports, re-enacts cultural rituals, culls details of authentic dress from friezes, coins, inscribed gems, and vase paintings. She describes weaponry and architecture with precision, and demonstrates fluency with the flora, fauna and landscape of the Mediterranean. In other words, more than a classical appreciation for the ancient world, H.D. exhibits an *anthropological* appreciation, filled with archaeological details. She engages antiquity outside the lines of classical mythology, which seems to be the *de facto* boundary for literary criticism. Other than an occasional critical nod to her travels, literary criticism hasn't dealt with the implications of these social sciences in and on her creative production.

Inclusion of these sources make clear the scope of H.D.'s poetic project as not only writing beyond the endings, but also (radically) writing back to, and altering, the very beginnings of western literature. I refer to this sociological attention as H.D.'s anthropoetics. And while the sources are rich beyond the scope of this essay, I will show these disciplines at work in an early poem, "Helen," that has been regarded conventionally as a mythological allusion, but which contains an important anthropoetic critique.

To begin, recall that H.D.'s early career sits at the start of the twentieth century and the crux of great change—the fall of various European aristocracies, the beginning of authentic rights for women, the burgeoning of social sciences such as psychology, anthropology and archaeology. It's within a flurry of manifestos, the dynamic turn of modern art, and the cultural devastation and personal losses of World War I. In all of these areas, even the war effort, everyone, not just intellectuals, was forced to question how to regard the precedents of history and the orthodox structures of culture.

The discipline of archaeology, in particular, was rapidly altering its modes of viewing the ancient past. Near the end of the nineteenth century, archaeologist Heinrich Schliemann, intent on finding "Homer's Troy," excavated from Mycenae Greece what he called the "treasures of Priam," the "jewels of Helen," and the golden "mask of Agamemnon" and he exhibited them throughout London (Hughes 180). In doing so, Schliemann placed stories hitherto relegated to the realm of myth under a new lens, suggesting that famous Homeric characters like Paris and Helen might be historical realities. The cultural surprise of Schliemann's project is difficult for us to comprehend—we have so deeply digested the overlap of ancient myth and history—but the astonishment, delight and excitement is palpable in contemporary accounts. Thus we find that at the beginning of literary modernism, the textual past was being both enhanced and challenged by material antiquity.

The British Museum became an important center of the debates about antiquity. With its frenzied period of acquisition throughout the prior centuries, by 1900 it had established itself as one of the largest and most influential cultural museums in the world. In this abundant storehouse of artifacts, H.D. was "studying daily," according to letters home in 1911 (Letter to Helen Wolle Dolittle, Nov 1911). It was here she was meeting Ezra Pound in its famous round library, under the painted border listing all the great male writers of the English literary tradition. There H.D. worked on translations, penned poems on Greek epigrams, checked out books for Richard Aldington (too young to do so himself), and rendezvoused with her new love at the Nereid monument, an excavated cliff temple that once sat upon a craggy Mediterranean shoreline (Silverstein's Chronology). Her days were full of taking in the images that furnish her first volume of poetry *Sea Garden* (1916). And as this visually astute poet absorbed the images around her she was also exposed to a conflict within the exhibits that ultimately surfaces in her poetry.

For also during this time frame, a quarrel percolated among curators about the proper method of exhibiting antiquities. Traditionally, artifacts were arranged according to their *aesthetic* value, a practice rooted in classical art history. Pressuring this time-honored custom was "a new breed" of archaeologists (Jenkins 9) aspiring to display artifacts in a way that educated visitors on how ancient societies actually functioned. The archaeologist-curators achieved a victory in 1908, just three years before H.D. arrived, with the opening of the Greek and Roman Life Room. Before the Life Room, all of the museum's holdings were arranged in a metaphoric "chain of art" depicting a hypothesized evolution. The chain began with so-called "primitive" cultures of India and South America and "progressed" to Persia and Egypt, on up through the Etruscans and Romans to the apex, Greek culture, the pinnacle of which was awe-inspiring Elgin marbles (Jenkins 23). Museum visitors figuratively traced the steps from "barbary" to "industry," to the full rise of civilization as they meandered towards the Elgin exhibit.

The opening of the Life Room in 1908 broke from this now theoretical chain and radically altered the form of exhibits. The archaeologist-curators displayed Greek and Roman cultures holistically, emphasizing how they lived instead of their greatest works of art. Practically, this meant displaying many artifacts that were not considered highly aesthetic: cooking pots, children's toys, tools, clothing, shoes and, because so many of the findings were from grave sites, a plethora of materials about the rituals of dying and burial customs. We might recognize in the aesthete model the outdated notions of judging all cultures based on a single western standard of civilization. Indeed, that that racist notion was debunked by the disciplines of archeology and anthropology hints at the critique of relativity H.D. finds under their influence. This museum context greatly informs H.D.'s early project as she frequently replicates the archaeological side of the debate. This slight distinction between ancient reality and myth has far reaching implications in interpreting her approach to the mythological figure of Helen.

Published in 1923, H.D.'s "Helen" demonstrates the tensions between the two approaches. From her earliest works to her last poem, H.D. puzzled over, studied and wrote about this ancient character. The poet's interest in Helen spans her entire writing career.[1] In literature, Helen is a part of what is known as the Trojan War cycle, a set of stories told and retold by various ancient authors—Homer, Hesiod, Virgil, and Ovid. The cycle occupies a central narrative in the mainstream classical tradition and, in Homer's hands, is considered the beginning of western literature. Helen's centrality to this story was perhaps best demonstrated by Christopher Marlowe's famous line, calling her "the face that launch'd a thousand ships" (12:80).

H.D. takes advantage of the character's fame, by titling the poem, simply, "Helen," eliding the usual possessive attachment to Paris "of Troy," after being "Helen of Sparta," while married to Menelaus. In each of the three short stanzas of H.D.'s poem, Helen stands centrally, yet has little agency. In each stanza, she is encircled by a viewing audience defining her in ways that are both familiar and difficult to pin down. The poem begins describing how "All Greece hates" her still eyes lodged in her white face (lines 1–2). The poem wastes no time pointing out Classical mythology's conflicted relationship with Helen, detesting what it loves and loving what it detests to the point of fetishism. In the next lines, "All Greece" focuses its seething gaze on her hands, eyes and face—those feminine features that the many authors in the written tradition have extolled in the most flowery of language.

We see in this opening scene something of a hostile beauty contest, alluding, as myths often do, to another mythic episode, the Judgment of Paris in which Aphrodite awards Helen in exchange for the verdict of most beautiful. In the poem's contest, however, the judge is a collective cultural gaze. Helen stands immobile, oiled up like an athlete; her skin radiates the "luster of olives." Yet H.D. underscores that this flowery attention to her beauty is in ironic opposition to the subtending hatred. If this is the western notion of beauty, she infers, it isn't all that pretty.

We can trace the poem's first line, "All Greece hates," to writings by the ancient playwright Euripides in his work *Orestes*. H.D. underlined that very phrase in her personal copy—the same book in which she penned her first draft of "Helen" in the flyleaf (Friedman "Serendipity" 7). So we know this ancient author was very much on her mind as she authored the poem. Yet Euripides did not invent this notion of collective hatred; it resounds throughout Homer's *Odyssey and Iliad,* Virgil's *Aeneas,* and Ovid's *Metamorphosis.* That the hatred for Helen is culturally conditioned and connected to the written tradition can be seen in an artifact held at the British Museum. An ancient papyrus shows a single line of Virgil's *Aeneid*—one line repeated seven times on seven separate lines: "It is not the hated face of Spartan Helen." The repeating lines lead curators to regard it as an ancient writing lesson.[2] The artifact exposes how young men while being taught to write using the stories of the Trojan War, are inculcated into a deeply negative attitude towards Helen, and perhaps women generally. The papyrus demonstrates how the hatred for Helen is ingrained from generation to generation through textual sources—a point that simmers in the subtext of H.D.'s poem.

The second stanza begins with a slight repetition of the first, describing how everyone reviles her pale face (lines 6–7). The absolute stillness of Helen's presence—her eyes, her stance—remain, but the force of hatred compounds to the point of suffocation. She "grows wan" and the once-lustrous Helen ossifies into an *objet d'art*. Helen's efforts to exert herself as a person are ineffective. The reader is led from her rigidly cast exterior of beauty, to a still functioning, yet weakened, interior—a memory that recalls "enchantments" and "ills" of the past (lines 10, 11). Helen's external self, her reputation, remains rigidly defined by "all Greece," which reduces it only to hatred—first the reviling, then hating it "deeper still" (line 8). The color white stands for a slow leaching of her humanity as she becomes an aesthete symbol in Classical myth, a statue.

H.D. became aware of the real-life history of Helen from the writings of Pausanias, who might be called an early archaeologist. Pausanias traveled around Greece in the first century BCE making notes on the vestiges of cities being wiped out by war and subsumed by the Roman Empire. He writes, for instance, about cult temples dedicated to Helen that testified to a great love and respectful allegiance. Pausanias showed H.D. something more than the "hated face." He speaks of beautiful shrines where fragments of her relics dangle in ribbons from the temple on the Spartan Acropolis (Hughes 27) and thousands of terracotta votive fragments before her altars. Artifacts within the British Museum similarly support a version of Helen as a beloved, not hated, cultural figure. For instance, on two large vases, ancient painters depict Helen in the fashion of goddesses, by painting her features in white, so that she stands out from the other figures on the red clay. Similarly the museum holds many personal artifacts for women—mirrors, combs, and bracelets—etched with Helen's name or likeness.

In her unpublished essay on Euripides, titled (like her final poem) "Helen in Egypt," H.D. sides with a little known text that says Helen never went to Troy, but spent those war years in Egypt. She describes Helen walking along a beach, saying: "her face is not in any Praxitelian sense beautiful. It is white and beautiful as a skull" (3). This movement from idealized sculpture of the ancient sculptor Praxiteles to stark human remains precisely prefigures the movement between stanzas two and three in "Helen."

The first two stanzas, as we've seen, show us the gradual devolution of Helen into a static form of an idealized sculpture—the mythological Helen we know, love and are given plenty of literary cause to hate. Repeating again, with slight variation, the rigid message of classical mythology appears a third time in the last stanza: "Greece sees unmoved" (line 12). H.D. then lays out a series of recognizably Homeric epithets praising her birth, "slenderest knees" and "cool feet" (lines 14, 15). But an awkward, grammatical shift interrupts the litany, switching from praise of "slenderest knees" to an insistence that the people could love this maid "Only if she were laid" among the cypresses (lines 15–18). The tone shifts from the sing-song of Homeric allusion to one of pronounced elegy as H.D. breaks the tradition's hold over the idealized Helen by giving her the one thing classical myth never did: a fitting burial. Greece could finally love her only if her corpse were laid to rest (lines 17–18). At the same moment we jag from the grammatical framework, we exit the literary tradition and enter a context that is clearly within the archaeological purview, a burial site. The last lines imagine Helen within the context of ancient funeral rituals associated with cypress trees. Her beautiful body, object of so much conflict, has been burned to ash. She has returned to being human.

In these three stanzas H.D. prods the cultural friction between the symbolic and the sociological, the mythological and the material. If we look to the textual tradition, we find little ink on the death of Helen. The authors of the Trojan War cycle—Homer, Hesiod, Virgil—are silent on the matter. The only ancient writer who broaches it is, notably, Euripides, the ancient author who spurred the poem. But Euripides offers Helen only a mythological death, depicting her as ascending to Olympus and being granted enthronement with the gods. In her essay on Euripides, H.D. fiercely quarrels with him for this simplistic finale, calling the ending "full of artificialities" and "silly" (NEPG, "Helen in Egypt" 12). A mythical ending is clearly not satisfying for the poet. The poem H.D. writes in response bestows on Helen a human burial, a sign of deep respect, an honoring of a life lived. In doing so, the poet moves Helen from the paradigm of the aesthetes to that of the archaeologists, from the written tradition to a sociological, cultural tradition. This is the very shift that she was absorbing through the exhibits at the British Museum.

The loving detail of putting Helen to rest in white ash surrounded by funeral cypresses is in keeping with ancient rituals and customs and links H.D.'s poem to twenty-four Helen-specific *burial* artifacts held at the British Museum. The Helen artifacts, which have mostly been exhumed from burial sites, are intricate, lovely, but don't demonstrate the high craftsmanship that would be exhibited outside the Life Room. These household artifacts express a fondness for Helen that reaffirms Pausanias' findings. Folded in the hands of women in their graves these objects honor a relationship that was personal and intimate, not rarified, not frozen. Whereas the written tradition elides Helen's death, the museum directly and repeatedly links Helen to the human burden of mortality. Thus, H.D.'s early poem moves us into a new sort of poetic relationship with the classical past, away from the static hatred, relentless repetition, the mythic grandeur, to the touching gestures of human burial. Within the poetic space, H.D. evokes a corporeal Helen—someone who would have had a cultural historicity and would have lived and died in a city or town, been attended by mourners, honored in a manner befitting her social stature. This is not a result of a cultivated aesthetic distance, but an anthropological closeness.

To return to the point with which I opened this essay, if H.D.'s treatment were a revisionist myth reading, the poet would employ tactics to imagine "beyond the ending," adding a new chapter to the traditional story we've inherited. But that doesn't happen in this poem. H.D. uses sociological knowledge to make a much stronger critique against written history and the literary tradition. Her poem connects us to an *alternate* history of Helen, a material history, and suggests quite powerfully that the things are not, and never were, the way we have been taught. Her poem strikes at the very beginning of the literary history, not the end. Throughout the poem, Helen does not act with a new, feminist agency, creating a new chapter in the myth, but she remains what she always was, an ancient Greek woman, much abused by culture and liberated in death. The anthropoetic critique emerges in the way the poet asks us to question the classical myth as we have inherited it. Her project questions how we inherited the frozen, aesthetic Helen and not the loved and revered one. And by naming "Greece" as the culpable hater of Helen, she also questions the strong alignment and identity that western culture has forged between itself and ancient Greece. H.D.'s archaeological empathy exposes a propagandist landslide of value assumptions passed, often unexamined, through mainstream literature.

While H.D.'s deep interest in archeology and anthropology is clearly evident in her library, letters, travel choices as well as her poetry and novels, the implications of these interests have rarely been called into the critical interpretations of her work. Bound to the literary tradition, literary critics continue to pour forth myth-based readings and in order to do so, they often must elide stanzas and lines that don't seem to fit. Ironically, for at least a half a century, university students have been presented with anthologies footnoting H.D.'s poems to classical texts, assuming Virgil's *Aeneid* or Homer's *Iliad* or *Odyssey* could help them to understand a poem like "Helen." This misdirection created the puzzlement and dismissal of her poems that we saw earlier in Thomas Swann's study of H.D.'s use of classical sources. Where, after failing to find H.D.'s sources, he merely dismissed poems as "insignificant." Swann is a critic confined to classical myth, while the poet is operating outside of the written tradition.

H.D.'s work in this early period, roughly 1911 to 1929, cannot be properly understood without considering the influence of sociological sources, specifically early archeology and the British Museum. Those sources construct the philosophic framework that informed her project within literary modernism. Importantly it also connects her work to the Modernists' preoccupation with tradition, history and culture. While Ezra Pound, Gertrude Stein and T.S. Eliot are often linked to those ideas, H.D. is not, but should be. When these material sources are reconnected to H.D.'s project, they illuminate the poet's sense of lyric immediacy, the richness of her intellectual inquiry, and her anthropoetic approach to antiquity.

Notes

1. Eileen Gregory argues that H.D.'s interest in Helen was piqued by reading May Sinclair's book *The Divine Fire* (1904) before she traveled to Europe, placing the date of her first interest as early as 1911. ("Euripides and H.D.'s Working Notebook" 85). The Trojan War cycle—its characters, places and scenes—can be found in nearly twenty of H.D.'s works: "Helen," "Leda," "After Troy," "Cassandra," "At Ithaca," "Calypso," "Circe," "Cuckoo's Song," "A Dead Priestess Speaks," "Helios," "The Islands," "Prayer," "Sea Heroes," "Why Have You Sought?" and "Thetis" (in two versions) as well as *NEPG* essays on Helen, *Winter Love* (1959) and her last epic poem *Helen in Egypt*.

2. According to the British Museum's database of artifacts, the papyrus contains "a line of Virgil's *Aeneid*, repeated seven times: probably a writing exercise." The text is *Aeneid* book II, line 60. The papyrus was acquired by London College in the 1890s, portions of this collection had been exhibited in London—including within the British Museum where it is displayed now.

WORKS CITED

DuPlessis, Rachel Blau. *Writing Beyond the Ending: Narrative Strategies of Twentieth-Century Women Writers*. Indiana: Indiana University Press, 1985.
Euripides. *Orestes*. Trans. William Arrowsmith. *Euripides IV. The Complete Greek Tragedies*. Eds. David Grene and Richmond Lattimore. Chicago: Chicago University Press, 1958. 105–208.
Friedman, Susan Stanford. "Serendipity: Finding a Draft Manuscript of H.D.'s 'Helen.'" *Sagetrieb* 14: 1&2 (1995). 7–11.
Gregory, Eileen. "Euripides and H.D.'s Working Notebook for Helen in Egypt." *Sagetrieb* 14:1&2 (1995). 83–87.
_____. *H.D. and Hellenism: Classic Lines*. Cambridge: Cambridge University Press, 1997.
H.D. *H.D. Collected Poems, 1912–1944*. Ed. Louis L. Martz. New York: New Directions, 1983.
_____. *Helen in Egypt*. New York: New Directions, 1961.
_____. Letter to Helen Wolle Doolittle. 17 Nov 1911. *H.D. Papers*. Beinecke Rare Book and Manuscript Library. Yale University, New Haven, CN.
_____. "Notes on Euripides, Pausanias, and Greek Lyric Poets." TS. *H.D. Papers*. Beinecke Rare Book and Manuscript Library, Yale University, New Haven, CN.
Hughes, Bettany. *Helen of Troy: Goddess, Princess, Whore*. New York: Knopf, 2005.
Jenkins, Ian. *Archaeologists & Aesthetes: In the Sculpture Galleries of the British Museum 1800–1939*. London: British Museum Press, 1992.
Marlowe, Christopher. *Doctor Faustus*. Ed. Sylvan Barnet. New York: Signet Classics, 1990.
Martz, Louis L. *"Introduction." H.D. Collected Poems, 1912–1944*. Ed. Louis L. Martz. New York: New Directions, 1983. xi–xxxvi.
Pausanias. *Guide to Greece: Vols. I & II*. Trans. Peter Levi. London: Penguin Books, 1971.
Silverstein, Louis. "H.D. Chronology." *Imagists.org*. 10 Dec 2006 http://www.imagists.org/hd/hdchron.html.
Smith, Arthur H. *A Guide to the Department of the Greek and Roman Antiquities in the British Museum. Fourth Edition*. London: British Museum Press, 1912.
Swann, Thomas Burnett. *The Classical World of H.D.* Lincoln: University of Nebraska Press, 1962.

The Needed Underworld
Modern Reactions to Symbolic Death

Rachel McCoppin

A popular theme in myths from around the world is the journey of the living protagonist to the underworld. In Sumerian myth, Inanna/Ishtar travels to the underworld and experiences death through the aid of her sister Ereshkigal, ruler of the underworld; in Japanese myth, Izanagi travels to the underworld to retrieve his resistant wife Izanami. The mythic underworld motif often signifies a transformation or rebirth of the protagonist; "In ancient times ... the underworld was not necessarily a place for the dead. Rather it was a ... place of learning, a cauldron for rebirth" (O'Hare-Lavin 202). In this spirit, modern women poets most commonly use the Greek myths of Demeter and Persephone and Orpheus and Eurydice to capture the underworld experience of symbolic death and renewal of the protagonist.

In ancient Greek culture, underworld myths portrayed an embrace of the cyclical nature of life—life must lead to death, but from death comes all birth. The myth of Demeter and Persephone inspired the Eleusinian mysteries, where worshippers embraced the fact that life and death were intermingled necessities; in the celebration of the myth, "each image of beauty and life is also an image of death. The golden wheat Demeter holds is synonymous in Greek with the sickle that harvests it" (Dobson 45).

Similarly, the ancient Greeks also worshipped the gods Apollo and Dionysus, whose pairing represented the necessary duality of life. Apollo, god of the sun and reason, represented all that is good, beautiful, and light, all that easily is embraced and accepted by most people, but the ancient Greeks also equally worshipped Dionysus, god of the fertility of nature, ecstasy, and intoxication, who represented the dark, mysterious, and often taboo sides of life. His worship involved drunken revelry, orgies, and tearing apart animals and consuming their raw flesh. The dichotomy portrayed in the worship of Apollo and Dionysus shows the Greeks' embrace of life as multifaceted. The embrace of Apollonian tenets—reason, illumination, and masculinity—were a clear and vital part of Greek culture, but the equal worship of Dionysus shows their acceptance of the Other, the unrestrained, dark, inexplicable, and feminine side of life. Dionysus is "also the god of death and of the underworld" (Downing 182). While he journeyed to the underworld and suffered dismemberment and death, as the god of fertility, he also resurrects with each grape harvest.

The myths of Dionysus and Demeter and Persephone focus on the cycles of nature, connecting the necessary birth, death, rebirth cycle to the lives of mortals. Christine Downing states, "Dionysus represents the sacredness and fearfulness of all boundary-dissolving experience: intoxication, sexual ecstasy, madness.... [He] exposes *us* to a kind of dismemberment and death" (182). Myths representing a living protagonist entering into and then emerging out of the underworld signify a "boundary-dissolving experience" where one embraces one's unconscious and the sides of life that many are afraid to face, the things defined as dark, mysterious, Other. Because of this journey, the protagonist is reborn, obtaining a fulfillment of self with the realization that life is as fleeting as the vicious cycle of nature, but it is also secure in its promise of continual resurrection.

Many modern women poets have revitalized these classic myths of the underworld, and interestingly, their modern renditions maintain the original Greek vision of the necessity of the Apollonian/Dionysian duality of life. The necessity of both life and death, "good" and "bad," and the spiritual rebirth that comes from this acceptance, is apparent in these modern poems in a similar way to how the Greeks captured it in these famous myths. Modern literature, in an era of extreme adversity with World War I and II, the influenza epidemic, the Great Depression, the Holocaust, and atomic warfare, still has a tendency to offer messages similar to the Greeks,' that hardship, even death, can bring an appreciation of life. But these modern women poets shed light on the secondary characters that Greek myth largely left silent; the Greeks worshipped Demeter and Orpheus, but largely forgot Persephone and Eurydice, just as the canon of Modernism mostly provides the male versions of stories of hardships and learning. Rita Dove in "Demeter's Prayer to Hades," Alice Jones in "Persephone," Denise Levertov in "A Tree Telling of Orpheus," Pamela White Hadas in "Eurydice," and H.D. in "Eurydice" enable these often silent characters to speak in order to remind modern audiences of the importance of Apollonian/Dionysian duality. These modern renditions of ancient works by women poets gives voices to ancient women, but also to women of the modern era. What these ancient women say reveals their underworld experience as a profound journey into themselves and their relation to the meaning of life—concepts that continue in all eras.

The Greek myth of Demeter and Persephone portrays Persephone, daughter of Demeter, goddess of the harvest and the fertility of the world, and granddaughter of Gaia, mother earth, out picking narcissus, when a snake bites her, and she is thrust to the underworld. Demeter is so enraged that she stops the cycles of nature in her demand for the return of her daughter, and because of Demeter's resistance, Persephone is allowed to leave the underworld and return to the world above with her mother each spring. The Eleusinian cults celebrated this myth because of its entirety; both Persephone's time in Hades each winter and her annual resurrection of life each spring were viewed as necessary. Central to the Greek's embrace of this myth is the fact that Persephone falls in love with Hades, ruler of the underworld (O'Hare-Lavin, 20); to many contemporary audiences, this is a contentious point, but it is this aspect of the myth that reveals its central meaning. Many contemporary versions focus on Demeter winning her daughter back, and view her annual death back to the underworld as a sad afterthought, failing to see the true importance of Persephone's embrace of her annual death; "her death implies power rather than loss, power that allows the seasons to keep turning" (Dobson 46). Persephone embraces her recurring death as much as she revels in her annual resurrection. This aspect of the necessity of an Apollonian/Dionysian view of life lends insight into Greek belief, and, indeed, the modern poems of Rita Dove and Alice Jones embrace the importance of this duality.

Rita Dove's "Demeter's Prayer to Hades" portrays an element of tension. The sadness and anger of Demeter at losing Persephone is there, but in this modern rendition, even in the first line of the poem, with her word "knowledge" (27), there is also the understanding that this experience both of Demeter and of her daughter Persephone provides a necessary knowledge about life. Dove portrays Persephone's leaving as a choice she has made, and it is this point within the poem that is key to tying it to the original Greek embrace of the duality of life. Persephone "was primarily the dread goddess of the underworld, not the innocent maidenly goddess of spring. There are no accounts of ... her playing a subordinate role to Hades" (Downing 181). In Dove's modern rendition, Persephone is shown, not as simply dying by a random snake bite, but as choosing a path that has harsh consequences, leading to her death, but eventually giving Persephone a wisdom that she has sought. The poem ends with a call to both "give up" and give in to fate and the natural cycles of nature but also to forge ahead and "believe in yourself" (27). In staying true to the Eleusinian cults' acceptance of the necessity of both the Apollonian and Dionysian sides of life, Dove provides both aspects within her poem. The poem accepts that "believ[ing] in yourself" has a cost, but that pain and struggle, like what both Demeter and Persephone experience as a result of Persephone's choice to love Hades, result in a spiritual knowledge and acceptance of the natural cycles of life. Similarly, Dove's poem "The Narcissus Flower" also speaks towards Persephone's death as her choosing to embrace what most define as horrible and fearful—the Dionysian. This poem shows the spiritual evolution of Persephone; she starts out innocent and possibly naïve, picking narcissus, but in the underworld she learns to embrace what she should abhor; "Persephone needed to become herself; she reached for that dark narcissus" (Downing 192). Thus Dove ends the poem with Persephone as queen, "liv[ing] beyond dying," suggesting the Eleusinian cults' belief that an embrace of duality provided a spiritual life beyond death.

Again in maintaining the Greek importance of the myth, Alice Jones' "Persephone" portrays Persephone as needing and embracing both her time in the underworld and her time on earth. Jones' poem begins similar to Dove's in that it portrays Persephone as choosing her fate, and again this is tantamount to the Greek meaning of the myth, that Persephone is not a victim, but is strong and has obtained spiritual wisdom. Early in the poem Jones portrays Persephone as being tired of remaining dependent upon her mother; in this poem she chooses to set herself free and move beyond the protection and control of Demeter, or of the known and safe earth. Jones entirely flips the popular telling of this myth, where Persephone is taken against her will to Hades, first in her initial death and then annually, as a tragic account; instead, Jones shows Persephone as longing for her death with the annual demise of nature, opening the door for her return to the underworld and Hades. Here, Jones is true to the important Greek tenet within the myth that Persephone loves Hades.

But the poem also moves beyond just Persephone longing to return to the underworld; it is far more complicated. Persephone longs to leave her mother, and life with all its beautiful fecundity behind; she longs for the death and sterility that the underworld brings her, but her coming desire to leave the underworld behind is also constant. When she is alive she longs for death, and when she is dead she waits for life. Jones' portrayal of Persephone does not leave her always dissatisfied though; instead, she is portrayed at the close of this poem as being capable of embracing her time of bright, beautiful life more because of her ability to accept death, and also conversely, she is capable of embracing the dying, darkening aspects of life more because of her ability to resurrect beyond it; she is thus a comfortable and natural transgressor between two worlds. Jones shows a Persephone who, at the end of the poem, fully loves and appreciates the beauty of her natural, giving mother—life, and the mysterious darkness of her equally natural husband—death.

The Greek myth of Orpheus and Eurydice has similar elements. Eurydice, on her wedding day to Orpheus, is also bitten by a snake and descends to the underworld. It is Orpheus who wishes to retrieve her back to the land of the living; he is renowned for being the best lyre player in the world, so he descends, alive, into the underworld, to play the lyre to Hades himself. Orpheus' beautiful song affects Persephone so much that she convinces Hades to let Eurydice go back with Orpheus, but Hades puts one caveat upon the deal—if Orpheus turns to look upon Eurydice, she must remain in the underworld forever. Orpheus goes the whole journey out of the underworld, trusting that Eurydice is behind him, but at the moment of release back to the upper world, he fails and turns, thrusting Eurydice back into the underworld. Most popular renditions of the myth today end at this point, leaving it a sad tale about never being able to escape the fact of death, but by examining the ancient Greek Orphic mystery cults' celebration of this myth, more can be revealed about its true meaning to the Greeks. These echoed the Eleusinian mysteries, revering both Persephone and Dionysus for their connection to the underworld and subsequent spiritual knowledge.

The continuation of the myth reveals the true meaning; Orpheus, losing Eurydice for the second time, sits and plays his lyre, but now with his experience of the underworld, his playing of his instrument has a new effect—all of nature responds to his song, and this reflects an integral aspect of the myth. Orpheus has learned something important as a result of his underworld experience, something that nature understands. It is this connection between Orpheus and nature that is vital to the myth; it is also what connects this tale to Demeter and Persephone, and why ancient Greeks worshipped both myths in their mystery cults. Nature and the underworld were intrinsically connected; death and life chased each other in nature's cyclical necessity; therefore, embracing both the aspects of life: beauty, fecundity, light, and the aspects of death: mystery, taboo, and darkness, led to spiritual wisdom.

Denise Levertov's "A Tree Telling of Orpheus" depicts Orpheus as enlightened because of his underworld experience. The poem opens with a tree watching Orpheus after he has emerged from the underworld; the tree is "deeply alert" (111) to him, as his sits in the tree's shadow and plays his renowned song of wisdom on his lyre. The song Orpheus plays inspires both "joy and fear" (112) in the tree; the tree feels the emotions Orpheus is playing and knows the "meaning" (112) that it shares. Levertov portrays what Orpheus' music reveals; his wordless song includes all aspects of life, both sublime and horrific; the song allows the tree to embrace and love what the tree fears most—fire (113). This modern rendition of the myth shows the Greek acceptance of the myth as a whole. Orpheus' song after he has left the underworld is filled with the Apollonian/Dionysian duality of life. The song Levertov has Orpheus play strips away the definitions of bad and good, and simply makes both natural; this is why Levertov has a tree as protagonist. The poem continues on to show the tree obtaining self-knowledge; the tree sees its own birth out of coal, and death, and rebirth, and the tree is no longer afraid, but values the cycle.

The tree, and all the trees around it, pull themselves from the ground that traps them and begin to dance to the music of Orpheus. This scene within the poem is integral to the Greek meaning of the myth. The Greek version of the myth continues with Orpheus being so immersed in his song that he fails to recognize that he has drawn the maenads, female worshippers of Dionysus, to him. They tear him apart, like Dionysus was, and spread the pieces of his body throughout the fields. Again, this often overlooked part of the myth is vital. The maenads' connection to Dionysus is important; they embody the Greek's worship of the darker, mysterious, wild side of life, and it is Orpheus' underworld experience that allows him to play a song to which nature and these wild women respond. The fact that they kill him in the same way Dionysus was killed places honor upon Orpheus and does not end the myth in a tragic way; instead, Orphic cults worshipped Orpheus because of this final point of the myth—Orpheus has obtained wisdom, and perhaps draws the maenads to him, accepting death, which is what he failed to do with Eurydice. With Eurydice, Orpheus wanted to defeat death, but this is impossible; instead, he must accept it, dying himself. In Levertov's allowing even the trees to defy what confines them and set themselves free, Levertov is showing that Orpheus has finally learned how to supersede death.

As a mortal, Orpheus tried to rescue Eurydice, not understanding anything yet about the cycles of nature, but once having experienced the underworld, he now sees it for what it is—natural, so his song afterward not only shows him finally free, but can also free those around him. Levertov portrays Orpheus as laughing and weeping as he watches the trees dance (114).

The Greek myth ends with Orpheus' severed head still emitting his song; this in itself suggests a resurrection, like Persephone's and Dionysus.' The pieces of his body that were scattered to the earth will now produce new life, and the cycle will continue; Carl Jung comments, "'Through dismemberment ... the divine spark got into everything, the divine soul entered the earth ... which guarantees a later resurrection'" (qtd. in Zabriskie 441). This myth in its entirety reveals the Greek's embrace of the duality of life; the failure to retrieve Eurydice is not the focal point of the myth; it is the wisdom that Orpheus obtains because of his underworld experience that made him worshipped.

Levertov's poem concludes as the myth does. The poem shows Orpheus helping the trees return to their place in the ground; then he goes to meet his fate with the maenads. Levertov portrays Orpheus as an enlightened man, as the Orphic cults defined him. This poem depicts the tree as being thankful to Orpheus because it was Orpheus' song that helped the tree accomplish the impossible by dispelling its fear of death and giving it wisdom that lies in accepting death. After hearing the song, the tree "see[s] more" clearly the intimate details of life and nature. The acceptance of death that the tree has acknowledged by listening to his song has made the tree value life, but Levertov does not end the poem with this simplicity—the tree, with this newfound insight also must endure "agony" at remembering the song (115). In combining "agony" with appreciation of life, Levertov ends the poem with the original Orphic cult meaning: that death, and all that is associated with it, must be embraced to fully live.

"Modern women writers ... reject woman's traditional Eurydicean role as long-suffering wife, abandoned lover, patient muse, and death filled archetype" (Sword 413); instead they give voice to her and see her value, showing that Eurydice holds just as much power as does Orpheus in this myth of enlightenment. Like Levertov, Pamela White Hadas and H.D. maintain the Greek integrity of the myth as a lesson of embracing both the Apollonian/Dionysian sides of life through contact with the underworld, though like Dove and Jones did with Persephone, they give voice to Eurydice to reveal her powerful role of welcoming the dark, mysterious Other of the underworld.

Hadas' "Eurydice" portrays Eurydice, not as a silent shadow, but as a woman who clearly wants to remain in the underworld. The poem reflects her death by snakebite, but immediately shifts to her requesting Orpheus to let her remain as she is, to "observe the rule he can't see" (17). It is this point in the poem that exposes Eurydice as having obtained knowledge in her underworld experience; she is almost scoffing at the ignorance of Orpheus in his attempt to cheat death.

Upon first entering the underworld, Orpheus did not realize the full magnitude of Eurydice's role; she is the fact of death, the mysteriousness of life; "Orpheus, who saw her only as *his* beloved, had ignored: namely, her 'in-herself-ness'" (Downing 189). Eurydice's silence in the Greek telling was not to declare her as unessential, as most popular versions of the myth portray; instead, Hadas shows that her silence, like Persephone's, simply makes her a representation of the mysterious, taboo, and feared aspects of mortality. Eurydice represents that which most are afraid to embrace; she "is not an utter void.... Her death holds the promise of dying into life with her vision cleared" (Goldensohn 44).

The poem continues on to show anger within Eurydice at Orpheus' attempt to save her; she feels condemned to silently follow him, and in this following, she is trapped. Hadas allows Eurydice to speak in the voice that was intended for her, and in the poem her words are what make Orpheus turn to her, which thus thrusts her back to death. Therefore, in the poem it is Eurydice who chose to remain in the underworld, refusing to be saved by Orpheus who does not, at this point in the myth, understand the laws of nature. The poem ends with Eurydice condemning Orpheus, already knowing the fate he is about to succumb to at the hands of the maenads. The anger that Hadas gives Eurydice shows that her position has given her wisdom about the workings of life and death, and this modern portrayal gives Eurydice the power she deserves.

In her poem "Eurydice," H.D. was "the first woman to give expression to Eurydice's experience from a woman's point of view" (Dawson 249). H.D. portrays Eurydice as turning from needing Orpheus' love to a place of power and identity in her embrace of the underworld. H.D.'s Eurydice is strong and brave enough to stay in the underworld and gain wisdom from the experience, to see the "splendor" of the underworld, just as Persephone fell in love with Hades. Again as with Hadas' version of "Eurydice," there is anger at Orpheus, but H.D.'s poem moves beyond just anger at his initial ignorance. H.D.'s Eurydice first blames Orpheus for condemning her to stay in the underworld, but the poem shifts to her understanding to embrace where she is. First Eurydice gains strength to no longer need Orpheus, but then the poem continues on to portray her as finding an inner peace and knowledge that she states elevates her beyond even the gods.

In her fully embracing death, Eurydice has nothing left to fear; therefore, like the celebration of the Orphic cults, H.D.'s Eurydice is resurrected; she ends the poem declaring that she has her "own spirit for light" (101). The Greek myth ends, allowing Orpheus to obtain the wisdom Eurydice helped teach him; once he dies a final time, he is better able to understand Eurydice, not trying to save her from something he does not comprehend, but standing beside her fully a part of the underworld.

The myths of Demeter and Persephone and Orpheus and Eurydice maintain "a mode of natural order" (Downing 191); they are not about anything extraordinary, just the cyclical nature of life. The myths of the underworld represent the unconscious; they "lead us to the *depths* of experience, to our own fears and longings about death, about failure, about loss and endings, to our own experiences of such journeys *within* life" (Downing 177). These modern women poets, through their own struggles in the modern era, have found the original intended voice of their ancient mythic selves. The mythic characters, both in ancient and modern times, who embrace the underworld allow us to face our worst, and see it as only natural, thus allowing us to resurrect ourselves.

Works Cited

Dawson, Terence. "The Orpheus Complex." *Journal of Analytical Psychology.* Vol. 45 (2000). 245–266.
Denicola, Deborah, ed. *Orpheus and Company.* Hanover, NH: University Press of New England, 1999.
Dobson, Marcia W. "Ritual Death, Patriarchal Violence, and Female Relationships in the Hymns to Demeter and Inanna." *NWSA Journal.* Vol. 4, No. 1 (Spring 1992). 42–58.

Dove, Rita. "Demeter's Prayer to Hades." 1952. Kossman 27–28.
_____. "The Narcissus Flower." 1993. *Orpheus and Company.* Ed. Deborah Denicola. Hanover, NH: University Press of New England, 1999. 148.
Downing, Christine. "Journeys to the Underworld." *Mythosphere* 1.2 (1999): 175–193.
Goldensohn, Barry. "Eurydice Looks Back." *American Poetry Review.* 23.6 (Nov/Dec 1994): 43–52.
Hadas, Pamela White. "Eurydice." 1979. In *Orpheus and Company*, ed., Denicola 17–18.
H.D. "Eurydice." 1941. *Gods and* Mortals, ed., Kossman 100–102.
Jones, Alice. "Persephone." 1990. In *Orpheus and Company*, ed., Denicola 158–159.
Kossman, Nina, ed. *Gods and Mortals.* Oxford: Oxford University Press, 2001.
Levertov, Denise. "A Tree Telling of Orpheus." 1970. Kossman 111–115.
O'Hare-Lavin, Mary Ellen. "Finding a 'Lower, Deeper Power' for Women in Recovery." *Counseling and Values.* 44.3 (Apr. 2000): 198–212.
Sword, Helen. "Orpheus and Eurydice in the Twentieth Century: Lawrence, H.D., and the Poetics of the Turn." *Twentieth Century Literature.* 35.4 (Winter 1989): 407–428.
Zabriskie, Beverly. "Orpheus and Eurydice: A Creative Agony." *Journal of Analytical Psychology* 45 (2000): 427–447.

From Persephone's Lips
Three Retellings by Louise Glück

VALERIE ESTELLE FRANKEL

Demeter and Persephone is one of the world's most well-known myths, but also one of the most problematic. It's the story of a girl questing into the underworld to grow from sweet flower princess to ruling queen of the dead, and of her mother who quests after her and must learn to let her go. In the end, Persephone becomes part of the cycle of nature, traveling forever in the pattern of the seasons. However, in Homer's original poem, Persephone doesn't quest willingly, but is kidnapped by Hades and torn away screaming. Demeter is a cold, grieving shrew, willing to destroy the world rather than listen to reason. One of the greatest women's tales in Greek mythology becomes trapped under a misogynist layer, as the male gods of the tale must force Persephone to grow up and Demeter to let go.

Louise Glück addresses these issues in her poetic adaptations, reenvisioning the tale through Persephone's eyes. "Persephone the Wanderer" analyzes Persephone through modern psychology, questioning whether she acquiesced to her rape. "The Myth of Innocence" sees Persephone seeking an escape from a life so close to her mother that she has no identity of her own. As such, she finds herself lost in love for the dark god, one who promises her a refuge out of sight of her family. As Persephone becomes the prize contested over by Demeter and Hades, the question remains—which is the best realm for her, heaven, hell, or earth? The pattern of the heroine's journey helps to supply an answer, for all myth is really humanity asking the deep questions of their souls as they struggle to find their place in the world.

Glück's opening describes the well-known myth as "the first version" (1) rather than the only or best one. This is intriguing, suggesting that this classic tale has far more to it than readers know. In fact, this "first version," best known from the Homeric Hymn to Demeter, is problematic from a gendered point of view. Persephone is kidnapped, helpless, sobbing for her father Zeus to save her (Homer 21–22). However, Zeus has callously handed her off to his brother, and neglected to inform Persephone or her mother of the fact. As the first line introduces the tale:

> I begin to sing of rich-haired Demeter, awful goddess—of her and her trim-ankled daughter whom Aidoneus [Hades] rapt away, given to him by all-seeing Zeus the loud-thunderer [Homer, 1–3].

Persephone lacks even a name here—she is little more than contested property.

Continuing with troubling aspects of the original tale, in an act of "negative creation" (10), as Glück calls it, Demeter withholds food from the earth after her beloved daughter Persephone is kidnapped. Here the feminine becomes vicious, letting seething rage conquer rationality and burning all of humanity because she cannot punish her brother, Hades. Glück calls this "consistent" with human behavior (5), but she might just as easily call it "stereotypical feminine behavior, succumbing to emotion and lashing out irrationally." This description, of course, is mitigated by the announcement that this is only the first version, the men's retelling of the story (and in fact, this story from Ovid's version to Homer's does come to us through male authors). Clearly, this first version is not the only one available, simply the best known: the tale of innocent flower princess, infuriated Demeter, grasping Hades. More is to come.

The title "Persephone the Wanderer" is intriguing in itself—Odysseus is called a "wanderer" in Greek myth, after ten years of travel. Hermes, Dionysus, and even Zeus are all male, all wanderers. The only female named "wanderer" in classic myth is Dido (whose name means wanderer), who ironically kills herself because she is forbidden to wander and follow her love. Perhaps stifled Persephone would have shared Dido's sad fate, torn between her birthplace and the love of a man, until, despairing, she cast herself on a pyre and perished. Only departing saves her.

Persephone, known for her single abduction, is not famous for her wanderings. However, the initial kidnap leads to the ongoing cycle of winter and warmth, steady as the lifecycle. Persephone, more than any other character in Greek myth, becomes the rhythm of the world and its seasons. Its pattern reflected people's most basic needs, physical and spiritual. Demetra George, author of *Mysteries of the Dark Moon: The Healing Power of the Dark Goddess*, notes:

> The light, visible full moon face of the Goddess is Demeter, who above earth gives the gift of food to nourish the living. The invisible dark moon face of the Goddess is Persephone, who, beneath the earth, gives the gift of renewal to regenerate the dead [George 252].

She becomes the force of the earth and with it, the heavens. The Greek term for "wanderer," *planētēs*, is the origin of the English word "planet." Here indeed is Persephone, traveling round and round on her journey.

In fact, after the intriguing connection to wandering in the title, the poem brings in a myriad of outside references, meant to construct a pebbled mosaic of an image when they are fitted together in their awkward jagged forms. Persephone has a brief visit to hell, a Christianized view of the place that makes her seem a saintly Beatrice only temporarily passing through its darkness while remaining pure and unsullied. Is she a victim of date-rape, like a teenager of today, "drugged, violated against her will / as happens so often now to modern girls"? (16–17). Or is this her choice, her willing scandal, which leaves her "stained with red juice like / a character in Hawthorne"? (22–23). Here she is Hester Prynne of *The Scarlet Letter*, of course, marked by the red badge of shame that emphasizes her culpability for the affair she willingly began out of passion, in defiance of the Puritan society that restricted her on all sides. These images conflict so wildly that a host of different Persephones stand side by side, all of them calling into doubt the original image of childlike daughter stolen and mother viciously scapegoating the world for this crime. Is she Dido? Beatrice? Hester Prynne? Or a yet older and more primal archetype waiting to burst forth and grow?

As revealed by the poem's end, this is not just the tale of an innocent princess dragged down to hell and sexuality by the dark god: "she has been a prisoner since she has been a daughter," Glück reveals (62). Demeter has been just as powerful a force in Persephone's life as Hades now is, smothering her with the overwhelming identity of mother and life force, the creator-goddess who feeds the entire world. Overshadowed by such a personality, how can Persephone grow beyond her role as child?

Further, the poem explains that the characters are not people but rather aspects to a conflict: id, ego, superego (36–38). Carl Jung and Joseph Campbell wrote of archetypes, seeing characters surrounding the hero as parts of him- or herself, concepts of the mind rather than characters. Here is the root of the tale—in archetype. Persephone is the naive child-princess all ready to embark on the classic heroine's journey, less publicized than the boy's tale, but echoing just as strongly back through ancient myth. Her name, Kore, simply means maiden, for she is the Divine Child, filled with glowing potential but awaiting a teacher to bring her to higher consciousness. The heroine's journey, like the hero's, sees the innocent child descending into the realm of death and discovering the hidden side of his or her nature, buried in the subconscious. By facing the Shadow, she triumphs over the rejected or unexplored half of herself—the devouring mother, killer of the innocent, and all the untried maiden is not. For Homer's Persephone, this figure is her mother.

Demeter in the "first version" of the tale as Glück identifies it is dismissed as the destructive mother, raging and destroying the earth when her role is to preserve it. However, in the Homeric version, she is the true "wanderer," questing across the world to find her child. Calling Persephone "the wanderer" emphasizes that she is an aspect of Demeter, mother and nature goddess, but the innocent part, the part that hasn't yet explored her own nature.

> Kore, meaning maiden, also means sprout, casting her as a "shoot" of her mother, both the same plant, as Persephone sinks into the ground and then revitalizes in spring. These figures are so similar-looking in ancient art that they could be considered the same goddess. Thus mother and daughter are a dual entity, one venturing below while the other wanders above [Frankel 261].

Persephone lives in the patriarchal religion of Zeus the sky god in a story retold by patriarchal Homer. Her role is to be demure, frightened, and acquiescent at her kidnaping into adulthood. Glück fashions a Persephone questing for more in life, rebellious even, as she prays for a path beyond her mother's immense shadow. She's eager for romance, titillated by Hades claiming her before Apollo, conflicted about leaving childhood behind. In short, Glück transforms her from object to person.

However, this is a story of separation, in which these goddesses, though so close, never interact. As Glück reveals, this tale is really a battle between mother and lover in which the daughter is "just meat" (87). Persephone's willingness or unwillingness—so important at the beginning of this poem—becomes meaningless, trapped as she is in a tug-of-war between mother and husband, the goddess of life and the god of death, primal forces of creation and destruction embodied. Persephone chooses both and neither, walking the balance that we call humanity—neither childishness nor death-dealing power, neither maiden nor queen, neither initiate nor judge of the dead, but all of these, shifting roles through the year is humanity itself must do, throughout the cycles that make up our lives.

> Persephone spends half her time as maiden and flower princess, helping Demeter as fertility goddess of the harvest. For the other half, she rules the dead as a crone. This dichotomy is perplexing, but less so if we understand the message contained here. Persephone is mistress of both life and death, using knowledge from one world to teach in the other. She is a true multifaceted and complete goddess [Frankel 181].

As Glück continues her poem-cycle, "A Myth of Innocence" describes "the horrible mantle / of daughterliness still clinging to her" (5–6). This makes Persephone sound like a gawky adolescent, embarrassed and outraged by her label of child, with no identity besides daughter to a goddess. To cast this off, she must go adventuring and become someone new, someone independent. This adolescent body is what she hates, the body of childishness, of the innocence of the poem's title, as she admits, *"I offered myself, I wanted / to escape my body"* (30–31). She wants to grow up, to be a woman, a goddess. So she chooses bridehood, chooses to leave the common world and venture below. As she prays for deliverance from her trapped, innocent state, Hades appears.

This juxtaposition shows Hades as called for and summoned, deliverer rather than kidnapper. Persephone is calling for a lover to bring her out of girlhood into the next phase of existence. This requires a descent into darkness, exploration of the subconscious shadow world. Hades becomes not only lover but guide as he whisks her into the underworld. She gives herself to "*Death, husband, god, stranger*" (37), and by opening herself to the wisdom they offer, she deepens.

Here is the heroine's journey, descending into death and returning with the new wisdom of adulthood. As Persephone notes, the girl is gone and will never return. Though the myth describes returning to daughterhood and girlhood each spring, this is a fallacy, for the new Persephone, though ever questing, ever wandering, has grown up. As such, she becomes a second Demeter, protecting the world of death as Demeter does the world of life. Both are guardians, beautiful in their divine femininity. Psychologist Erich Neumann describes the true mystery of the tale:

> The daughter becomes identical with the mother; she becomes a mother and is so transformed into Demeter. Precisely because Demeter and Kore are archetypal poles of the Eternal Womanly, the mature woman and the virgin, the mystery of the Feminine is susceptible of endless renewal [308–09].

The third poem in this cycle, "A Myth of Devotion," tells the story from Hades' perspective. In myth, he is the mysterious, unknowable god, with his voice and motives often shrouded. Glück's poem demystifies him, revealing his thoughts concerning the immature maiden. He lays a mirage of earth over the underworld for her, with everything the same as it is above, adding only a bed. To help her adjust, and he names this place "*Persephone's Girlhood*" (40). There, Persephone can experience sex, easing her from the reassuring childish world to a place of experience. From there, he will coax away the stars, the moon. This echoes another moment of the original Homeric hymn as Persephone is trapped in the underworld:

> And so long as she, the goddess [Persephone], yet beheld earth and starry heaven and the strong-flowing sea where fishes shoal, and the rays of the sun, and still hoped to see her dear mother and the tribes of the eternal gods, so long hope calmed her great heart [33–39].

While Persephone is still connected to earth, she is a part of it and her mother can hear her cries. But Persephone must at last part from daylight as she parts from girlhood and innocence. Hades proves her guide in all these things as he tells her the truth: He cannot tell her that nothing can hurt her anymore, for that is a lie, and Persephone is no longer the innocent found in the other poems—she has passed beyond. In the end, he tells her the more truthful, "*you're dead, nothing can hurt you*" (46). The underworld offers no comforting illusions, no childish safety. It is a place of stark reality and knowledge together, a place Persephone must visit within herself if she wishes to grow up.

> On an outer level the story of Persephone's annual disappearance and return was an allegory of the spring sprouting of the dormant winter seed, explaining the changing of the seasons to the peasants. On an inner level the reenactment of this ritual drama gave humanity access to the archetypal themes of loss and return. And on a secret level, as celebrated by the initiates of the Eleusinian Mysteries, this ritual revealed the great transformation mystery: the cycle of birth, death, and renewal [George 241].

In ancient Greece, the Eleusinian Mysteries reenacted the deeper emotions of this story in a sacred annual ritual. It offered a way for both men and women to connect with the sacred feminine. Upon arriving at Eleusis, the worshippers would fast, echoing Demeter's grief and withdrawal after the abduction. For nine days they imitated Demeter, offering sacrifices and drinking sacred barley-water by Demeter's well. Following this, initiates filed into the omphalos, navel of the world. Entering was like entering the dark stillness of death. Within, the priests began the Greater Mysteries, frightening the initiates with all the horrors of dying. After, a light shone, indicating the return to life. With it came a joyous shout: "The queen of the dead herself has given birth in fire to a mighty son!" (George 242–247; Kerenyi 93). Persephone's descent results in life, and with it the renewal of the world. Only through Hades, the force of death, can Persephone become the creator of life and continuer of the cycle.

> Demeter's mythic drama of separation, loss, and reunion with her child became a symbol for the continuity of life that circles and connects the world of the living to the world of the dead. The basic theme of the Mysteries was the eternal coming of life from death; the repeated celebration of these mysteries continued this cosmic event [George 251].

In Homer's version, she is a weeping child, kidnapped and dragged forcibly into adulthood. Glück's version sees her discontented with her lot, struggling to escape "the horrible mantle / of daughterliness" ("Myth of Innocence," 5–6) and summoning her dark guide in a prayer. He guides her gently into the underworld, offering her a magical bed in the underworld with the daylight world laid over it in a comforting illusion. Only after Persephone has absorbed this new life stage will Hades draw her in further to a world of knowledge and experience. Thus empowered, Persephone can return to the world, a goddess rather than an innocent.

WORKS CITED

Frankel, Valerie Estelle. *From Girl to Goddess: The Heroine's Journey through Myth and Legend.* Jefferson, NC: McFarland, 2010. Print.
George, Demetra. *Mysteries of the Dark Moon: The Healing Power of the Dark Goddess.* New York: HarperCollins, 1992. Print.
Glück, Louise. "A Myth of Devotion." *Averno: Poems.* USA: Macmillan, 2007. 58–59. Print.
_____. "A Myth of Innocence." *Averno: Poems.* USA: Macmillan, 2007. 50–51. Print.
_____. "Persephone the Wanderer." *Averno: Poems.* USA: Macmillan, 2007. 16–19. Print.

Hesiod. *Homeric Hymns. Homerica*. Trans. H G. Evelyn-White. *Loeb Classical Library Volume 57*. Cambridge, MA: Harvard University Press, 1914. Web. http://www.theoi.com/Text/HomericHymns1.html.
Kerenyi, Karl. *Eleusis: An Archetypal Image of Mother and Daughter*. Trans. Ralph Manheim. New York: Schocken, 1977. Print.
Neumann, Erich. *The Great Mother*. Trans. Ralph Manheim. Whitefish, MT: Kessinger, 2004. Print.

Reimagining Myth and the Maternal with Ruth Fainlight, Margaret Atwood and Katie Donovan

CHARLOTTE BEYER

Introduction: Myth and Women's Poetry

The critic Estella Lauter has asked the pertinent questions: "what is the *raison d'être* of myth for contemporary women? What leads women poets or artists to engage in mythmaking?" (209). This essay explores these and related questions regarding the use of mythology in contemporary women's poetry, drawing on selected examples from different cultural contexts in works by Ruth Fainlight (America/Britain), Margaret Atwood (Canada), and Katie Donovan (Ireland).[1] Myth is poignant to many contemporary women poets, and this significance is borne out by numerous conscious and unconscious links between writing and lived experience, as Halldis Leira and Madelien Krips suggest: "Mythology and historical psycho-cultural patterns have always influenced and dominated our lives, even though we are not always aware of the fact" (83). Such ideas and "patterns" are also central to poetry, although, as Sanja Bahun-Radunović and Julie V. G. Rajan note: "Traditionally, myth has reflected socio-political negotiations of femininity that privilege masculinity" (9). Commenting on the resonance of myth in women's creative endeavors, Leira and Krips state: "Themes from ancient mythology still command our attention, and these same themes are retold in modern literature and the arts" (83). Such questions have also been examined by Alicia Ostriker. Addressing the topic of the female poet's perspective and her willingness to seek inspiration in diverse places, Ostriker enquires: "Does the marginal position of the woman poet generate a different way of thinking about politics or history, or even language itself?" (5). Certainly, this questioning of convention is evident in the work of the women poets discussed here, particularly when it comes to the subject of myth and women's responses to it. My essay focuses on the representations and implications of the revision of myth in women's poetry, including in teaching contexts, with a particular emphasis on representations of femininity, the body and maternal figures, and draws on a range of critical and theoretical approaches, including feminist literary theory. Through these discussions, I suggest that contemporary women's poetry recasts myth to challenge and subvert dominant cultural narratives and representations, and thereby offers complex and empowering portrayals of female identity which interrogate the gender coding inscribed in mythology.

Explorations of Mythic Resonances

Contemporary women poets recast myths in a number of ways, from exploring particular figures of mythic resonance, to revising ideas and patterns. As I have shown elsewhere, the poetic form is uniquely adaptable to women's exploration and revision of patriarchal discourses due to its imaginative potential (Beyer, "Feminist Revisionist Mythology" 277). Through their poems, women reimagine oppressive depictions of females and one-dimensional constructions of femininity. Importantly, such textual revisionings also expand the parameters of the literary canon to include marginalized female poetic voices, as argued by Lauter, Ostriker, Yorke, and others. This endeavor is discussed by Heather Walton (543), Liz Yorke (14), and Ostriker (105) who all cite Adrienne Rich's essay "When We Dead Awaken: Writing as Re-Vision" as an important critical reflection on strategies for resisting the dominant ideology and literary establishment and presenting counter-discursive alternatives.[2] Ostriker's analysis of contemporary women's poetry and explorations of gender and creativity, in her book *Writing Like a Woman*, also offers an insightful examination of women's rewriting of myth (132).[3] Commenting on the significance of these aspects of cultural and literary production, Yorke states: "The revisionary task of reminiscence and retrieval also involves *re-inscription*, a process in which the old narratives, stories, scripts, mythologies, become transvalued, re-presented in different terms" (1). Such strategies are emulated and creatively developed in women's poetic representations of myth. This section of my essay focuses on the poetic contexts and practices of recasting myths and tales that present one-dimensional constructions of femininity, the female body and identity, and their reworking in contemporary women's poetry by reimagining mythic or powerful figures.

These discussions are explored through reference to selected poems by Ruth Fainlight and Katie Donovan.

The first poem in this part of my discussion examines problematizations of knowledge, creativity and female identity. In her 1980 collection *Sibyls and Others*,[4] the American-born British poet Ruth Fainlight (Duffy) explores the evocative mythic figure of the sibyl in a series of reflective poems (Beyer, "Ruth Fainlight" 129–130). This move, according to Fiona Cox, could be seen as Fainlight's response to finding herself "on the edge" both of the canon and British culture (49). In classical mythology, a sibyl represents various dimensions—she is a prophetess (Morford and Lenardon 170), but also an author (Parker and Stanton 200) who writes her prophesies on leaves (Morford and Lenardon 170). The sibyl therefore emerges as a multi-faceted and creative figure representing female authority. Fainlight's poems use the sibyl to highlight these connections and examine their gender political dimensions, the significance of which critics have reflected on in more general terms:

> Tales of this and other Sibyls have repeatedly been re-appropriated to forge an image of the female artist as a visionary whose fate could be seen as paradigmatic of the female artist in a chiefly male-organized official culture [Bahun-Radunović and Rajan 4].

Such allusions are echoed in Fainlight's use of the sibyl motif. Commenting on Fainlight's employment of the sibyl, the critic Lidia Vianu, in her interview with the poet herself, observes: "The sibyl is a favorite mask, maybe the only one, with you. The sibyl is the poet, the seer, sensibility, tragedy, art, the whole wide and doomed world" ("Writers" 121). The final poem of the sequence, entitled "Introspection of a Sibyl," reflects on the inner thoughts of the sibyl persona through a first person perspective (169–170). Referring to the emotional significance of the figure, Fainlight states in her interview with Vianu: "The Sibyl was a perfect vehicle to express some of my deepest feelings" ("Writers" 125). The affective dimension of the figure adds to the poignancy of Fainlight's poems. Her "sibyl" poems thus rework a specific motif and persona from myth in a variety of ways, in order to investigate aspects of femininity, corporeality, and creativity (Beyer "Ruth Fainlight" 130). Or, as Cox states in her analysis of Fainlight's "sibyl" poems: "The sibyl is an exemplar of [...] a woman too disruptive and disturbing to be allowed (or to want) full access into society" (49). The sibyl comes to represent the female poet, her wisdom and insight, but also to problematize the gender politics of creativity.

The second poem specifically reimagines the female body through myth. The Irish poet Katie Donovan's poem "At Queen Medb's Cairn" from her 1993 collection *Watermelon Man* (87)[5] is rooted in the poetic persona's personal process of discovery. As Gerold Sedlmayr argues, Donovan's poetry portrays "the ageing body, myth and language" (272). Importantly, this portrayal of Medb uncovers a powerful symbolic female figure who reflects a specifically

Irish cultural and literary heritage, a topic also treated elsewhere in Donovan's poetry (Beyer, "Katie Donovan" 91). As Brendan Kennelly further states:

> The history, or herstory, of Irish women is rather like that of the Irish language—much talked about but little heard. Of recent years, however, Irish women have been discovering, or re-discovering, their own voices, with beneficial consequences [Donovan, Jeffares, and Kennelly xx].

Medb challenges conventional feminine stereotypes of feminine subservience. Drawing on the figure of Medb, a "queen and warrior-goddess" (Parker and Stanton 226), Donovan creates an image of a defiant female figure whose body possesses enormous powers when released. Using a symbolically resonant location, the poem "At Queen Medb's Cairn" describes the speaker's act of honoring Medb's female power, as Donovan explains ("Interview"). In her interview with Melissa Thompson, Donovan reflects on her fascination with Medb and the physical power of the female body, describing how: "urine actually comes out with a lot of force, especially in Medb's case. It came out with spectacular force. Three rivers worth" ("Interview"). Heather Walton observes, in referring to Ostriker's discussions of feminist revisionist myth and the female body: "a woman poet using transgressive bodily metaphors in the retelling of authoritative narratives can have a particularly disturbing impact upon received understandings" (547). Thus, towards the poem's end, the poetic persona's sense of solidarity and physical identification suggests that Medb's symbolic power has communicated itself to the speaker (Donovan 87), in a confirmation of continuity underpinned by mythic resonance.

These representations of the female body, knowledge and power are important, because they reflect the richness of myth and foreground strong, complex female figures. Yorke's point echoes this. She argues:

> Women writers and poets are creating fictional work—stories, myths, tales—that are rooted in the historical body, in the materiality of women's experience in real life. In doing so, they are giving voice to a largely unlistened-to dimension of experience [4].

By recasting mythology, contemporary women poets illustrate the relevance of these ancient texts and widen their continued appeal to a broad readership, because of what they say about female strength, but also because of what they suggest about the limitations imposed on women.

Reimaging the Maternal

In contemporary women's poetry, motifs and figures from myth are used in creative recastings of motherhood and maternal figures. These endeavors have culminated in complex and thought-provoking reimaginings of maternal authority. Contemporary women poets' engagements with myth rethink how motherhood and the maternal body have conventionally been understood, including their representation in what Leira and Krips call "cultural myths" (83). My discussion of myth and mothers involves a reflection on the significance of such "cultural myths" and popular conceptions of the mother figure and maternal experience.[6] In her discussion of these dimensions, and referring to a range of feminist critics, Meryle Mahrer Kaplan states: "The idea of a socially supported and defined 'myth' or 'institution' of motherhood is shared by many feminist writers" (7).[7] However, because "mythological themes and figures are human constructions" (Halldis and Krips 85), when used or evoked in women's poetry, they may engender a complex and nuanced engagement from readers and students of poetry. I have previously commented on the importance of reader identification and emotional engagement in teaching and learning (Beyer, "Exploring Postcolonial" 98–99; Beyer, "The Stuff of Legend" 400–401).[8] This point also relates to the "flash of connection" which frequently inspires women's revisions of myth in poetry, according to Ostriker (133). Examining the role of mythology in reimagining how maternal experience (and female experience more generally) has been represented and communicated leads to the opening up of new areas of critical discussion of women's poetry. With this in mind, I consider three different poetic interpretations of maternal figures in myth by Margaret Atwood, Ruth Fainlight and Katie Donovan.

In Margaret Atwood's poem "A Red Shirt" from the 1978 collection *Two-Headed Poems*,[9] the emphasis is on an instructive dimension, which highlights the aspects of intergenerational relationships between females and issues of communication.[10] "A Red Shirt" portrays the speaker and her sister sewing a garment for her young daughter. Sharon Wilson states that the poem, in reflecting on the symbolic allusions of the color red, makes reference to H.C. Andersen's fairy-tale "The Red Shoes" (121) and its "moralistic story line" (125), as well as to a range of female-centered myths evoked by the speaker to counter those messages, such as the "goddess myth" (132). Atwood's "A Red Shirt" illustrates how individual poems using motifs or elements from myth may also facilitate a maternal speaking voice within the mother-child relationship. The poem furthermore suggests that poetry may be shared and enable further communication between different generations of females, and between mother and daughter, thereby encouraging feminist consciousness-raising and reconnection.[11]

The project of re-imagining the maternal body through the prism of myth is the focus for the next two poems in my discussion. These texts use motifs from mythology in order to explore different allusions associated with maternal corporeality. Ruth Fainlight's poem "Squatting at the Womb's Mouth" (364), from her 1991 poem sequence *Twelve Sibyls*,[12] is centered on the startlingly physical image of the sibyl bringing forth her own emergent persona. This empowering vision is encapsulated in the physical imagery suggested by the poem's title. Through the commanding figure of the sibyl, the poem engenders a double perspective whereby the sibyl, observed by the speaker, is both delivering and being delivered. The poem's use of organic metaphors and imagery adds further dimension to Fainlight's representation of the sibyl recreating herself through this corporeal deed. "Squatting at the Womb's Mouth" echoes the act of self-creation, both in its linguistic act of articulation, and in reclaiming this intriguing and powerful sibyl figure. The bringing forth of one's own being suggests a measure of symbolic and physical autonomy from male-defined structures, and an ability to regenerate and recast the self, which also chimes more widely with the use of revisionist mythology in contemporary women's poetry.

In the third poem to be examined, Katie Donovan makes specific reference to Irish mythology and its depiction of maternal figures. Donovan uses the Irish myth of Macha to re-imagine female strength and the mother in her powerful poem "Macha's Curse" (133–136), from the collection *Entering the Mare* (1997).[13] In the ancient Irish myth of Macha, this female figure is depicted as a pawn used by her husband Crunnchu, and forced to race against the King's horses although she is pregnant, as Penny McCracken explains: "Running alongside the chariot pulled by King's horses, [Macha] gives birth to twins and curses the men who would not defer the race" (26). I have suggested elsewhere that, in the poem "Macha's Curse," Donovan's "tone and vocabulary emulates a folk tale or folk song, re-imagining this ancient tale of female authority and strength" (Beyer, "Katie Donovan" 92). This display of authority extends beyond the myth and individual female figure in its implications and appeal. Donovan's poem looks to Irish myth to identify creative "foremothers," female figures who embody resistance and power, and who present examples of the realities of maternal experience.

Brendan Kennelly comments on the tradition within Irish myth of portraying female authority, stating: "The ancient mythology of Ireland features many powerful, aggressive women who take the sexual initiative, run the show and dictate the fun" (Donovan, Jeffares, and Kenelly xxi). In Donovan's poem "Macha's Curse," Macha resists attempts to subject her to patriarchal domination, through insisting on her physical power and perseverance (136). Instead, she finds the inner resources which allow her to prevail; the poem itself becomes a linguistic extension of her strength, by adopting the manner of a spell (136), which contributes to its resonance and depth. In an interview, Donovan comments on her poetic portrayal of Macha, and what this mythic figure represents to her: "I love Macha and I love the idea of a woman getting her revenge because women aren't supposed to have low thoughts like this" ("Interview"). This is an important act of revision, as Kennelly suggests: "The articulate consciousness of many Irish women is re-interpreting the past and deeply influencing the present. There's a freshness in these deliberate acts of re-interpretation, as well as a note of passionate understanding" (Donovan, Jeffares, and Kenelly xxiii).

Exploring these poetic representations of maternal experience and corporeality, the depictions of the mother-daughter relationship, and their grounding in mythology, enables us to assess the multi-dimensional quality of contemporary women's poetry. Furthermore, Leira and Krips argue, such myths are "compelling because they mirror our own lives and the dramas which are enacted in our minds and experiences" (83). This last assessment reflects the link between mythological motifs and narratives, and their enduring creative significance for women, but also raises further questions about mainstream responses to, and inclusion of, women's perspectives in poetry.

Conclusion: Creativity in Poetry

Drawing on selected examples, my essay has examined how contemporary women's poetry illustrates diverse recastings of myth and elements from myth. Commenting on the creative innovation that this represents, Bahun-Radunović and Rajan state that "female artists re-appropriate myth, a traditional tool of patriarchy, as a mode of expressing their own creativity in innovative [...] ways" (15). Thus, we have seen how contemporary women's poetry employs myth to represent complex ideas regarding female identity, the body, affect, creativity, and maternal experience. The emphasis in contemporary women's poetry, in relation to myth, is on reimagining motifs and constructions of gendered identity, Yorke states. She has it that: "'writing the experience' and 'writing the body' are both revisionary projects, and both are essential strategies for a feminist poetic" (Yorke 2). Bahun-Radunović and Rajan echo this assertion, arguing that contemporary women poets use myth in personal and subjective ways, but also "to speak to global and local historical and political experiences" (5). These are important questions for women, both in private and personal relations, and in creative and instructive contexts. Yorke reminds us that, far from being elitist or obscure, such recastings of myth can have a real bearing on women's lives: "The concept of *re-vision* also carries suggestive possibilities for the construction within culture of an alternative field of identification, inviting a new attitude or exploring a fresh perspective for 'real-life' women" (15). This acknowledgment is perhaps the most significant aspect of the employment of myth in contemporary women's poetry, particularly seen from a teaching and learning perspective. It is precisely the ability of these poetic texts to speak to individuals and collectives, and offer them new inspirations and prospects, which is so poignant and has such resonance for women as educators, readers, and poets.

Notes

1. My essay refers to manifestations of myth from various cultural contexts and employs a broad definition of the term. The poems I use as examples are intended to be illustrative.
2. I also discuss Rich's essay, in Beyer, "Feminist Revisionist Mythology" p. 279. The essay is also cited in Cox p. 12.
3. In Beyer, "Feminist Revisionist Mythology," which examines Atwood's poems in *Interlunar* and *Morning in the Burned House*, I also discuss Ostriker's examinations of myth and revisionism, see pp. 278–9.
4. Reprinted in *New & Collected Poems* (2010). Page references to this edition.
5. Reprinted in *Rootling: New and Selected Poems* (2010). Page references to this edition.
6. I also examined mothering and dimensions of the maternal in Jackie Kay's poetry; see Beyer, "Exploring Postcolonial and Feminist Issues."
7. Kaplan references Carolyn G. Heilbrun, *Reinventing Womanhood*, Julia Kristeva, "Women's Time," Adrienne Rich *Of Woman Born*, and Sara Ruddick *Maternal Thinking: Towards a Politics of Peace*, among others.
8. I have discussed aspects of undergraduate teaching and learning and mythological material in a recent article; see Beyer, "The Stuff of Legend."
9. Reprinted in *Selected Poems II: 1976–1986*, pp. 47–51.
10. Palmer (p. 112) and (p. 126) presents a wider discussion of these issues in contemporary women's writing.
11. See also Groen (pp. 103–4) for illuminating discussions of this topic.
12. Reprinted in *New & Collected Poems*. Page references to this edition.
13. Reprinted in *Rootling: New and Selected Poems*. Page references to this edition.

Works Cited

Atwood, Margaret. *Selected Poems II: 1976–1986*. Boston: Houghton Mifflin Co, 1987.
Bahun-Radunović, Sanja and Rajan, and V. G. Julie. "Introduction: Cassandra's Gift." *Myth and Violence in the Contemporary Female Text: New Cassandras*. Sanja Bahun-Radunović and Rajan, V. G. Julie, eds. Farnham: Ashgate, 2011. 1–18.
_____, _____, and _____, eds. *Myth and Violence in the Contemporary Female Text: New Cassandras*. Farnham: Ashgate, 2011.
Beyer, Charlotte. "Exploring Postcolonial and Feminist Issues: Rabbit-Proof Fence in a Teaching Context." *Changing English: Studies in Culture and Education* 17.1 (2010): 93–101.
_____. "Feminist Revisionist Mythology and Female Identity in Margaret Atwood's Recent Poetry." *Literature and Theology* 14.3 (2000).
_____. "Imagining Mother: Representations of Contested Maternal Identities and Loss in Jackie Kay's *The Adoption Papers* and Isha McKenzie-Mavinga's 'Yearning To Belong.'" *MP: An Online Feminist Journal* 2.6 (2010): 72–83. Web. 20 July 2014.
_____. "Katie Donovan, *Rootling: New and Selected Poems*." Review. *Iota* 90, 2011. 91–92.
_____. "Ruth Fainlight, *New & Collected Poems*." Review. *Iota* 93 (2013): 128–131.
_____. "The Stuff of Legend, or Unpacking Cultural Baggage? Introducing First-year English Literature and Humanities Students to Foundational Literary Texts." *Changing English: Studies in Culture & Education* 20.4 (2013): 395–403. Cox, Fiona. *Sibylline Sisters: Virgil's Presence in Contemporary Women's Writing*. Oxford: Oxford University Press, 2011.

Donovan, Katie. "Interview with Katie Donovan, November 8, 1998." Interview with Melissa Thompson. *Mary Mary: A Documentary About Women, Ireland and Change.* 18 April 2014. http://www.tallgirlshorts.net/marymary/katietext.html.
_____. *Rootling: New and Selected Poems.* Tarset: Bloodaxe Books Ltd, 2010.
_____, A. Norman Jeffares, and Kennelly, Brendan, eds. "Introductions by the Editors." *Ireland's Women: Writings Past and Present.* London: W.W. Norton & Co., 1994. xvii–xii.
Duffy, Carol Ann. "Older and Wiser: Carol Ann Duffy Introduces Poems of Ageing." *The Guardian* 13 March 2010. 18 April 2014. http://www.guardian.co.uk/books/2010/mar/13/carol-ann-duffy-poems-ageing.
Fainlight, Ruth. *New & Collected Poems.* Tarset: Bloodaxe Books, 2010.
_____. "Writers Can Have Some Effect on the World at Large." Two Interviews with Lidia Vianu. *Desperado Essay-Interviews.* Ed. Vianu Lidia Bucharest: Editura Pentru Literatură Contemporană. Contemporary Literature Press. 2009. 109–129. http://www.unibuc.ro/n/resurse/docs/2011/feb/28_11_55_21lidiavianu.desp-interviews.pdf.
Groen, Martine. "Mother-Daughter, the Black Continent: Is a Multicultural Future Possible?" Verhulst, Schreurs, and Woertman 94–105.
Kaplan, Meryle Mahrer. *Mothers' Images of Motherhood: Case Studies of Twelve Mothers.* London: Routledge, 1992.
Lauter, Estella. *Women as Mythmakers: Poetry and Visual Art by Twentieth-Century Women.* Bloomington: Indiana University Press, 1984.
Leira, Halldis and Madelien Krips. "Revealing Cultural Myths on Motherhood." Verhulst, Schreurs, and Woertman 80–83.
McCracken, Penny. *The Curse of Eve, the Wound of the Hero: Blood, Gender, and Medieval Literature.* Philadelphia: University of Pennsylvania Press, 2003.
Morford, Mark P. O. and Lenardon, Robert J. *Classical Mythology, Sixth Edition.* Oxford: Oxford University Press, 1971, 1999.
Ostriker, Alicia. *Writing Like a Woman.* Ann Arbor: University of Michigan Press, 1983.
Palmer, Paulina, *Contemporary Women's Fiction: Narrative Practice and Feminist Theory.* London: Harvester, 1989.
Parker, Janet and Julie Stanton, eds. *Mythology: Myths, Legends and Fantasies.* Cape Town, South Africa: Struik, 2006.
Rich, Adrienne. "When We Dead Awaken: Writing as Re-Vision." *On Lies, Secrets and Silence: Selected Prose 1966–1978.* New York: Norton, 1979. 33–49.
Sedlmayr, Gerold. "Sexuality, Monstrosity and Mythology in Contemporary Irish Women's Poetry." *The Body and the Book: Writings on Poetry and Sexuality.* Glennis Byron and Andrew J. Sneddon, eds. Amsterdam: Rodopi, 2008. 257–273.
Verhulst, Janneke van Mens; Karlein Schreurs, and Liesbeth Woertman, eds. *Daughtering and Mothering: Female Subjectivity Reanalysed.* London: Routledge, 1993, 1998.
Walton, Heather. "Feminist Revisioning." *The Oxford Handbook of Literature and Theology.* Andrew W. Hass, David Jasper, and Elizabeth Jay, eds. Oxford: Oxford University Press, 2007. 543–557.
Wilson, Sharon Rose. *Margaret Atwood's Fairy-Tale Sexual Politics.* Jackson: University Press of Mississippi, 1993.
Yorke, Liz. *Impertinent Voices: Subversive Strategies in Contemporary Women's Poetry.* London: Taylor & Francis, 1991.

"Out of the Ash I Rise"
Sylvia Plath and the Rebirth of the Woman Poet

Kate Williams

Sylvia Plath is a necessary writer to bring into the conversation about the mythology of women writers in the twentieth century because Plath herself has become a mythical figure. Readers and critics are obsessed with her life and more importantly her death by suicide, which is generally accepted as a self-fulfilling prophesy. Knowing that her poetry is being read as personal, Plath creates her speakers as mythological figures who pervert the traditional structure of man as hero and woman as muse. Most menacingly in her *Ariel* poem "Lady Lazarus," Plath invokes the Biblical legend of Lazarus and the mythological figure of the Phoenix to create a poem that is as chilling as it is empowering. Here, Plath seeks to regain total autonomy over her voice and body by creating a vengeful figure that forces her voyeuristic audience to watch her reveal her true independent self. "Lady Lazarus" is useful to read when considering Plath's use of mythology because it is the figure she seems to have most internalized in the months leading up to her suicide. Like Lady Lazarus, Plath's power lies in her ability to terrify her audience, and she uses horrifying images in her poem to create a new mythological experience in literature: the rebirth of the modern woman poet.

Plath is placed in the school of confessional poetry among writers like Robert Lowell, John Berryman, and Anne Sexton. The concept of poetry as confessional is not new to the twentieth century. Women poets had been thought of as personal and confessional since the nineteenth century even though, as Elizabeth Petrino argues, "writing in an era of political, religious, and artistic ferment, nineteenth-century American women writers were vitally engaged in bringing about social and political change" (123–4). And yet their work was, for the most part, unappreciated by men. Women were viewed as emotional, and their poems were construed as being "affective, 'natural,' and spontaneous," not artistic. Critics esteemed women as "unconscious wellsprings of emotion," not as poets (Petrino 124).

By the end of the nineteenth century, women poets were beginning to write in what we now consider to be a modernist style: "the modernism in imagist poets, such as Amy Lowell and H.D., who stress imagery, aesthetic restraint, and an increasingly open poetic form, is already evident in poets from the 1870s and 1880s" (Petrino 136). Women were stepping outside of the private sphere and their role as the "angel in the house," and into the more public sphere by stating their opinions candidly to whomever would read their words. Petrino writes that, "although they cultivated a public persona and were widely known for poems that appealed to the masses, many female poets also wrote lyrics that expressed emotions barely considered printable in their eras" (123). Such women writers as Helen Hunt Jackson, Lizette Woodworth Reese, and Emily Dickinson took risks by defying the notion that they were the weaker sex and rejected a culture that insisted that they limit themselves to the confines of the private, domestic sphere. As we can see from such early modernists as Amy Lowell, H.D. and Gertrude Stein, by the twentieth century women openly rejected hiding in the privacy of their domestic space while men ruled the public sphere.

These early women modernists proved that they were no longer acquiescent to male poets, not only through their poetry and their candid discussions of society and politics, but also through their very lifestyles. Being a wife, mother and poet did not seem to be a possibility in the nineteenth and early twentieth centuries because women were still expected to devote their lives to their husband and children with little or no outside interests during this time. Marianne Moore, for example, never married and Mina Loy left her children for years while she pursued her writing career across the Atlantic.

This idea that motherhood had to be separated from authorship was changing by the mid-twentieth century. Plath insisted on her own maternity, and she writes in her *Journals* that if she could not have children "I would be dead. Dead to my woman's body. Intercourse would be dead, a dead-end. My pleasure no pleasure, a mockery. My writing a hollow and failing substitute for real life, real feeling, instead of a pleasant extra, a bonus flowering and fruiting. Ted should be a patriarch. I a mother" (500). Plath desperately wanted to have children, an ambition that women poets earlier in the century were often willing to forfeit for the career of poetry. Womanhood, especially motherhood, in poetry continued to be defined as odd and unimportant, and tension emerged in not only the day-to-day lives of women poets who found themselves torn between their domestic responsibilities and their artistic strivings but also in the way that female experience was not accorded the status of universality. In contrast to earlier women writers, women in the twentieth century were not afraid to write about motherhood, pregnancy and abortion in direct and often non-sentimental ways. Yet when they did so, their writing was construed as overtly emotional and confessional rather than as serious and objective because their experiences were particular to women. The fact that women were read as personal rather than universal, then, has much more to do with subject matter than with style. Because so many poems she wrote were based on her life story, many critics accepted that Plath only wrote about on her own experiences, thus her dark *Ariel* poems are often read as only the inner workings of a suicidal mind instead of as the work of a masterful poet.

Considering that the confessional movement to which Plath belonged was founded by Robert Lowell, twentieth-century women's poetry is not alone in being read as personal. The difference, however, is that Lowell is a self-proclaimed confessional poet. His poetry is defined by its intentionally personal nature. Women writers, on the other hand, have historically been read as personal poets regardless of whether or not they actively write poetry about their real-life experiences. Sandra Gilbert writes:

> While the male poet, even at his most wretched and alienated, can at least solace himself with his open or secret creativity, his mythmaking power, the female poet must come to terms with the fact that as a female she is that which is mythologized, the incarnation of otherness ... and hence the object of anthologies full of male metaphors [447].

I argue that the fact that women's being so mythologized by male writers is precisely why Plath mythologizes herself—she purposely puts her speakers in the same role that a man would, only instead of being the quiet muse or the goddess, she is the angry phoenix, ready to eat her prey. Her speakers are needed by the male figures of authority, though they are not seen as muses. Instead, the speakers have the ability to either keep the patriarch in power or destroy him completely. The mythologized woman, then, becomes the powerful figure who has the patriarch as her muse.

Plath most deliberately and forcefully perverts standard notions of mythology in the poem "Lady Lazarus." Lady Lazarus is a modern female version of the male Lazarus whom Jesus raised from the dead. The feminized Lazarus, however, is less sympathetic than the Biblical one. In the Bible, Lazarus dies from an illness and Jesus raises him from the dead to prove his supernatural ability. There are two important distinctions here between the two Lazarus.' Biblical Lazarus needed a divine figure to bring him back to life. Lady Lazarus, by contrast, has the self-generated ability to raise herself from the dead. Also unlike the Biblical Lazarus, Lady Lazarus is responsible for her close encounters with death instead of dying by illness, calling her ability to die repeatedly "an art," which she performs "exceptionally well" (43–45).

Lady Lazarus has survived three suicide attempts, and she imagines her escapes from death, as much as her close encounters with it, as enviable accomplishments to be revered. To Lady Lazarus, the ultimate glory is in returning from the dead, and she revels in her audience's proclamation of her survival as "a miracle!" (55). Lady Lazarus's attempted suicide is not a cry for help, yet she does not actually want to die. She instead wants the attention of her audience and the awe that accompanies seeing a person raise herself from the dead. In this way, she is more aligned with Jesus than with the Biblical Lazarus because both Lady Lazarus and Jesus use their powers to prove to disbelievers that they truly have this divine power.

Lady Lazarus further aligns herself with Jesus in her miraculous ability to heal other people. After witnessing the miracle that Lady Lazarus performs, she imagines people will crowd around her wanting to hear her speak, or to touch a piece of her hair or clothing. Similarly, Jesus' followers believe that he has the power to heal a person just by his touch. However, unlike with Jesus, it is unclear who levies the charge and profits from it with Lady Lazarus. It seems likely that Herr Doktor nominates profits from displaying her as a medical miracle. Lady Lazarus recognizes that she is being used by the doctors to advance their science and seems to revel in her status as a miracle. She wants people to believe that she really is able to heal them just by touching them. She becomes a demonic Jesus figure, a more human version of the man who, according to Christian doctrine, scarified his own life to save the world from sin. Lady Lazarus sacrifices her life for her own gain, which is why she warns God and Lucifer: "Out of the ash / I rise with my red hair / And I eat men like air" (81–84).

By warning both God and Lucifer, Lady Lazarus demonstrates that she is not a force of evil or good. She is something else entirely, otherworldly, more powerful than the most controlling forces in the universe. Like God, she has the power to heal people. Like Lucifer, she wants to use her power for her own advantage rather than to actually help people. She has traits of the two most powerful beings and, on top of that, she is human. As Alicia Striker Ostriker argues, "'Lady Lazarus' reduces Lucifer, God, the killer of the Jews, and the poet's doctor to a single brutal exploitative figure" (102). She is God, Lucifer, and Jesus all rolled into one person. And this is a very dangerous combination. According to Christian doctrine, God and Lucifer are the supreme, immortal forces who control the world. By warning them that she is going to rise from the ash, Lady Lazarus threatens the most powerful forces of good and evil. They should fear her immortality and recognize her as a separate, unnatural force.

Although she credits herself with the accomplishment of rising from the dead, Lady Lazarus is actually saved by human doctors. Rather than divine intervention, then, this modern Lazarus receives medical intervention. She is not in control of her own body but is at the mercy of the male doctor who brings her back to life and unbandages her. Lady Lazarus does not view her doctor as her savior, however, and insists that she is responsible, at least this third time, for her defeat over death. Herr Doktor makes the decision to save Lady Lazarus's life. He interferes with her suicide attempt, thereby snatching her autonomy away from her.

Herr Doktor's "unmasking" of Lady Lazarus should, by all logic, reveal her naked and therefore true self. Yet it is precisely her nakedness that is most artificial. Katherine Margaret Lant asserts that, "for the male writers, the unclothed body of the male speaker betokens joyous transcendence, freedom, power," but in Plath's work "the body stands not as a shimmering emblem of the soul's glory but seems, rather, an embarrassing reminder of the self's failures, an icon of the poet's vulnerability" (624, 625). Lady Lazarus's nakedness does not give her physical power. When her bandages are removed she is a terrifying figure of "skin and bone," a reminder of what she has attempted to do and the fact that she could not even succeed in killing herself (39). Lant states that, "what seemed most difficult for [Plath] to overcome was her very real awareness of the female body as vulnerable" (633). Throughout her *Journals* and poems Plath constantly refers to the female body as victimized because, as Lant explains, "the unclothed male body is—in terms of the dominant figurative systems of Western discourse—powerful in that it is sexually potent, sexually armed; the naked female body is ... vulnerable in that it is sexually accessible, susceptible to penetration, exploitation, rape, pregnancy" (626). In order to cover up this vulnerability, Plath creates the persona of Lady Lazarus who asserts complete control over her own body. She can bring herself back from the dead and use it to seduce, awe, terrify, and eat her audience. The persona of Lady Lazarus allows Plath to articulate both vulnerability and a desire for invulnerability. Her power lies in her awareness that her physical presence is terrifying.

Lady Lazarus's reference to the phoenix in the final lines of the poem is clearly an invocation of ancient mythology, which demonstrates that she is intent on mythologizing the female experience. By the end of the poem, the reader wants to believe that Lady Lazarus really is a phoenix. Readers are the "peanut crunching crowd" who wait with eager anticipation to see this dead woman re-birth herself and rise from the dead in the purely mythological form of the phoenix (32). Readers act as voyeurs to Lady Lazarus's transformation and want her to turn into a mythological creature in order to justify the mythologizing image of the woman that has undoubtedly been created in the mind.

Because of the dramatic conditions surrounding her death, Plath's later poems are often read solely in terms of her suicide. Plath thus becomes a mythological figure herself, a symbol for women who struggle to be both successful career women and loving mothers and wives. The reification of the woman poet is not unique to Plath, but she is the poet who seems to have internalized the professional/domestic dichotomy to the greatest degree in her work and personal life. She was obsessed with the tension between being a woman and a poet, and she struggled to strike a balance between the requirements of art and domesticity throughout her poetic career. The dual obligation of poetry and motherhood is one that Plath did not take lightly, and she made it her life's work to achieve both. She was not alone in her struggle to maintain a household and a career. Suzanne Juhasz argues, "Poets until mid-century, like Moore, striving for public recognition, try to live out the split demanded of them between 'woman' and 'poet'—to play by the boys' rules. This necessitates leaving feminine experience out of art; leaving it at home and in the kitchen. By doing so, some women get themselves admitted into the fraternity" (4). However, Juhasz continues, "throughout the century, women have sought to find voices in which they could speak as poets. Some of the difficulty that they have experienced in being heard comes from the strain of trying to make one sound out of two conflicted selves" (5). According to Juhasz, the woman poet exists as a divided self: woman and poet are separate entities that coexist but cannot reconcile. She can never be simultaneously a woman and a poet because as a woman she has to attend to her domestic duties that do not include creatively engaging in a man's world. Juhasz defines Plath as "the woman poet of our century who sees the problem, the situation of trying to be a woman poet with the coldest and most unredeeming clarity, and who, try as she might, finds no solution" (114). This double bind, the warring of two separate selves living within one entity, Juhasz argues, ultimately led Plath to take her life.

Plath felt a special kinship with Lady Lazarus because she too survived a suicide attempt. Like Lady Lazarus, Plath was impressed with her own escape from death. In the Cambridge section of her *Journals*, written in the years 1955–57, she writes, "I feel like Lazarus: that story has such fascination. Being dead, I rose up again, and even resort to the mere sensation value of being suicidal, of getting so close, of coming out of the grave with the scars and the marring mark on my cheek which (is it my imagination?) grows more prominent" (99). It is difficult to ignore Plath's suicide efforts when reading her poems, yet it is reductive to read her poems only in relation to the way her life ended. Plath's close friend and critic A. Alvarez understands Plath's poems as being partly responsible for her depression and suicide rather than as symptom of Plath's mental state, arguing that "for the artist himself art is not necessarily therapeutic; he is not automatically relieved of his fantasies by expressing them. Instead, by some perverse logic of creation, the act of formal expression may simply make the dredged-up material more readily available to him" (38). Alvarez suggests that Plath decided to kill herself precisely because she created personae that killed themselves in her poetry. Plath really saw herself as Lady Lazarus and thought that she would once again survive this attempt. This theory suggests that Plath assumed the mask of "Lady Lazarus," and what initially began as a fictional persona became a true identity. Plath sought to enter and return from the world of the dead, becoming a literal Aeneas or Dante, thus blurring for herself the lines between her poetry and her life, myth and reality.

Sylvia Plath is a talented poet who has found her place in the canon of twentieth-century poetry primarily through the myth created by her suicide. She mythologized her female speakers in an effort to direct how she would be mythologized herself. Her use of mythology in her writing, particularly in "Lady Lazarus," demonstrates that her poetry should be read as more than just insight to her psyche during the last few months of her life. Plath's work is an example of the anxiety male poets felt toward women and a justification for their fear. The mythological phoenix figure she re-imagines in "Lady Lazarus" is a warrior figure, a woman who is prepared to fight for her poetic voice to be heard. By "eat[ing] men like air," Lady Lazarus and Sylvia Plath demonstrate the power of words to give new life to the realm of modern women's poetry.

WORKS CITED

Alvarez, A. *The Savage God: A Study of Suicide*. New York: Random House, 1972. Print.
Gilbert, Sandra M. "'My Name Is Darkness': The Poetry of Self-Definition." *Contemporary Literature*. 18.4. (1977): 443–57. Print.
Hughes, Ted. "Sylvia Plath and Her Journals" *Grand Street* 1. 3 (1982): 86–99. Print.
_____, and Frances McCullough, ed. *The Journals of Sylvia Plath*. New York: Dial Press, 1982. Print.
Juhasz, Susan. *Naked and Fiery Forms: Modern American Poetry by Women*. New York: Octagon Books, 1976. Print.
Lant, Katherine Margaret. "The Big Strip Tease: Female Bodies and Male Power in the Poetry of Sylvia Plath." *Contemporary Literature*. 34.4 (1993): 620–669. Print.
Petrino, Elizabeth. "Nineteenth-century American Women's Writing." *The Cambridge Companion to Nineteenth-Century American Women's Writing*. Ed. Dale M. Bauer and Philip Gould. Cambridge: Cambridge University Press, 2001. 122–142. Print.
Plath, Sylvia. "Lady Lazarus." *Ariel*. New York: Harper and Row, 1966. Print.

PART II: OUTSIDE THE GREEK TRADITION—
FROM THE NEAR EAST TO THE AZTECS

Coatlicue and Chicana Grrl Power

SARAH R. WAKEFIELD

In 1920, philosopher Hartley Burr Alexander dramatically observed, "It is indeed doubtful whether the human imagination has ever elsewhere conjured up such soul-satisfying devils as are the gods of the Aztec pantheon. Beside them Old World demons seem prankishly amiable sprites ... their material characters, ugly, ghastly, foul, afford unalloyed shudders which time cannot still nor custom stale" (49–50). For such gratifying creatures, the Aztec pantheon never seems to enter the classroom. Perhaps their demonic nature repels some, or perhaps it's because their names offer pronunciation challenges. Whatever the reason, Aztec gods and goddesses receive little attention from English teachers when compared with their Greek and Roman counterparts.

Certainly the zoomorphic statues from ancient Mexico strike contemporary American students as bizarre. They are used to bulked-up superhero gods from comics and graphic novels, and the imposing eight-foot stone statue of the Mother Goddess Coatlicue looks nothing like Wonder Woman. Yet academics and Chicana activists have adopted this member of the Aztec pantheon as a symbol of ethnic struggle. With her serpent skirt and necklace crafted from human sacrifices, Coatlicue represents the ability to give life and death. Even her name encompasses this duality, for coátl means both snake and twin. Although she is mother to 400 sons known as the Centzon Huitznalwa and also to a powerful daughter, Coatlicue is best known in Aztec mythology for her youngest son, the warrior god Huitzilopochtli, conceived from a bundle of hummingbird feathers that fell from the sky. Jealous and appalled by the miraculous pregnancy/mystical rape, the goddess's many children "were very angry, they were very agitated, as if the heart had gone out of them. Coyolxauhqui incited them, she inflamed the anger of her brothers, so that they should kill her mother" (Carrasco 60). Coyolxauhqui, Coatlicue's only daughter, cuts off her mother's head, and Huitzilopochtli, already a grown warrior, bursts from his mother to slay his instigating sister. Her dismembered head becomes the moon, his 400 brothers become the stars, and Huitzilopochtli represents the sun.

Coatlicue began as an earth goddess representing the circle of life, but her ancient symbology changed with the rise of the Aztec empire. Susanna Rostas observes, "She was the female equivalent in many respects of Quetzalcoatl. Although her myth of giving birth to Huitzilopochtli was obviously a recent one, her form ties her into the mythic scenarios of Mayahual and Itzapapolotl" (383). In other words, Coatlicue includes aspects of Quetzalcoatl, the feathered-serpent god of wind and learning; Mayahual, a fertility goddess; and Itzapapolotl, the "Obsidian Butterfly" warrior-goddess who reigns in the paradise where humans were created. She changed even more as years passed:

> But by the time we get to the sixteenth century, the militant Mexica have transformed Coatlicue (another version of the Mother) into a ghastly, hostile deity. The death aspect of the dual power of the Mother—fertility and death—had taken over. Around her neck a necklace of men's hearts and hands was symbolic of her insatiable thirst for human sacrifice. Let's keep in mind that that image of Coatlicue was created in the context of a war-oriented, conquest driven society, that of the Aztecs [Castillo, *Massacre of the Dreamers* 11].

Patriarchy emphasizes the bloodthirsty side of the goddess and throws off her careful balance. The myth of Huitzilopochtli offers a good measure of gore, explaining celestial bodies through a series of beheadings, and reduces Coatlicue to a womb for a great Aztec warrior.

Despite the fact that other myths have virgin births and children springing forth in full armor, like Athena from Zeus's head, Coatlicue sits in obscurity. Latina feminist critics know her well, however, from Gloria Anzaldúa's 1987 *Borderlands/La Frontera*, a fluidly bilingual text that includes the author's poems about the goddess, whom she views as a Jungian psychic archetype. "*Coatlicue da luz a todo y a todo devora*. [Coatlicue gives birth to all and devours all]" she writes (46). But the Aztec deity moves beyond oppositions because "she represents duality in life, a synthesis of duality, and a third perspective—something more than mere duality or a synthesis of duality" (68). This is the key to Anzaldúa's concept of the "Coatlicue state," a necessary step towards a mestiza's self-awareness where she accepts that her traumas hold the source of her power.

Acceptance means moving past fear, however, and the poems in *La Frontera* often touch on the anxiety of non-identity:

> She has this fear that she has no names that she
> has many names that she doesn't know her names She has

> this fear that she's an image that comes and goes
> clearing and darkening [43].

Coatlicue herself suffers from no such terror, but "Coyolxauhqui, Coatlicue's daughter, represents for Anzaldúa the trashed figure's feeling of being torn apart by internalized shame and guilt from being spurned by society, embodying the contradictions of the dominant culture within one's own being" (Hartley 42). The fragmented Coyolxauhqui, determined to save her family's reputation through murder and subsequently murdered by her youngest warrior brother, must be reconstituted for Mexico and its women to move forward.

Literary projects that seek to put the goddess and her daughter back together again face several challenges. What form should the deities take? After centuries of bloodthirsty revisions, do we even know their "original" faces, and can the mythological figures be freed from patriarchal constraints? Should modern Chicanas even look to Coatlicue and Coyolxauhqui as grrl power role models? Such questions appear in Ana Castillo's 1997 poem "Coatlicue's Legacy," in which a victim of domestic violence struggles to embrace her power, whether it stems from childbirth, child rearing, or revenge. Coatlicue appears only as a shadow in "Emplumada" (1982) by Lorna Dee Cervantes, with its two warrior hummingbirds and lament over the coming autumn. Where instructors often turn to Anzaldúa's poems on the Aztec goddess, this essay provides close readings of two additional poems on female estrangement and empowerment to broaden understanding of myth beyond Greco-Roman tradition.

"Coatlicue's daughter" narrates Castillo's poem ("Coatlicue's Legacy" 1–3). In myth, Coyolxanliqui, infuriated by her mother's mystical pregnancy, betrayed the goddess and, after her death at the hands of her half-brother Huitzilopochtli, the princess became the moon. Metaphorically, all Chicanas can claim status as Coatlicue's daughters by virtue of race. Being the goddess' daughters make them complicit, however, in the destruction of their own matriarchal heritage.

Castillo's speaker pays dearly for matricide. She endures domestic violence because, as she says repeatedly, she cannot remember how to escape the situation. Yet somewhere, she holds the word that would slay her mortal abuser to the point that medical intervention would be impossible. In Egyptian mythology, the goddess Isis tricks her grandfather, the sun god Re, by planting a poisonous snake in his path and then refusing to heal its bite until he reveals his secret name—with his name comes all of his power. Castillo's poem similarly echoes the supremacy of The Word, for if her speaker simply lets it out, even unconsciously, "life is at the hem of my stone skirt ... four hundred warriors strong" (17, 19). With this image, the speaker recalls being Coatlicue herself, "She of the Stone Skirt" and mother of the Centzon Huitznalwa. But where the original goddess gives birth through beheading, Coatlicue's daughter experiences labor pains strong enough to spin the world. Once the child arrives, the speaker revels in the choices available to a new mother. She can sever the umbilical cord or not, "spit out ... or shit them out—" (36–37).

The correspondence of excretion and childbirth brings to mind Tlazolteotl, goddess of sex and childbirth, another key figure in Anzaldúa's *Borderlands/La Frontera*. As Chicanas move from fear to self-acceptance, "one privileged moment in this Coatlicue process is paying homage to Tlazolteotl, the goddess of lust and filth who figures as one of Coatlicue's aspects or manifestations" (Hartley 41). Like Coatlicue, Tlazolteotl embodies oppositions: filth-eating and purification, death and life. Her iconography may challenge American students even more than the mother-goddess's snake-headed statue. In an image from the *Codex Borbonicus* from early colonial Mexico, the deity squats while the head of an adult emerges from the birth canal; the maize fronds at the top could represent her connection to agriculture or brooms for sweeping away sins. Tlazolteotl shows a balance of traditional manuscript colors, carmine red and carbon black, that represent "the metaphor for knowledge or wisdom" (Boone 21). Bloodthirsty Aztec influence also comes through in her wardrobe, the skin of a sacrifice victim most noticeable in the extra set of hands hanging loosely from the goddess's limbs. Death surrounds new life, just as in the case of Coatlicue, and Castillo's speaker fantasizes about bringing Tlazolteotl-style punishments upon her abuser.

Castillo's image of Coatlicue's daughter highlights duality, bringer of life as well as death, but the speaker's anger and desire for punishment mirrors the goddess as revised in Aztec society. To reclaim a powerful female icon as a Xicanista weapon ironically requires more of the gruesome aspects of the goddess—the patriarchal misprisioning of Coatlicue—to help her daughters "robbed and raped / to numbness" (42–43).

In contrast to celebrating the power of an unbalanced Coatlicue, Lorna Dee Cervantes's poem "Emplumada" accepts that the ancient earth goddess is lost, replaced by warrior sons who also lack power in modern society. Critic Ada Savin describes Cervantes's work as "an eloquent literary expression of the Chicanos' paradigmatic quest for self-definition ... the existential quandary is made explicit: the feeling is one of overwhelming estrangement from one's essential identity markers: name, physical appearance, and language," very similar to critiques of Gloria Anzaldúa's poetry (218). "Emplumada" concludes the author's eponymous 1981 collection, coming at the end of the third section in which a female speaker expresses longing for a beloved who often has abandoned her. Impermanence and nostalgia fill the piece, which gestures obliquely to Coatlicue's story, now so ancient that only the smallest of reminders remain.

While Castillo's poem features a woman who forgets her goddess heritage, Cervantes's female speaker is even more estranged from the power of the Coatlicue myth. The poem presents nature in its classic cycle of life and death, when summer eases into autumn, but rather than a sense of connection and balance, there is a focus on transience. First, the speaker laments the death of the snapdragons with "their shrill-colored mouths" (Cervantes 3), perhaps a symbol of women's voices, now silenced and faded to brown. Her reflection does not lead, however, to a clichéd realization that flowers bloom again each spring. The snapdragons simply are gone.

The great Mother Coatlicue is gone, too. Instead, traces of her son Huitzilopochtli, conceived from a bundle of hummingbird feathers, remain as two of those birds fiercely couple, seeking something positive as "warriors / distancing themselves from history" (14–15). History definitely worked its magic on Huitzilopochtli, as the Aztecs transformed him from a sun deity to "a national divinity, their militant patron god … [who] sits rather uncomfortably in the pantheon" (Conrad and Demarest 27). Thus elevated from the godly masses, Coatlicue's youngest child follows his mother down a similarly bloody path. The dualistic goddess skews towards viciousness, and Huitzilopochtli demands massive human sacrifices: "It was specifically the Mexicas' sacred duty to pursue a course of endless warfare, conquest and sacrifice to preserve the universe from the daily threat of annihilation" (38). The Hummingbird God helped the tribe from Tenochtitlan rise to dominance in an Aztec empire, changing history in Mesoamerica.

How the mighty have fallen … or have they? If we read the joined hummingbirds in "Emplumada" as symbolic of Huitzilopochtli, the god reclaims his mother's fertile side. The "grim determination" to continue a race serves as its own declaration of war on the bloody patriarchal past. Snapdragons may be faded and silent, but the ancient balance of life/death is restored.

Tiny hummingbirds are a far cry from the nine-foot stone statue of the terrifying Coatlicue. About the carving of the goddess, Ann De León writes, "Through her body, its fractures, mutilations, earthly and cosmic connections, Coatlicue symbolizes and narrates the violent birth of the Aztecs" (260). Hundreds of years after their ascendance, what symbolism does she offer to modern Chicanas? When a ball of feathers falls from the sky—Coatlicue literally is emplumada, or feathered—the path of the goddess changes, dramatically, without her consent. She gives birth to a warrior and then becomes more warrior than mother herself. In their poems, Ana Castillo and Lorna Dee Cervantes reclaim some of the fractured pieces of Coatlicue's life-giving side. Their works emphasize that even though the goddess has faded from memory, her daughters remain, however downtrodden, and even her famed son continues to preserve Mexico from annihilation, however small his effort. It may be clichéd to say so, but through literature Coatlicue continues to give birth to new creations. As Gloria Anzaldua declares, "Let the wound caused by the serpent be cured by the serpent" (46), or in this case, let the serpent goddess remove some of the venom by reminding women of the power they hold as potential mothers.

Works Cited

Alexander, Hartley Burr. *The Mythology of All Races: Latin-American.* Boston: Marshall Jones Company, 1920. Print.
Anzaldúa, Gloria. *Borderlands/La Frontera: The New Mestiza.* San Francisco: Aunt Lute Books, 2007. Print.
Boone, Elizabeth Hill. *Stories in Red and Black: Pictorial Histories of the Axtec and Mixtec.* Austin: University of Texas Press, 2008. Print.
Carrasco, David. *City of Sacrifice: The Aztec Empire and the Role of Violence in Civilization.* Boston: Beacon Press, 1999. NetLibrary eBook. Web. 10 Nov. 2015.
Castillo, Ana. "Coatlicue's Legacy." *I Ask the Impossible: Poems.* New York: Anchor Books, 2001. Print.
_____. *Massacre of the Dreamers: Essays on Xicanisma.* Albuquerque: University of New Mexico Press, 1994. Print.
Cervantes, Lorna Dee. "Emplumada." *Emplumada.* Pittsburgh: University of Pittsburgh Press, 1981. 66–67. Print.
Conrad, Geoffrey W. and Arthur A. Demarest. *Religion and Empire: The Dynamics of Aztec and Inca Expansionism.* Cambridge: Cambridge University Press, 1988. Print.
De León, Ann. "Coatlicue or How to Write the Dismembered Body." *Modern Language Notes* 125.2 (Mar. 2010): 259–86. Print.
Hartley, George. "'Matriz sin tumba': The Trash Goddess and the Healing Matrix of Gloria Anzaldúa's Reclaimed Womb." *MELUS* 35.3 (Fall 2010): 41–61. Print.
Rostas. Susanna. "Divine Androgyny but 'His' Story; The Female in Aztec Mythology." *The Feminist Companion to Mythology.* Ed. Carolyne Larrington. London: Pandora, 1992. 362–387. Print.
Savin, Ada. "Bilingualism and Dialogism: Another Reading of Lorna Dee Cervantes's Poetry." *An Other Tongue: Nation and Ethnicity in the Linguistic Borderlands.* Ed. Alfred Arteaga. Durham & London: Duke University Press, 1994. 215–223. Print.

Conduits and Conjurers
Heroic Characters, Sacred Nature and Social Order in Kelly Norman Ellis, Nikky Finney and Patricia Smith

JANINE HARRISON

In their two most recent chapbooks, poets Kelly Norman Ellis, in *Tougaloo Blues* and *Offerings of Desire*; Nikky Finney in *The World Is Round* and *Head Off & Split*, and Patricia Smith in *Blood Dazzler* and *Shoulda Been Jimi Savannah*, employ the conceptual frameworks of heroic characters, sacred nature, and social value that are involved in defining myth.

"Heroic characters" in the forms of gods, proto-humans or superhumans, are often included in mythic narratives, according to Mary Magoulick, Folklorist and Professor of English and Interdisciplinary Studies at Georgia College & State University, in "What Is Myth?" Heroes serve as mediators of disconcerting dualities, helping cultures' members to resolve realities and build patterns to live by (2). This symbolic mediation offers encouragement to members to accept reality, to heal, and to flourish (5). Whereas historically poets have mainly alluded to mythological Greek and Roman gods for these purposes, in the works of Kelly Norman Ellis and Nikky Finney, the majority of references are to *matriarchal* heroic characters, specifically, goddesses from African and Asian mythologies.

Kelly Norman Ellis, who uses the most direct references to mythology, introduces African mythological figures in both *Tougaloo Blues* and *Offerings of Desire*. In *Tougaloo Blues*, the most allusions are to deities from Nigerian tribal myths and indicate a direct lineage from deities to African-American women. To illustrate, Ellis reinforces the connection of mythical African ancestor to contemporary black female in both "Mammy Water's Prayer" and "Daughters." In "Mammy Water's Prayer," she appropriates Mammy as "…the mermaid goddess / of the ascagoula," a city in Mississippi (19–20). Ellis' Great-grandmother Agnes appears to be communicating through "some ibo ancestor's gift to her" (25) via telepathic chant, to Mammy Water, for a good catch while crabbing in the Gulf of Mexico. In "Daughters," a text involving Professor Ellis instructing daughters with missing mothers and serving as medium from them to their children, a murdered mother, Lori, asks Ellis to show her daughter how to write poetry. In response, Ellis "…tell[s] the girl to make altars to / a mermaid goddess named yemonja" (34–35). She then channels, "she told me to tell you / you are mermaid and lion / fertile and black" and to write about it (40–44). Ellis asks this girl to honor the divinity, whom her mother has implied is ancestral.

In "Yemonja's Heart," written about a trip Ellis makes to New Orleans with two female students, she mentions Oshun, a river goddess and a wife of Shango, orisha of lightning (Belcher 309). She pens, "Oshun is watching us like mothers do. She is singing water, / …. We are her / goddesses on a moon ride" (35–38). Soon, Yemonja whispers to "speak our secrets … / [seeing]signs for Gulfport and I tell them she is coming…" (65 and 67). The second morning, after Yemonja awakens them with the sun, they leave to meet Ellis' former student, Ellen Hagan, and "Yemonya whispers with her sister Oshun Go meet the other / girl, the fourth one browned with Kentucky sun. Ride into / my heart, ride into the light.…" Ellis considers New Orleans a "home," and it is apparent that to the poet that mother figures Oshun and Yemonja want Ellis, students, and Finney present. Yet again, the lineage from goddesses to African-American females is addressed and, in fact, the humans *become* goddesses.

The four goddesses that Kelly Norman Ellis references in *Tougaloo Blues* originated in Africa, with three from Yoruba tribal mythology. Three are also water spirits, lending to rebirth symbolism, as if the deities are reborn in each generation of African-American female descendants.

In *Offerings of Desire*, Ellis' mythological focus is again upon goddesses. In "Superhero," for instance, she refers to Lasyrenn, a mermaid associated with Mammy Water, describing "Lasyrenn's hair / like a rope" (lines 1–2); she is considered to be *iwa* or queen of the ocean, presiding over love, particularly maternal love (Sparks and Conner 59). She then compares Oya to her, adding that Oya's hair is the new rope. Oya is an orisha worshipped by the Yoruba tribe; she is a river and another wife of Shango (Belcher 309). Shortly thereafter, the persona maintains, "I am Oya rocking hurricanes. / I am the protector of your dead" (4–5) and "I am the earth shaker / protector of women" (8–9). The remainder of the work is then devoted to developing Oya's identity as a guardian, citing Oya as "protector of scribbling women" (22), "defender of drag queens, of the butch and the femme" (34), "[protector of] plum women / the lynched / the raped" (49–51). The poem ends "I am / Sapphire" (68–69), paying homage to African-American female author and poet Romona

Lofton, who wrote *Push*, later made into the film *Precious*, covering the social issues of abuse and incest. The poem is an offering—of acceptance, healing, and thriving, to readers. It attests to the fact that even though various minority groups have been historically wronged, the issues involved are now being voiced.

Later, in "Pontchartrain," a poem about Hurricane Katrina's impact on the predominantly poor black Lower Ninth and its post-disaster neglect as compared to the restoration care given to the touristy Bourbon Street area, the poet again refers to Oya. Part III is written as a plea to the goddess, as well as to her storm sisters, Oshun and Yemonja, to "Protect the dead and the living" (74), and to "Talk to Jesus / Tell him his mothers live here / Tell him his sisters sleep here" (84–86). "Pontchartrain," then, navigates dual realities of reconstruction in areas post–Hurricane Katrina based upon socioeconomic importance, and offers soothing as an imploration to a guardian to watch over those who have been ill-treated. In both chapbooks, Ellis uses mythology as a vehicle for empowerment and healing.

In *Head Off & Split*, Nikky Finney uses direct references to African and Asian mythology, and as with Ellis, to matriarchal heroic characters. In "Segregation, Forever," Finney posits that due to slavery and continued racism, African-Americans have been severed from their organic support systems and that, even though time has passed, the repercussions of separation, of segregation, are still evident in negative media portrayal, which sells the educated persona back into slavery. Still, Finney alludes to Oshun, stating:

> Oshun's
> fingers, six million years long suspend
> each of their high notes. Three [Black boy]
> bodies dervish and dangle, their ancient
> sound fills every sidewalk crack in the
> new world [lines 10–15].

In her use of Oshun, a Yoruba tribal goddess known for benevolent love (Wilkinson 249), Finney may be arguing that even with separation and negative press, Oshun's power is still extensive enough to reach the boys and to transform their pure joy into leveling of the foundation between blacks and whites.

Furthermore, Finney refers to the Chinese Buddhist goddess of mercy, Guanyin, who responds to calls for help and is known for watching and listening, in her work, "Shaker: Wilma Rudolph Appears While Riding the Althea Gibson Highway Home," about a romantic relationship between two women that is likely ending. During intercourse, in which the persona, a runner, is "arched just under the broken-hearted woman" (33). Finney writes:

> The ghost calf taking in her milk while Guanyin
> floats above them both, Zen guard of the firing

> line, of every win or lose, rooted in the margin lane,
> bowing to me and whispering to Wilma, *Don't dare
> let her win.* Her sky-blue hat and thick black gun
> pointing & ready to target when to burst [34–39].

The poem ends with the runner ready to risk all for the "try try again of love" (46), ready to run. Guanyin serves in the role of Starter, biased toward Wilma, who desires help ending the relationship, but is merciful enough to allow another chance for the persona to win at the race of love. Finney's choices in both instances are goddesses who are charitable in nature.

In addition to mythological allusions, Nikky Finney views Black female elders as matriarchal heroic characters indirectly, particularly in *The World is Round*. In "Assam," for example, an ode to an old black woman who is sitting on the shoreline, her "throne" (10):

> things still pull to her,
> the uncalled water
> knocks softly
> bubbling about
> her flat out thighs,
> the salt water wanting in,
> no matter [lines 14–20].

The poem ends, "*without you I whisper / the world is plain / tap water*" (35–37). Even though the back story of this elderly woman, beyond being one who used to swing her hips, and who embraced grandchildren who ran into her arms, which may be imagined, is never explained, the persona, apparently a stranger to the woman, honors her.

This is even more marked when Finney discusses her grandmother. First, in "Chapter One: Counting Straws," of the segmented prose poem, "Hurricane Beulah," she notes:

> She does not see me
> leaning into the door wishing she wouldn't shave away her
> golden woman chin straw. *This is my research material!* I
> want to scream. She does not know that I believe these hairs
> hold the key to all her powers. She never sees me counting,
> pulling, on the tiny hairs beneath my own chin, wondering
> when, when can I count on being just like her? [13–19].

Later, in "Chapter Three: The Bra," Section 3, after recounting fond childhood memories of living with her grandmother, Finney explains, "if you could still look up in the world and still see yourself in / the eyes of the one who is the very reason you are still graciously free / of madness, then you would do whatever you had to for her" (159–161). Her grandmother later dies of cancer. Finney tells readers that Beulah had taught her to believe in that which extends beyond the five senses. In "Chapter Four: The Cancer," Section

9, the work concludes, "I felt the warm heavy wind of the Great Mother lift the plain / dutiful life of another mother to the beyond" (304–306). Throughout the work, it is apparent that Finney views her grandmother as a wise woman role model and is grateful for her. She also values the concept of "mother." Rather than "God" taking her grandmother, it is the "Great Mother," whose influence is kindly and powerful, who takes another into the afterworld. "Mother," too, is perceived as matriarchal heroic character, similarly to Ellis' references to maternal mythological goddesses. In yet another poem, "Fishing Among the Learned," Finney refers to her grandmother as a "Human University" (15) who could accomplish more while fishing for an afternoon than Congress ever could (7–13). She then cites lessons that her grandmother taught her about teaching as analogous to fishing, such as "To educate means to lead out" (31), that being a teacher means doing "...more than talk about it, she / can see it beyond the convincing skinny pages / of any flattened tree" (41–43), and to assume that others will follow, so she must "Put something back whenever [she] can" (61). These instructions further explain Finney's awe of Grandma Beulah, to the extent that she can be perceived as a heroic character.

While Patricia Smith does not use direct references to mythology, in *Blood Dazzler*, she personifies New Orleans as a powerful woman, a heroic character, capable of withstanding multiple hurricanes. In the Prologue, "And Then She Owns You," New Orleans is painted as a temptress who "tells you *Leave your life*. Pack your little suitcase / flee what is rigid" (35–36). She leads a person away from his or her mundane existence, "out into the darkness / and makes you drink rain" (47–48), a form of rebirth. In "Why New Orleans Is," this perspective is further supported when Smith states, "Every damned body needs a midnight stage" (6); everyone requires a forum for their darkest thoughts and emotions. Thus, the city is depicted as a place to purge, a purifier, albeit a primal, but *necessary* mechanism for human release. New Orleans is, however, portrayed as a complex character. In "And Then She Owns You," the city is described as "wavering," uncertain how much longer she "can stomach the introduction of needles, / the brash, boozed warbling of bums with neon crowns, / necklaces raining" (17–20). She does not know the limits of her strength. She is also a mother; in "34," Section 23, a persona recalls fondly that the Big Easy, "without flinching, / called me [her] child" (8–9). She is undaunted as well. In "Rebuilding," there are "the busy sounds of lifting what is damned. / Paint the rubble pretty, hues gone berserk / with dry hope" (10–12). In Smith's portrayal, New Orleans is strong enough to bear suffering, hurricanes, and rebuilding and is, moreover, heroic.

Ellis, Finney, and Smith use direct or indirect references to matriarchal heroic characters in their poetry. Such myths are designed to give hope to women that their status as second-class citizens need not be permanent, thereby functioning as world-creating and world-affirming (Magoulick 6–7). Whether through use of empowering ancestral lineages that heal or heroic characters who are role models of strength and forgiveness, qualities reputedly female, and in particular, maternal, are advocated; the three poets thus accomplish the goal of providing hope.

"Sacred nature" is another concept that is used to explain mythology. Often associated with significant "ritual," these narratives are mostly connected with religions and are thought to be true, literally or metaphorically, within their faith systems (Magoulick 1–2). In "Ritual," Victor Turner posits that ritual is a type of symbolic language that assists members of a society in understanding any event in relation to the society's broader range of symbols (373). According to Anthropologist Mary Douglas, in "Deciphering a Meal," ritual as myth may include everyday ritual, which can exemplify a culture (417). Ellis and Smith use everyday ritual in the forms of hair, food, and music.

In *Tougaloo Blues*, "Kitchen Witches," Ellis discusses having her hair done in the kitchen by "auntees," who simultaneously cook and gossip, explaining, "right here, I learn to love woman / -ish worlds" (16–17). She continues, "the kitchen witches taught me their rituals under black / women's moons. / nights of nappy edges coil tight..." (18–20). In addition, she asserts, "where naps no longer bow, but whose pressed memory I / still wear" (22–23). In her essay, "Beauty Shop Literacies: Nikky Finney and the Sacred Beauty Hour," Alexis Pauline Gumbs states that beauty shops are places where, for black women, "hair is not a problem, but rather an opportunity for intimacy and self-love" (170). Ellis' home kitchen "beauty shop" seems to also allow for this type of bonding and self-nurturing during her formative years and later, as memory. Gumbs continues that such an experience is helpful not only for the beauty shop clients but also "hopefully, the readers are prepped for profound change" (170). Ellis' work, too, allows readers to see black women's space anew as sacred place and ritual.

She explores ritual again in "Offerings," a poem about black women cooking chicken for dinner, by stating, "and the child is initiated / into the ancient woman art / of sacrifice and offering" (22–24). Ellis turns everyday ritual into rite of passage, thereby elevating it to the realm of sacred.

In *Shoulda Been Jimi Savannah*, "A Colored Girl Will Slice You If You Talk Wrong About Motown," Smith reviews the lives of children of young adults who had become parents too soon, arguing that the children learned, "what we needed, not from our parents and their rumored / South, but from the gospel seeping through the sad gap / in Mary Well's grin" (30–32). After further Motown references, canvassing different facets of their present and future, Smith explains, "Every lyric, growled or sweet from / perfect brown throats, was instruction..." (38–39). In a personal interview, Patricia Smith discussed that *Jimi Savannah* "...is about the experience of being first generation up north." Because her parents migrated to Chicago from the south, they "...were initially intimidated by their new environment, and didn't really know the 'rules' of raising a child in the city." Consequently, Smith was "not only an only child, but ... isolated from everything a child should and could be doing ... [and] looked to the music for guidance." She further stated, "All my ideas about the way life and love were supposed to progress came from whatever Motown song was out at the time. As you might imagine, this led to a warped, ultimately disappointing mindset. But the possibilities thrilled every cell of my body, and the lyrics rapidly became religion. That process is important because I seldom read about little colored girls who came up during that time, how we crafted whole lives from bits and pieces of songs." In other words, Motown music serves as a rite of passage into adulthood for black girls.

Sacred ritual, then, as used by Ellis and Smith, helps readers to see the everyday rituals of hair styling, cooking, and listening to Motown through fresh eyes as rite of passage and sacred space within an African-American cultural context.

Another concept associated with mythic narratives is myth reflective of social value within a particular culture (Magoulick 2). A corresponding trait is "charter for social action," in which the narrative conveys how to live and may include assumptions, values, and central definitions of individuals, families, and communities (3). In the black creative writing tradition, writing is viewed as service—a means to advocate social change. This tradition is prevalent in the works of all three poets in the form of persona poetry.

Many black poets write persona and tribute poems about slaves to, according to Brian Connif, contribute "to the *social need* within black culture of presenting heroic ex-slaves ... keeping the spirits of these beloved fugitive slaves on the minds of the living" (qtd. in Rambsy 551). Each poet keeps this tradition alive through her presentation of more modern black historical figures. This extension of the slave narrative, therefore, exemplifies the myth of social value.

Kelly Norman Ellis provides social value in *Offerings of Desire*, "Superhero," the previously discussed poem written using a first-person narrative in the voice of Romona Lofton, a modern-day role model for voicing injustice and promoting social betterment. Superhero Sapphire is the "protector.... / of translucent truth" (63–64).

Nikky Finney also uses the persona poem to teach about revolutionary figures in recent history. Specifically, in *Head Off & Split*, "Red Velvet," she writes middle sections in second-person point of view, placing readers in the shoes of Rosa Parks during the time when she refuses to move to the back of the bus and must face the consequences. Parks was a seamstress, and Finney describes her entering the courthouse, "you walk up the sidewalk /

in a long-sleeved black dress, your white collar / and deep perfect cuffs holding you high..." (94–96). Transitioning to third-person point of view, she states, "...A woman made of all this is never to / be taken for granted, never to be asked to move / to the back of anything, never to be arrested" (112–114). The poet concludes, "A fastened woman / can be messed with, one too many times" (127–128), soon continuing:

> through her softly clenched teeth
> she will tell you, without ever looking
> your way
> You do what you need to do &
> So will I [133–137].

By placing readers in the position of both the oppressed and the oppressor, they are allowed to see Parks' strong will and determination.

When asked if the black persona poem continues the tradition of the slave narrative and about its purpose, "Red Velvet" in particular, in a personal interview Nikky Finney stated:

> I've always been deeply engaged with history. Even as a girl I noticed the history that we talked about in school was not the history that we talked about at home around the dinner table. I also noticed the books in the tiny Carnegie Library in my small southern town were not the same books that my father and mother made sure were on our shelves. The reality of two distinct worlds—Black and white—was my reality from the first. In college I started to read the Slave Narratives and then the WPA interviews that took place around the turn of the 20th century. I always wondered about what wasn't being said in those well-meaning interviews. From a position of power, race-secrecy, and history, Black people have never told all of what happened to us as a People. Our religion has encouraged us to keep moving beyond that pain and horror. Our desire to never relive the horrors of being one of the enslaved has taught us that Black classic line my grandmother used to say, "Ohh now, let's not go back into all that mess."

Finney continued:

> I think my desire to bring forward the voice of Rosa Parks is a desire to see her voice in the mix of this 21st century contemporary narrative. We would not be on the page we are on without her. We cannot go one step into the future without her great historical shoes. I wanted to write of her life from not only the great woman who 'refused to move' but also the regular woman who had a whole other "regular" life based on things that other human beings based their lives on. I think the personae poem is indeed in the tradition of the Slave Narrative. I do think we MUST make the distinction that the slave narrative is a FIRST person narrative and the personae poem is an interpretation, by another, of that life. Very important distinction.

The entirety of Patricia Smith's *Blood Dazzler* demonstrates the need for social change by focusing on the injustices committed toward poor blacks living in or near New Orleans during the aftermath of Hurricane Katrina. One such poem, "34," is written in the individual voices of the 34 residents of St. Rita's Nursing Home in St. Bernard Parish who were not evacuated. A refrain, which also serves as the conclusion, is "*Leave them*" (71, 131, and 164–165). The theme of betrayal continues when victim 29 accuses, "Louisiana, / goddamn. / You lied to me so lush" (143–145), and when victim 31 explains, "They left us to our God, / but our God was mesmerized elsewhere, / watching His rain" (154–156). Her poem shows the betrayal, literally, of workers abandoning the nursing home patients as well as abandonment on larger scales, both state and deity.

According to Howard Rambsy II, in "Holy Ghosts: The Diverse Manifestations of Black Persona Poetry," when black poets write persona poems in the voices of slaves, "The poems serve as tributes and continuations to the legacies of heroic slaves, and the works showcase poets' interests in taking interactive approaches to black history by adopting the very spirits of their slave ancestors ... black poets and their supporters ... present their works continually liberate slaves and runagates from the confines of the past and transport their spirits to contemporary readerships" (555). Writing in the voices of strong black females both contemporary and in recent history as well as writing in the voices of victims of socioeconomic inequities is yet another form of keeping such figures and events in the minds of modern readers and their descendants. Whereas slavery may seem too far back in history for these generations to find relevant, examples from within the last 50 years may prove more relatable. Only by doing so, by understanding both historic strengths and wrongs, can current and future generations know what is possible in terms of how to support social advancement.

In retrospect, whether the use of mythology is direct or indirect, integral to matriarchal heroic characters, to ritual as sacred nature, or to the persona poem as social value, two characteristics define the poetry conjured by Kelly Norman Ellis, Nikky Finney, and Patricia Smith: ancestry and service. Sonia Sanchez stated, "I write to keep in contact with our ancestors and to spread truth to people" ("Family Tree"). In an environment that, by enslaving Africans, produced a nearly rootless African American culture, regaining ties in such forms as mythical matriarchs, elderly Black females, place, ritual, or modern historical figures, is paramount. As is truth. Ellis,' Finney's, and Smith's works exemplify poetry as an agent of social advancement—as protector, as healer, as equalizer—as truth, as power, as hope, and as possibility. What, after all, could be more vital?

Acknowledgments

Patricia Smith's excerpts from *Shoulda Been Jimi Savannah* (Minneapolis: Coffee House Press, 2012) are reprinted by permission. Copyright © 2012 by Patricia Smith. Published 2012 by Coffee House Press.

Patricia Smith's excerpts from *Blood Dazzler* (Minneapolis: Coffee House Press, 2008) are reprinted by permission. Copyright © 2008 by Patricia Smith. Published 2012 by Coffee House Press.

Kelly Norman Ellis' poetry appears in *TOUGALOO BLUES* (Chicago: Third World Press Foundation, 2003) and is reprinted by permission. Copyright © 2003 by Kelly Norman Ellis. Published 2003 by Third World Press Foundation.

Nikky Finney's "Segregation Forever," "Shaker: William Rudolph Appears While Riding the Althea Gibson Highway Home," and "Red Velvet" appear in *Head Off & Split: Poems* (Evanston, IL: TriQuarterly Books/Northwestern University Press, 2011). Reprinted by permission. Copyright © 2011 by Nikky Finney. Published 2011 by TriQuarterly Books/Northwestern University Press. All rights reserved.

Nikky Finney's "Assam," "Hurricane Beulah," and "Fishing Among the Learned" appear in *The World is Round* (Evanston, IL: TriQuarterly Books/Northwestern University Press, 2013). Reprinted by permission. Copyright © 2013 by Nikky Finney. First edition copyright © 2003 by Lynn Carol Nikky Finney. First published in the United States in 2003 by InnerLight Publishing. This edition published in 2013 by TriQuarterly Books/Northwestern University Press by arrangement with Nikky Finney. All rights reserved.

WORKS CITED

Allan, Tony, Fergus Fleming, and Charles Phillips. *Voices of the Ancestors: African Myth*. London: Duncan Baird, 1999. Print.
Belcher, Stephen, ed. *African Myths of Origin*. London: Penguin, 2005. Print.
Douglas, Mary. "Deciphering a Meal." Thury, Eva M., and Margaret K. Devinney 417. *Introduction to Mythology: Contemporary Approaches to Classical and World Myths*. New York: Oxford University Press, 2009. Print.
Ellis, Kelly Norman. *Offerings of Desire*. Detroit: Willow Books, 2012. Print.
———. *Tougaloo Blues*. Chicago: Third World Press, 2003. Print.
Family Tree Quotes. Web. 14 Nov. 2012. http://truemiracleswithgenealogy.com/genealogy-quote-of-the-week-sonia-sanchez
Finney, Nikky. *Head Off & Split*. Evanston: TriQuarterly/Northwestern University Press, 2011. Print.
———. Personal interview. 3 Dec. 2012.
———. *The World Is Round*. Atlanta: InnerLight, 2003. Print.
Magoulick, Mary. "What Is Myth?" *Folklore Connections*. Georgia College & State University. Web. 13 March 2012.
Rambsy II, Howard. "Catching Ghosts: The Diverse Manifestations of Black Persona Poetry." *African American Review* 42, (2008): 549–564. Print.
Smith, Patricia. *Blood Dazzler*. Minneapolis: Coffee House Press, 2008. Print.
———. Personal interview. 3 March 2013.
———. *Shoulda Been Jimi Savannah*. Minneapolis: Coffee House Press, 2012. Print.
Sparks, David, and Randy Conner. *Queering Creole Spiritual Traditions*. Kentucky: Routledge, 2004. Print.
Turner, Victor. "Ritual." Thury, Eva M., and Margaret K. Devinney 373.
Wilkinson, Philip, ed. *Myths & Legends*. New York: DK, 2011. Print.
Zogbé, Mama. "Mami Wata: From Myth to Divine Reality." *Mami Water West African Diaspora Vodoun*. Mami Water West African Diaspora Vodoun, 2010. Web. 16 Oct. 2012.

When Pele Blows
Trask's Repositioning of the Hawaiian Creation Epic

JAMES A. WREN

Ua mau ke ea o ka 'aina i ka pono.
(The life of the land is preserved in righteousness.)
—motto of the state of Hawai'i

The physical ravages of disease (e.g., influenza, smallpox, measles and syphilis) and the accompanying violence and banishment. The traumatic displacement, forced migration, and homelessness following on the heels of betrayal. The oppression of dissenting voices and psychic trauma as a sense of identity deconstructs. Be the genocide social, psychical or cultural in nature, from hunger, corruption and casual cruelty through youthful suicide and the loss of language, to the pangs of racism and beyond, the very social realities shaping the contemporary lives of *kānaka maoli* (as indigenous Hawaiians recognize themselves) arose in the accumulation of some two and a half centuries of colonial exploitation, cultural suppression, and military occupation. Whether peripherally nudging or fully violating and deeply penetrating, the trauma inherent to the destruction of Hawaiian lives, land and culture has, doubtless, given way to a collective or cultural unconscious inscribed within a larger, crushing "culture of trauma."

Against this background, redoubtable feminist, internationally-respected voice for the downtrodden, and prolific poet Haunani-Kay Trask has taken up her pen.

Obsessed less with a wistful nostalgia for a simpler time before February 18, 1778, when Captain James Cook and his ships arrived in the Islands, or the debilitating demands of day-to-day living, Trask is possessed of a single, awe-inspiring need: that Hawai'i rediscover a voice of her own so that she might recreate an indigenous civilization built upon truth, remembrance and reconciliation of a sort. Arguing for an aggressive and portentous alternative view of Hawaiian history as well as a dark and menacing critique of an alien history and anthropology beyond the Islands, she concomitantly undertakes a wider, rich literary exploration of the mythical, ritualistic, and folkloric representations of gender and sexuality found in the native mythology of creation. Insofar as she taps into ancient Hawaiian religious myths and provides contemporary interpretations, her carefully controlled manipulation and repositioning of the traditional *mele*, or songs integrating music, poetry, and *hula* within political contexts, recontextualizes the pathways by which their ancient ancestors first sang their world into being. Doing so provides both the vehicle of resistance and the supporting iterations within political claims to a racially based sovereignty.

But in order to understand her perspective and the original inhabitants of Hawai'i, Trask asks us first to accept that *They* see—by extension, experience—their world very differently from *Us*; of necessity, they relate a very distinct tale of their history. For them, it all began Pele who was exiled from her home and left to follow a star from the northeast as she found her way across the seas. One day, awakened by the smell of something familiar in the air, she saw in the distance a high mountain, its peak hidden within a smoky haze. This would, she knew, be her new home. Carrying her magic stick *Pa'oa* as she ascended the mountain to a place where the earth had collapsed into the ground, she thrust her stick downward, deep into the ground, and therewith named the surrounding land Hawai'i. Once inside the Kilauea Crater, she found a large pit she called *Halema'uma'u* (*hale* or "dwelling"; *ma'uma'u*, "the fern jungle that surrounds the volcano"), and there she took shelter. Now an integral part of the natural world around her, she came to be recognized as the goddess of fire, lightning, and volcanoes. She was also known for her creative power, her deep passions and her overwhelming love (Kalākaua 32, 130–148).

Using the myth of Pele to structure her writing, Trask moves quickly to underscore an emphatic and intimate familial relationship of the native Islanders both to the *land* and to the *gods*, as she employs heavily cadenced, musical language to argue that the gods gave birth to the Hawaiian islands and then gave birth to her Hawaiian forefathers. And while her words lend credence to a deeper understanding—of the deep connection to the islands and to the sustaining strengths of family and love, it is her adroit maneuverings within an immensely difficult poetic genre, the political poem, that heralds her first works as the cornerstone of an emerging indigenous Hawaiian poetry.

Many of her early poems in *Light in the Crevice Never Seen* (1994), not unlike the volcanoes that gave way to her beloved native islands, erupt upon the page. In their vigorous and encroaching force and their strength of purpose, they spew fire. Even the titles of each verse illustrate the enormity of the pain and displacement of a colonized people that she feels in herself. But it is her appropriation and the subsequent proliferation of a special speaking voice, the traditional *haku mele*, that simultaneously emboldens her with the power to compose verse and to summons her audience before her as she creates shared membership in an imagined "way of life" (Žižek 201–202). Deeply chagrined at the development of tourism, which she believes to have accelerated the decay of native island culture and language already apparent with the Japanese and Americans' subjugation of Hawai'i, Trask's first volume of poetry harkens back to the use of chants of *hula* to propagandize, to suggest an overthrow (Kahananui 20).

Trask's combination of insightful imagery—"green chatter-chatter of coconut leaves," for example—alongside of bilingual phrases, tantamount to an unconscious code-switching between Hawaiian and English, results in a synergy that conveys her larger, profound feelings for the land. These poems enable us to recognize, to "hear" in the world around us "a constant, inconsolable/grief."

Moreover, through the integration of voice, repetition and gesture, she exposes us not just to her brilliantly incantatory poems but to the power of larger archetypal patterns that have emerged over time. Put differently, as she invokes the spiritual and mythological in these uncertain times of transition, she conceives of trauma as a space, an opportunity, to make life and behavioral changes necessary to support psychological and emotional growth. Reminiscent of Mircea Eliade's reading of the "Myth of the Eternal Return" (32–34), Trask suggests that such actions become reality only insofar as they repeat an archetype. In this instance, with an overarching rhythm that responds to the innate solar clock and circadian rhythm as well as the calendar time, she calls into question a linear perspective on life and living, one that betrays the inherent contradiction of biological drives we might possess to compete, to isolate, and to fail to recognize our present actions within larger connections to the past or to the future. Not just for the sake of the aesthetic but to underscore the rediscovery of continuities long buried, life in the Islands is for Trask a continuum, a dialogic between opposing forces, evolving and dissolving, seeking balance and fulfillment.

Ever-present is that sense of social relevance, most noticeably in her implied call for a devout and heroic commitment rather than submission to the aimless lack of meaning in its absence. In this sense, her writings are completely "presentative": that is, instead of stating an abstract "message," they project a host of nuanced effects and voices that evoke and suggest the promise of redemption.

It is this belief in redemption that provides focus to her second volume, *Night Is a Sharkskin Drum* (2002). After almost a decade since her first work appeared, Trask moves beyond the now-familiar fires of Pele to reclaim—and revel in—the unexpected power of the word. Bursting with the seductive allure of her earthen rhythms, ripe and spilling their juices as they themselves copulate and recreate, her lyrics are every bit as much incantation as they are instigation and provocation. Beyond the predictable and vulgar cliché of the ubiquitous American or the pretentious and condescending reminders of the crassly dogmatic imposed from without, Trask's words become both, as emboldened feathers of former chieftains and their *kahuna* (the official keepers of the ancient knowledge and profound wisdom of the early Hawaiians), and as their cudgels. The title itself suggests the depth of meaning and entendre found in most of her verses, in this instance calling upon the combined powers of Pele and night and chants of war. Trask's allusion recalls a version of the creation myth wherein Pele's sexual advances are obfuscated as sea thrice pours down upon her head. In fact, the ritual implied in her chanted words connects to the ancestors and to their natural world, to the very archetypes that had once assured their never-ending connection to humanity.

This connection is made concrete later with another allusion, this time as Pele warns others across the sea of "lakes of flames," "Pôloa's breadfruit" and "rain and storm and piercing cold."[1] The matter of tonal values, of a precise and fastidious sense of the possibilities of phrasing, and of an intricate yet instinctive feeling for the dynamic of the structure are obvious, as art, dance, music and poetry are highly integrated into every aspect of life, to a degree far beyond that of contemporary society, and Trask makes the most of this sense of integration as she relies upon the power of the *hula*. In fact, when read together, her poetic sequences reveal the larger hidden nature of a dance sustained, interlocking: verbal nuances, at once compelling and full of life, lend themselves to a well-defined progression from beginning with *eruptions* and *flames*, to end or "climax" in *night* and *darkness*, only to return to a new beginning of *rain* and *piercing cold*. The sophisticated dimensions of the words—the mythological aspects, cultural implications, and ecological setting—provide an unprecedented glimpse into her deeper layers of nuance.

In fact, the entirety of Trask's second volume builds upon Island traditions, moving as it does through song-chants and the dance of *hula*, intimately connecting Pele and her sister Hi'iaka to the volcanic landscape of Hawai'i and other phenomena of nature.[2] Her mythological epic ties primal elements together, and the resulting power of the lyric and its dramatic effect are unsurpassed, as she captures the inherent poetry of Hawaiian places, the feel of the Hawaiian landscape—in particular, those volcanic features viewed as the handiwork of Pele herself—and the unique mood of a Hawaiian nation long past. As she dances, sings, commemorates, Trask reminds us of the potential of renewal, of renewed relationships to the continuum of time and to the universe, dynamic, responsive, evolving. Insofar as any once-isolated sense of self *becomes* integrated, communal, one gains a truly *transformational* relationship to the physical and the social environments. Perhaps more to the point, her visual and auditory mirroring of repetitive gestures and songs have a positive impact on those individuals once isolated, alone and disrupted.

Put differently, repetition or participation for the poet form the sole basis for reality, and only by ceasing to be alone, shunning any sense of individuality outside of a larger communal identity, can reality be addressed.[3] Inherent to the limitations of archetypes and its paradigmatic gestures, we *become* as we borrow from the past, as we undertake an archetypal role and allow ourselves to participate in the ritual. Trask reminds us that only when we *embrace* and *honor* our place in the ever-spiraling continuum are we, therefore, empowered to experience ourselves as component to a greater reality. No longer are we alone.

Composed in spare stanzas, this volume becomes in the end a lyrical evocation of Hawai'i by an angry poet whose ancestral lands have fallen before the false gods of tourist dollars, increased militarization, and uncurbed urbanization. More important, the stanzas echo in effect the many chants, the war dance (*Hula ku'i moloka'i*) performed to a repetitive beating of the communal drum, or *pahu hula* (Kahananui 28). Grounded in the ancient grandeur and beauty of Hawai'i, this collection is both the hunt and the haunting love song for a beloved homeland under assault. It is safe to say that in both volumes, Trask is at her strongest when she manages to balance craft with anger and defiance. Taken together, her anthologies of poetry equates the native Hawaiian experience in its historical context as no more than colonialism, initiated by military invasion and sustained through military and economic occupation and oppression. Uncompromising, she goes a considerable distance with her poetry as she speaks fervently in favor of the rights of native peoples the world over.

Poetry, then, is not only crucial to her activism; it is the vehicle that propels her arguments forward. For Trask believes in and utilizes her art for change. She could do no less. There is, in fact, a cost to speaking without anger of the deaths and dislocation that Native Hawaiians suffered in postcontact Hawai'i. On the simple, communicative level, any failure to express the pain created by this legacy obscures the depth of individual feeling and discounts the subordination experienced by the larger community. More significantly, the use of polite, rational tones when feeling violation underscores an overwhelming betrayal of the self.

In the absence of an audience moved by her exhortations, Trask can do no more than lament what she perceives as apathy among native Hawaiians who eschew "small fortunes" in favor of "observing the parade."

Later, her lamentations give way to an ugly cruelty and abuse in the form of personal attacks. At one point, she lambasts Daniel Inouye, the U.S.

senator from Hawai'i.[4] Under her acerbic pen, the "armless" senator as typical of all Japanese Americans in the Islands is smugly rendered, diminished, then denounced as a preposterous manikin, "feigning an accent."

It is not without a certain sense of irony that the third and strongest section, "Chants of Dawn," immediately follows such vicious and insidious attacks. Life, she tacitly seems to recognize on some level at least, cannot be sustained in isolation; therefore, compelled toward health and survival, it seeks connection to others. Searching for balance and integration is a dynamic process, the opposite of the static state of physical, emotional spiritual or cognitive imbalance. Her anger, thus, resolves as love poems and celebrations of the land—often in spare stanzas that travel toward "sovereign suns" and the intoxicating "mana/of Hawai'i."

As she balances craft with defiance, the rhythms of Nature reconnect. We find integration, balance, and ultimately a promise that the health of an entire people might find encouragement and restoration (Franklin and Lyons 222–249). Simultaneously, we are left with to question whether the interweaving of multiple storylines detracts from or perhaps even erases the gravity of meaning of the original myths, or whether it contributes to a multifaceted engagement with the subject.[5]

Believing that native Hawaiians have been shunted off to the margins of society, she employs her words as weapons against what she perceives to be the oppressor. Aside from marking out the differences between European nationalism and postcolonial ones, Trask indicates the ways in which an elitist nationalism spoke for the "fragments" of the colony, such as women, peasants, and other outcasts. Decades after the formation, national governments in the region continue to transmit deeply structured and powerfully conflicting expectations from its citizenry of belonging and allegiance to the nation-state. Clearly, the tensions surrounding these expectations as well as the shifting nature of globalization and geopolitics can be seen in a myriad of cultural expressions that require a reassessment of marginalization and privilege.

By problematizing the cultural longevity of Hawai'i in a time of increased trans- and post national creativity, she forces her audience to question not the legitimacy but the primacy of indigenous Island culture. She opens a debate on the place of citizenship, as well as whether those select, newly privileged "citizens" ought embrace, co-opt, or perhaps abandon the Other, those who once enjoyed privilege but now are by definition denigrated as "marginalized communities" in order to sustain their own legitimacy.

But is sovereignty necessarily the answer? Does it in some way repair the lingering effects of cultural trauma? Might it restore function, to compensate for a fault, or can the concept be expanded to account for a general condition whereby a constitutive fault is repaired by art, justice or invention?[6]

Although Pele lives to this day in the Hawaiian imagination and inside her volcanoes, her exuberant spirit remains uncontained, at times dangerous and dehumanizing, at others, creative and explosive in abundance. Never able to win a clear victory as she explores the ebb and flow of desire, memory, belief, it is the tension of opposing forces maintains balance. Likewise, it is this continuous movement that suggests an eventual sensitivity to the literal and the metaphysical flow of energy into and out of the body (Macy 51–79). Celebrating the rhythmic unity of all things in Nature, as personified by the goddess Pele, these movements recall on a metaphoric level—as metaphorical conceit—ancient rituals and archetypes; they are simultaneously tribal and divine.

In the end, Trask's vision of creation *ex nihilo* mirrors as it proposes its own caveat: in the absence of any sense of repairing, combining, and retooling materials already at hand, her alternative vision forces us to reconsider the foundations of modernism as we replace myths of rupture and perfection with a celebration of the potential, the repair and its material traces.

Certainly, Trask's method has its dangers but is a way of establishing a context with many overtones of association and significance. Like the volcano's lava that creates new land, the goddess Pele reminds us that even fiery eruptions and emotional upheavals are followed by new life and change. At the least, we await the promise inherent to the indomitable human spirit, ever hopeful, that inscribes these archetypal dances and indeed all true healing. She has insisted on finding a poetic line and diction that are intrinsically Hawaiian even as she betrays a revulsion against all that has happened, a tale of discarded traditions in the absence of new values worthy of civilization.

NOTES

1. In order to appreciate a sense of the rhythms original to Pele's chant, it bears repeating here: *Kîpû iho la i ka lau o ke ahi;/Pala 'e'ehu i ka lâ/'ulu o Pôloa, e!/Pô wale ho'i; e ho'opô mai ana ka 'oe iâ'u./I ka hoa o ka ua, o kea nu, o ke ko'eko'e!* (Kahananui 11).

2. Following Isadora Duncan's understanding of the "movement of waves, of wind, of the earth ... [as] ... ever in the same lasting harmony" (*The Art of the Dance*), we might appreciate the extent to which our lives are so defined in a unidirectional temporality that remain unconscious of the cycles of nature, inured as it were to the "cycles within ourselves" (Dossey 25).

3. Whereas early missionaries discouraged *hula* as vulgar, indigenous Hawaiians failed to renounce the practice even as they accepted an alien Christianity. And because they continued the tradition in secret until such time as they could practice them openly again, today they are preserved in memory and in the poems and the dances learned from their *kupuna*, or ancestors.

4. Her description takes on additional meaning, as well. Hitherto, Hawaiian characters in literature and film often embody the problematic role of the "Other" and are usually forced into a stereotype reflecting an unmistakable Western bias perspective as an epitome of fundamentalism and hatred versus the civilization and modernity represented by white, wealthy westerners.

5. In what has come to be one of the defining twenty-first century issues, *inter alia*, multifarious approaches to this issue, Hawaiian independence activists argue that since the overthrow and annexation were both illegal, the independence of Hawai'i should as a matter of course be restored. Since the United States overthrew the Royal family and annexed their territory, the United States must voluntarily and peacefully withdraw from the Islands. But should independence and sovereignty be re-established, what becomes of the 80 percent of the population who have no Hawaiian blood?

6. In *The Portrait of the Artist as a Young Man*, for example, James Joyce writes of going forth to "forge in the smithy of my soul the uncreated conscience of my race" (134). His gesture goes a long way in positioning art as a consciousness-shaping agency.

Works Cited

Amos, Tori. "Mohammad, My Friend." On *Boys from Pele*. (Track 8). Atlantic Records, 1996.
Dossey, Larry. *Space, Time and Medicine*. Boston: Shambhala, 1982.
Duncan, Isadora. *The Art of the Dance*. New York: Theatre Arts Books, 1928.
Eliade, Mircea. *The Myth of the Eternal Return*. Princeton: Princeton University Press, 1954.
Emerson, Nathaniel B. *Pele and Hi'iaka: A Myth from Hawaii*. VT: Tuttle, 2013.
_____. *Unwritten Literature of Hawaii: The Sacred Songs of the Hula*. Honolulu: Forgotten Books, 2008.
Franklin, Cynthia and Laura E. Lyons. "Land, Leadership, and Nation: Haunani-Kay Trask on the Testimonial Uses of Life Writing in Hawai'i." *Biography* 27.1 (2004): 222–249.
Joyce, James. *A Portrait of an Artist as a Young Man*. New York: CreateSpace Independent Publishing, 2014.
Kahananui, Dorothy M. *Music of Ancient Hawaii*. Hilo, HI: The Petroglyph Press, 1962.
Kalākaua, David. *The Legends and Myths of Hawaii*. New York: Mutual Publishing Co., 1990.
Macy, Robert D. "Healing in Familiar Settings." *New Directions for Youth Development: Youth Facing Threat and Terror*. Summer 51–79. *Youth Facing Threat and Terror: Supporting Preparedness and Resilience: New Directions for Youth Development*, No. 98. Ed. Robert D. Macy, Susanna Barry, and Gil G. Noam. San Francisco: Jossey-Bass, 2003.
Trask, Haunani-Kay. *Light in the Crevice Never Seen*. Corvallis: Calyx Books, 1994.
_____. *Native Daughter: Colonialism and Sovereignty in Hawaii*. Honolulu: Common Courage Press, 1993.
_____. *Night Is a Sharkskin Drum*. Honolulu: University of Hawai'i Press, 2002.
Žižek, Slavoj. *Tarrying with the Negative: Kant, Hegel and the Critique of Ideology*. Durham, NC: Duke University Press, 1993.

Mythic Reenactment from Sandra Alcosser and Pattiann Rogers

Tami Haaland

In her *Short History of Myth,* Karen Armstrong says that myths "help us to cope with the problematic human predicament." They show us our origins, teach us about death and offer explanations about moments of transcendence (6). According to Joseph Campbell, myth functions "to initiate the individual into the order of realities of [the] psyche," which leads to "spiritual enrichment and realization" (*Occidental Mythology* 521-22).

Contemporary, industrialized and technologized society offers few opportunities for the kind of mythic reenactments or initiation ceremonies common in traditional societies. Mircea Eliade points out that we view ourselves as essentially secular, despite the implicit effect of various myths and archetypes upon our behavior. "Modern man's originality, his newness in comparison with traditional societies, lies precisely in his determination to regard himself as a purely historical being, in his wish to live in a basically desacralized cosmos" (*Rites and Symbols of Initiation* ix). According to Armstrong, "our modern alienation from myth is unprecedented" (10). She points out that our heavy reliance on rational thought to the exclusion of myth has led to divisiveness, including the violence of world wars and other catastrophes of the modern world (Armstrong 132-35).

Though not writing specifically about myth, Martin Heidegger describes a similar problem with contemporary existence: human beings have "'spirit and reason' and [are] destined to think," but have accustomed themselves to only one kind of thought, namely, calculative thought, which is the primary thought process involved in science and the development of technology. Meditative thought, on the other hand, ponders, and dwells "upon that which concerns us ... here and now." Such thinking lends itself to the contemplation of symbol, archetype and myth as they play upon our lives. But we run away from this latter kind of thinking, Heidegger argues, in part because we are inundated by technological devices (44).

Emerging from this historical context, from this present, secularized condition, some contemporary writers provide readers with intimate access to myth. Among them are Sandra Alcosser and Pattiann Rogers who recreate the sensory detail that breathes life into old stories. The poems become reenactments that entice the community of readers to participate in the world of myth and the possibility of transformed identity.

In *Except by Nature*, Sandra Alcosser takes up the theme of initiation in "Wildcat Path," a poem focused on a woman who encounters a cougar. Instead of portraying a terrifying event, she creates a voice that speaks of fascination and discovery, the voice of a woman tracking a mystery. Alcosser thus portrays a woman strengthened and remade by her connection with this powerful natural force.

As the poem begins, the speaker, presumably a teacher, has stepped from a school bus and is walking through a wooded area while a small mountain lion follows her. When her husband shoots at and misses the animal, a tuft of hair remains on a nearby aspen. The experience of this event contradicts the expectations of her family and neighbors as well as the stereotypical assumptions about women in distress. Neighbors and family imagine that her fear was unbearable, that she only wanted her husband to rescue her. Yet she is confident in her own ability to frighten the animal away and says, "I wanted her close. Breathing in my face" (46). She doesn't fully define this quality that draws her close to the cat, but by the end of the poem, the speaker wears the tuft of cat hair "pressed in a locket covering the faces of my family. / Nothing else will ever give me such pleasure in my body" (55–56).

The husband with the gun, the school bus, the house and neighbors all represent modern civilization and what is acceptable in the eyes of the community. The speaker walks away from all of this and toward the wild land which is associated symbolically with chaos. The cougar can take away life, and her closeness to it implies a symbolic death, one of the essential elements of an initiatory experience. We see her entering into this "death" as her dress is shredded and destroyed. Then, she walks naked in the forest, implicitly reborn into her new existence.

No longer just the calming and nurturing lady she has always been, she recognizes less visible elements of her personality. She has "wanted to scream / like that every day of [her] life. Take the world / with one swipe. Delicate-like, chew on its bones" (18–20). The speaker takes on qualities that society values much less than the "gentleness" she exhibited before. As she presses the hair over the faces of her family, she asserts her autonomy from them and the primacy of this experience in her life. It is common that a person transformed by an animal spirit takes on the qualities of that animal. In this instance, the speaker discovers both power and ferocity within herself as she assumes this new identity. She has become "the woman who walked with a lion" (50).

In *Firekeeper: New and Selected Poems*, Pattiann Rogers frequently writes about mythical themes by approaching them tangentially, without naming characters or story, though both are often implied. In "There is a Way to Walk on Water," for instance, she creates a mesmerizing scene in which both speaker and reader are drawn into the experience. Taken first by the idea of the impossible—defying natural law by stepping onto the surface of water—the reader moves further into the details of the moment until, apparently, natural laws are suspended all together. The person on the water becomes as pliable as the air above the sea, yet conscious of "migrating petrels" moving through the body.

Rogers draws upon a Christian myth as subject for the poem, but through her detailed description, she allows readers to imaginatively reenact that experience as they are drawn into the sensory detail. This and other poems by Rogers can be seen as similar to the mythic retellings used as one of the tools of shamans and visionaries to acquire passage into another state of being. The poem establishes a sense of awe and allows the reader to participate in an imagined mythical experience, which suggests that poetry and other creative arts can fulfill many if not all of the functions of myth (see Eliade, Armstrong, and Campbell, below).

In another of her poems, "The Laying-on of Hands" whose title refers again to a Christian miracle, Rogers allows us both to suspend disbelief and explore human limitations. "There's a gentleness we haven't learned yet, but we've seen it" (1–2), and "there's a subtlety we haven't mastered yet, but we recognize it" (9–10). Rather than invoking only Jesus' laying on of hands to create healing or miracle, Rogers moves further back, invoking the tree of knowledge—woman and tree—and by extension, the idea of the cosmic tree, a myth that exists in one form or another in various cultures: the trees of knowledge and life in Genesis, the cross of the New Testament, Yggdrasil of Scandinavian myth, the tree at the center of the sun dance lodge that serves as an axis to connect heaven and earth. In this vein, the poem gives us a contemporary example of an age-old symbol that is situated at the center of many creation myths as a means of connecting the divine world to the human world. And what comes through most importantly in this poem is the sense of connection between self and tree implying an intimate intertwining of self and myth.

Rogers moves a step further along this path by creating another mythical scene, one the reader is again invited to enter. In "Eating Death," she addresses finality at the same time that she invokes the beginning: "Suppose I had never distinguished myself / to myself from the landscape" (1–2). Here the supposition eliminates any premise of dualism, of subject and object, and the speaker becomes, at least imaginatively, indistinct from the world she inhabits. She is no longer the separate entity longing for reunion, and in this context, even death is not a threat.

"Eating Death" serves as both a reenactment of the beginning of consciousness and an initiation into death. According to Eliade, any kind of initiation involves a death of the old self which makes room for the new self to emerge (*Myths, Dreams, and Mysteries* 208). One common way that this death occurs in stories from ancient and traditional cultures is for the initiate to be swallowed by a monster and subsequently reborn out of that experience.[1] In Rogers' poem, the speaker puts her arms "around its neck, to draw [it] in, sucking, / swallowing" (40–41); because the speaker and death are inseparable, there seems to be a mutual consumption in which both are destroyed. As Eliade speaks about it, being swallowed by a monster is a mystery

> that involves the most terrible of initiatory ordeals, that of death, but which also constitutes the only possible way of abolishing temporal duration—in other words, of annulling historic existence—and of re-entering into the primordial situation. Evidently, this re-entry into the germinal state of 'the beginnings' is itself equivalent to death: in effect, one 'kills' one's own profane historic existence, now outworn, to re-enter into an immaculate, open existence, untainted by Time [*Myths, Dreams, and Mysteries* 223].

Paradoxically, Roger's poem recreates this experience by following the thread of a supposition that portrays the speaker in what appears to be a primordial state in which there is no separation. This means that she would have no need to "return" since she is already "there." But as she meets death, its "grin" is "the white stone" of the speaker's "history" (33), which suggests that her condition is not so much primordial, but both inside and outside of time. On the one hand, the supposition invites us to imagine this speaker and the landscape as identical, so unified that there is no separateness or passage of time; on the other hand, the speaker has a separate consciousness that allows her to recognize death coming towards her.

To have history, according to Eliade, Armstrong, and Campbell, is to live beyond mythical origins in the secular, everyday world. As she meets death, then, mouth to mouth, first kissing and then consuming it in the "last event of [her] life" (43), the speaker partakes in the annulment of her own history. In one way, this last scene reverses the mystery in which the monster swallows the initiate. Here, the initiate consumes death, the monster. But the opening supposition of this poem establishes that the speaker is not other than anything that she encounters, or to put it another way, all things extend from her. Therefore her consumption of death is no different from death consuming her.

What happens to the reader who encounters such a startling account of death? My guess is that it shocks, fascinates, lures one into the idea that the end can be so lovingly welcomed. But beyond the most literal possibilities, the poem provides a vicarious initiation for the reader, one that opens the reader's mind and spirit into "the order of realities of his own psyche, guiding him toward his own spiritual enrichment and realization" (Campbell, *Occidental Mythology* 522).

In their recreation of mythical scenes, both Alcosser and Rogers rely upon precise images from nature, allowing the reader to imagine via specific sensory detail the world in which the myth can occur. The interconnection between myth and nature stretches as far back as myth itself. The sense that the numinous lies behind the natural world is not only a Romantic and post-Romantic idea, but is common in the worldview of many oral and traditional cultures worldwide. Nature becomes a place of revelation, populated by divine attributes and sometimes spirits—like personified death—replete with lessons and experiences that expand the horizon of participants. For the most part, the traditional, initiatory experience sends the initiate back into the natural world that she has come from in order to be reborn.

Eliade remarked that during the medieval period of western history, the "ritual reality" of initiation lost its potency and instead the "spiritual message" of the experience was addressed directly to the imagination through literature (*Rites and Symbols of Initiation* 125–26). Armstrong discusses literature at length, indicating that writers "are operating at the same level of consciousness as mythmakers," and as a result, they dwell on similar themes (142). But it is perhaps Campbell who has the most to say about those who come upon "signs and symbols," then translate them for others. These people

> are the sensitized, creative, living minds that once were known as seers, but now as poets and creative artists. More important, more effective for the future of a culture than its statesmen or its armies are these masters of the spiritual breath by which the clay of man wakes to life [519].

In this light, Alcosser and Rogers, like many artists, are playing a critical role. Their poems offer passage into the world of "signs and symbols" and present readers with the opportunity to engage in initiatory journeys and the possibility of transformation.

NOTE

1. For examples of this phenomenon, see Joan Halifax, *Shamanic Voices*, especially the account of Sanimuinak (110–113).

WORKS CITED

Alcosser, Sandra. *Except by Nature*. St. Paul: Graywolf, 1998.
Armstrong, Karen. *A Short History of Myth*. New York: Canongate, 2005.

Campbell, Joseph. *The Hero with a Thousand Faces*. 3rd. ed. Princeton: Bollinger, 1973.
_____. *The Masks of God: Occidental Mythology*. 4th ed. New York: Viking, 1972.
Eliade, Mircea. *Myths, Dreams, and Mysteries*. Trans. Philip Mairet. New York: Harper & Row, 1960.
_____. *Rites and Symbols of Initiation: The Mysteries of Birth and Rebirth*. Trans. Willard R. Trask. New York: Harper & Row, 1965.
Halifax, Joan. *Shamanic Voices: A Survey of Visionary Narratives*. New York: Penguin, 1979.
Heidegger, Martin. "Memorial Address." *Discourse on Thinking*. Trans. John M. Anderson and E. Hans Freund. New York: Harper & Row, 1966. 43–57.
Rogers, Pattiann. *Firekeeper: New and Selected Poems*. Minneapolis: Milkweed Editions, 1994.

Utilizing and Disrupting Legends in Indian Poetry

PRAMILA VENKATESWARAN

In the tradition of Indian poetry, using mythology for creative self-articulation or as analogy for experiences of the individual and the world is an accepted convention. So is the retelling of the myths, because the audience never tires of such retelling, from the mouth of a storyteller at the temple or from the printed words of a poet. But in the last few decades, with the growth of many movements, such as postcolonialism, feminist movements, and postmodernism in the arts, the critique of received mythology is alive in everything from poetry to film. In poetry, we see the retelling of the myths particularly by Indian poets from the points of view of female characters, or from the point of view of the poet who is looking at myths in a new way, thus enabling her to paint a reality applicable to our present day travails or use myths for aesthetic purposes.

In a dialogue between the narrator and Dhurjati Babu about holy men posing as charlatans in Satyajit Ray's short story, "Khagama," Dhurjati Babu criticizes society's naive acceptance of the *Ramayana*[1] and the *Mahabharata*[2] without critique. He calls these epics a bunch of weird tales that people, educated or not, have been swallowing whole for centuries (Ray 77). Babu's skepticism of mythology is tested in this story that climaxes in the strange transformation of Babu into the cobra, the holy man's (Imli Baba's) pet, which he kills: thus his cynicism makes Babu become a weird myth himself!

Ray is obviously playing with the conservative idea that one should not question myth but accept it as devoutly as something divine; at the same time, Ray relishes mischievously in the idea of creating a new myth out of transforming the naysayer into the cobra that he kills, so now people can actually gossip about the new myth that is spawned out of the old one about the holy man, Imli Baba. Thus one tale ends and a new tale is born out of the old, as if to say myths don't just die but live on.

Such an interaction with mythology, which could involve retelling or questioning, is prevalent among contemporary Indian poets. The result is both a fascination with mythology and a pressing need to rewrite some of the myths. Mythology in India is the stock genre available for narration in the home and the temple. It is the stock-in-trade of bedtime storytelling as well as the subject matter in large assemblies gathered for instructional storytelling (*katha kalakshemam*). Myth informs daily life, the cultural life of the people—it is everywhere, in temples, in dance and sculpture, poetry, covers of textbooks and festivals. It becomes reenacted in families, so much so that mythology seems more real than reality itself. The speaking deer, the compassionate monkey, the talking tree, humans transforming into natural objects are accepted as tangible. The suspension of disbelief that Samuel Taylor Coleridge urges among readers of poetry is so germane to the Indian psyche that rationalists like Satyajit Ray's character, Dhurjati Babu, have a difficult time eschewing it. The old quandary of whether fiction mirrors life or life fiction is moot when we see the lines between imagination and reality collapsing in mythology infusing the daily life of a people.

We can argue that myth is a paradigm inhabiting our collective unconscious that we tap into from time to time as a way of keeping us on the path. A. K. Ramanujan in "The Ring of Memory," discusses how all great stories are about forgetting and remembering. Myth is perhaps what we remember especially when we are coming out of amnesia, like King Dushyanta in Kalidasa's *Abignyana Sakuntala*. The king forgets his promise to Sakuntala that they will marry after his travels, and only when he retrieves the ring—swallowed by a fish and found by a fisherman who is charged with stealing the king's ring—does he remember his love. Just as the ring in this instance, or the absent lover evoked by a landscape, object or memory "will [a person] into being" (Ramanujan, *Uncollected Poems* 98), so does myth serve this function of "re-cognition." We can think of references to names in myths as metonyms. They conjure up our memory of the whole story, but we can carry that metonym "everywhere to conjure up the original at will" (99). Poets from Srinivas Iyengar to Dom Moraes, Kamala Das, and A.K. Ramanujan have not only written about a poetics that fashions itself in new ways in a decolonizing world of post-independent India, but their poems enact this poetics. The poets' re-enactment of myth and their framing of new mythologies through such a re-cognition and re-vision creates a mythopoetics of reality.

Reginald Shepherd points out the three uses of myth in modern poetry: retell the myth, relive it by entering it on a personal level as a moment or a character, or revise it in order to enlighten readers about some aspect of it that is clouded or oppressive (Shepherd).

It is rare that a modern Indian poet retells mythological stories blindly. But the poems that do retell myths add a new element to our understanding of the story. For example, R. Parthasarathy's "Kannagi" is beautiful in terms of both content and form. (Kannagi is the heroine of the Tamil epic *Cillapatikaram* by Illango Adigal). The poet describes Kannagi's rage at the injustice meted out to her husband by the king. She plucks out her breast and hurls it over the city of Madurai, an act that makes the flames leap up and engulf the city. The poet asks at the end of the poem if Kannagi knew before this act that makes the divine beings raise her up to heaven what would become of her land. Metrically spare, and syntactically tight, the poem advances within a few clauses to this overwhelming question the poet asks Kannagi: "What would become / of her sweet Tamil country?" (Parthasarathy 54). The question, we realize, is the poet's own, as we read his poem, "The Attar of Tamil." In this poem, Parthasarathy refers to the mythology of India as the island of the rose apple tree, one of the seven islands that make up the world. This is a personal poem where the poet talks of his return to his country after being away from it and realizes that just like the rose apple tree (i.e., India) has been unscathed, so is he despite his exile (Parthasarathy 55). He comes back readily to his language and his land despite his hiatus from both; memory is fueled by desire. Both the mythical Kannagi and he are deeply attached to their land and their mother tongue. Leaving them means death. The male poet empathizes with his mythic heroine and shares with her the emotion of place and language, both iterated as feminine.

Sitayana is an example of a modern Indian poet rewriting the *Ramayana* from Sita's[3] point of view, thus giving Sita voice, because its author, Srinivasa Iyengar feels this main protagonist is rendered voiceless in this powerful myth that informs a patriarchal culture. Therefore giving Sita voice turns the tide against patriarchy. Iyengar enters the feminine psyche with the power of his imagination in this elaborate volume, thus "re-marking" the myth by retracing his path back to Sita and her life of further exile from Rama after the test of fire (Iyengar).

Another example of recognizing mythology and remaking it is Nirendranath Chakrabarthi's "Fatal Evening." This poem is written in the voice of Arjuna,[4] who toward the end of the *Mahabharatha*, loses some of his divine power bestowed on him by Krishna, is unable to protect his people, and is defeated by a gang of thieves. The poet has a different take on Arjuna. While Vyasa, the author of the *Mahabharatha*, believes that Arjuna's fate is predestined, Chakrabarthi's Arjuna asserts that he is a creature of will, not fate. This philosophical emphasis on will can be read as a product of the crisis of colonialism followed by independence. The poet's character is despondent that he is unable to use his divine Gandiva (weapon) against a bunch of thieves. He feels he has forsaken his people. The hero of the epic thus becomes an anti-hero in the poem. Interestingly, midway in the poem, the poet addresses Arjuna in the third person and assumes a voice in the poem, almost as if becoming the mythological character now transposed into reality in twentieth century India (Chakrabarti 52).

In modern Indian poetry, one seldom finds a mere retelling of mythological stories. Instead, there is a preponderance of using the myth to enter one's own experience, so the myth becomes a gateway to personal discovery. As Reginald Shepherd explains, "Myth can also be used to place one's own experiences, thoughts, and feelings in a larger context, opening them up to realms beyond the individual, making them less purely personal and idiosyncratic," so even if the poet is talking about her own private experience, couching it in a particular mythological story makes the poem accessible to the reader and lifts it from the purely private. Shepherd shows how Louise Glück does this by using the Ulysses myth to talk about her personal experience in her family. Contemporary Indian poets and South Asian diasporic poets have interesting takes on Indian mythology and use them in inventive ways to write about their lives: Poets such as Usha Akella, Chitra Divakaruni, Reetika Vazirani, Meena Alexander, Suniti Namjoshi, Usha Kishore, Debjani Chatterjee, and prominent women poets thus rewrite and reflect on their personal lives or contemporary issues through mythology.

One important turning point in Indian poetry in the 1970s was the assertion of voice by Indian poets as they became more conscious of themselves as independent. Irony and realism were the twin strategies that became the hallmarks of late twentieth century Indian poetry. Paradox, wit, humor, self-mockery, the use of colloquial English, a breakdown of forms, and a questioning of tradition characterize modern Indian poetry. The feminist voice in Indian poetry became resounding after the 1970s in poets like Kamala Das and Eunice DeSouza, followed in the 1990s by poets like Rukmini Bhaya Nair, Meena Alexander, and numerous others. These poets dived into the wreck of patriarchy to retrieve the book of myths to find their names. "Like the speaker in Adrienne Rich's 'Diving into the Wreck,' whose discovery of her submerged self is a discovery that she is a 'we' for whom even the distinction between subject and object dissolves," with the result that the heroines in revisionist mythology are more "fluid than solid" (Ostriker 237).

Rukmini Bhaya Nair's "Genderole" needs to be read in this light. She critiques received tradition as voiced by the myths and as encapsulated by some of the saints, such as Sankara.[5] Sankara himself, a quasi-mythological figure, due to his intellectual prowess and his divine inspiration and strength making him an enlightened figure in a drab environment, who dies at the young age of 32 after a prolific output, is a subject central to many of the debates in Hindu philosophy. In "Genderrole," Nair flouts English meter and syntax, and questions Sankara's message in his poems, such as "Bhaja Govindam."

Nair reproduces in English the run-on graphemic style of Sanskrit poetic meter that Sankara uses in his poem, "Bhaja Govindam," while at the same time questioning Sankara's assumptions. She quarrels with Sankara about his idea that women are part of the fleeting splendor that man encounters in the world and therefore man needs to abrogate desire in order to achieve salvation. Nair argues, using postmodern slang, that woman is the "basic text" that fills in the "gaps" in Sankara's misogynistic philosophy that denies women their material being and spiritual aspirations (Nair 67).

While Nair's language may sound mocking and irreverent to the ears of the religious who revere Sankara as a god, her openness within the margins of the poetic text falls soundly within the Indian tradition of *bhashya*, or commentary: No theory is considered beyond argument. Thus, while Indian poets use myth, they feel free to disrupt it and play with it. Feminist poets understand and employ jouissance to rewrite mythical texts and shape them to empower themselves and the female collective.

Myth also allows for poets to use language in interesting and "strange" ways. The abnormality of mythology flows seamlessly with the abstraction in poetry and more so with disruptions of form and quirkiness of syntax. Reetika Vazirani's use of the Radha-Krishna[6] myth to talk of her own experience in *Radha Says* is worth exploring. Perhaps of many contemporary books, Vazirani's posthumous volume best exemplifies the disruption of mythology to create a new mythology of the speaker or reader of the poem. For example, "Hotel Moghul and Housekeeping" is probably about a woman in a hotel who is clad in a petticoat and sari blouse receiving a call from her lover who is betraying her. Her sense of exile is evoked by the metonymic references to the *Ramayana*—"14 years," and the name "Sita" three-quarters of the way into the poem—as well as the lover saying he has to "take another call." The housekeeping the woman does is like that done by Sita and Radha of myth: the line between the characters has dissolved (Vazirani 34). In "Reader of Lawbooks and Radha," Vazirani juxtaposes the law books against Radha's actions to show how she flouts convention: "do not take another man's wife / but Krishna takes Radha and her thousand." The syntactic arrangement of the lines in order to show opposites becomes disrupted in "She Knows Krishna Will Leave." Adding "I am sunbrowned…" the speaker's personal experience with her lover is superimposed and filters through the affair between Krishna and Radha. In myth, Radha is in love with Krishna but is often jealous when he does not show up and feels complete only when he is with her. Their relationship is characterized by quarrel, passion, longing, and joy. In Vazirani's poem, despite the jagged lines, the story reveals itself pulling us toward her declaration, "I savor the jilted / havoc of my breath … sometimes we / murder what will save us" (Vazirani 32). We are shaken by her use of the word "murder"; argument *is* like murdering the person we love most, so the myth which is about the joining of lovers after the quarrel may not become our reality. Outside the frame of the poem, Vazirani tragically murders her child and commits suicide, the poetic text becoming a palimpsest of her mythobiography! Like Rukmini Bhaya Nair, Vazirani abandons plain English syntax for lines that fragment, slip into new sentence-parts without pause, and run on mapping the stream of our minds. The strangeness of her lines as a result resembles the strangeness of myth: and as readers we accept both equally because of our fascination with stories and our willingness to suspend disbelief for pleasure.

Contemporary poets create mythology using lived experience in strange and complex ways. A.K. Ramanujan's "Breaded Fish" for example is a poem that, although it does not refer directly to a particular myth, becomes a myth in itself: the dead woman who has been washed up on the beach covered with sand appears like breaded fish (Ramanujan 4). The image, despite the sadness and mystery of the death, becomes the stuff of our senses by evoking a delicacy as well as Visnu's avatar as fish or "matsya." Perhaps, the poet suggests, this death is not an end but the regeneration of the soul into a new life. Consumption and renewal—the twin foundations of creation—keep us going, even if the speaker in this poem is too stunned to be able to swallow, let alone savor, anything. Here again, like in Vazirani's poems, the poet's life of being married to a Christian who eats fish that he finds difficult to savor due to his strict Brahminical upbringing haunts the margins of the poem.

Similarly, Usha Akella creates myth out of people she meets and the places she visits. For example, in her poem, "Song for Gulsoma," the poet infuses the child, Gulsoma, with light—"Shine on little girl"; in the poem, the girl is transformed into a bird and a rose, thus disrupting the misery that is meted out to her by her family (Akella 108). In Akella's poems, places also transform, so the readers can imagine possibilities that are available to us. Jerusalem lies "under the fingertips of a golden menorah" (Akella 102). In Iraq, she can hear the bells ring instead of bombs (Akella 107). Nicaragua is a "lost poem" the poet retrieves (Akella 77).

Each time a poet uses or disrupts a myth, we get an interesting and new creation. In Vijay Seshadri's "The Long Meadow," Yuddhisthira, near the end of his life, approaches heaven to find his enemy being glorified there, not his brothers, the Pandavas! What is touching is that his dog is his only companion that wades with him toward the final scene where he ponders this "last illusion." The poet uses this detail to segue into his own wandering with his mutt in the Long Meadow by his house in New York. The dog, although "rescued from a crack house," is, touchingly, the rescuer of both Yuddhisthira and the poet (Seshadri 57). This detail is echoed by the speaker, a dog, in Arun Kolatkar's *Pi-Dog*, who traces his line back to Yuddhisthira's dog: "my ancestor became the only dog / to have made it to heaven / in recorded history"

(Kolatkar 519). The mythical dog also recites the Vedas and in his contemporary form is now cognizant of every smell and taste in his kingdom in the middle of a crowded metropolis. Through the use of myth, Kolatkar comments on contemporary India, as in *Sarpa Sastra*. Using colloquial language to recreate this classical Sanskrit text, a section of the *Mahabharata*, Kolatkar offers "a liberal or common sense revisioning of what in India has become a text used to justify the violence of reactionary Hinduism" (King 381). Similarly, Rukmini Bhaya Nair in *The Ayodhya Cantos*, uses the voices of Hanuman, Sita, and Vishnu to talk about the violence of Hindu nationalists destroying the Babri Masjid, a Muslim shrine in modern Ayodhya, in 1992. Nair's characters are contemporary using everyday language to address the goddess Bhavani, an immanent presence. "Vishnu sniggers. Wake up, Sitara! Hanumanji, / Flashback time is over.... Vishnu at / Your service, ready to produce his own B-grade movie" (Nair 34). Nair shows that myth does not necessarily dwell within a religious sphere but can be used to disrupt a violence emanating out of narrow definition of religion. The Hindu nationalists' claim that a Muslim holy place occupies Lord Rama's land is ultimately a philosophical impossibility, if indeed one believes that God cannot be pinned down to a few square meters! In this volume, because myth and reality intersect in the violence, the poet uses myth to break the continuing violence, showing that myth that is used as poison by one group can be used as antidote by another.

The disruption of mythology to talk about both personal life and contemporary issues is best done by Dalit poet activist, Meena Kandasamy. Her irreverence for Hindu mythology, as well as political figures who are mythologized, is startling. Her poems are hard-hitting, pointing out the built-in casteism in the myths. The last lines of "Ekalavyan," deliver their punch. She cleverly transports the figure of the discriminated Ekalavyan from the *Mahabharatha* into the modern context of the discriminated Dalit—is his trigger finger cut off by Dronacharya, the arch patriarch, for he will pull the trigger (release the arrow)? Her answer: "You don't need your right thumb / To pull a trigger or hurl a bomb" (Kandasamy). Although Nair and Kandasamy are separated by caste characteristics they are born with, they share similar politics and aesthetics. In fact, all the feminist poets this essay includes use mythology in a way that is useful to their feminist politics. What is also interesting is that many of the male poets referred to here also share the same politics. In my poem, "Draupadi's Dharma," the classical heroine of the *Mahabharatha* could be any woman who is in a war-torn modern setting, fed up with war and longing for an ordinary life. At the end of the poem, Draupadi turns to her husband, Yuddhishtira, and says, "I'm tired of your cock-eyed dharma" (Venkateswaran); her irreverence for the ethics of dharma or right action is meaningful, for it has proven to be its opposite in her context—a woman who is being stripped of her dignity.

Looking at mythology with the awareness of our personal experiences and from our vantage point in history, we can bring the spirit of play to myth thus increasing the jouissance of the page on which we write and our spirits. As Nair, Vazirani, Kandasamy, Seshadri and a host of South Asian poets, both women and men, show, we can look at mythology obliquely to tell its truth, allude to it, fragment it, shake a bit of it onto our experience or on a poem and stir the contents to see a new myth taking shape. Myth entices, but it does not have to rule us like a religion. As poets, we can enter and leave it at will, or shake up its contents to see what falls on our laps. As myth and poetry infuse each other, we are allowed insights that will break our fall, whether it is the violence in the country, family, or self.

NOTES

1. The classical Indian epic about the Prince Rama of Ayodhya exiled for 14 years by his father. During his exile, where he is accompanied by his wife Sita and his brother Lakshmana, Sita is kidnapped by Ravana. Rama with the help of Hanuman and an army of monkeys rescues Sita from Ravana after a long battle.
2. The classical Indian epic about the war between the Pandavas and the Kauravas over stolen land.
3. Heroine of the *Ramayana*.
4. One of the five Pandava brothers in the *Mahabharatha*.
5. A philosopher who composed many poems and philosophical treatises in Sanskrit.
6. One of the milkmaids who is the lover of Lord Krishna. Krishna, an avatar of Vishnu, advises the Pandavas in their war against the Kauravas. The *gopikas* or milkmaids sport with him in love play.

WORKS CITED

Akella, Usha. *The Rosary of Latitudes*. Houston: Transcendent Zero Press, 2015. Print.
Chakrabarti, Nirendranath. "Fatal Evening." *Another India: An Anthology of Contemporary Indian Fiction and Poetry*. Ed. Nissim Ezekiel and Meenakshi Mukherjee. New Delhi: Penguin, 1990. Print.
Iyengar, Srinivasa. *Sitayana*. Madras: Samata Books, 1987. Print.
Kandasamy, Meena. "Ekalavyan." *Poem Hunter*. http://poemhunter.com. Web.
King, Bruce. "2004: Ezekiel, Moraes, Kolatkar." *Fulcrum: An Annual of Poetry and Aesthetics*. No. 4. 2005. 366–381. Print.
Kolatkar, Arun. "from *Pi-Dog*." *Fulcrum: An Annual of Poetry and Aesthetics*. No. 4. 2005. 517–529. Print.
Nair, Rukmini Bhaya. *The Ayodhya Cantos*. New Delhi: Viking, 1999. Print.
_____. "Genderrole." *The Penguin New Writing in India*. Ed. Aditya Behl and David Nichols. Penguin Books India, 1994. Print.
Ostriker, Alicia. *Stealing the Language: The Emergence of Women's Poetry in America*. Boston: Beacon Press, 1986. Print.
Parthasarathy, R. "The Attar of Tamil." *The Penguin New Writing in India*. Ed. Aditya Behl and David Nichols. Penguin Books India, 1994. Print.
_____. "Kannagi." *The Penguin New Writing in India*. Ed. Aditya Behl and David Nichols. Penguin Books India, 1994. Print.
Ramanujan, A. K. "A Ring of Memory." *Uncollected Poems and Prose*. Ed Molly

Daniels-Ramanujan and Keith Harrison. New Delhi: Oxford University Press, 1991. Print.
_____. *Selected Poems*. New Delhi: Oxford University Press, 1976. Print.
Ray, Satyajit. "Khagama." *The Penguin New Writing in India*. Ed. Aditya Behl and David Nichols. Penguin Books India, 1994. Print.
Seshadri, Vijay. *The Long Meadow*. Minnesota: Gray Wolf Press, 2004. Print.
Shepherd, Reginald. "Mythology in Poetry." http://reginaldshepherd.blogspot.com/2007/08/mythology-in-poetry.html. Web.
Vazirani, Reetika. *Radha Says*. Ed. Leslie McGrath and Ravi Shankar. Connecticut: Drunken Boat, 2010. Print.
Venkateswaran, Pramila. "Draupadi." *Indivisible: An Anthology of Contemporary South Asian American Poetry*. Fayetteville: University of Arkansas Press, 2010. Print.

The Mything Link
The Feminine Voice in the Shifting Australian National Myth

PHIL FITZSIMMONS

An Introduction to the Context and Causation

It is generally recognized by social commentators that Australia is currently in the grip of an identity crisis. While the general populace is well aware of the growing recognition of a new emerging Australian spirit, so too the national mythic narrative is still is caught in a hazy tacit knowledge that revolves around the supposed collective heroism of the "bloody" Gallipoli impasse that began at dawn April 25, 1915. At the heart of this male-centered war narrative is the concept of "the Anzac digger," the "pioneer and bushman-soldier" (Day 76) whose sheer determination, fighting spirit and the "digging of trenches" engendered the Australian concept of "mateship." Such was the socio-political need for a national story and a national heroic figurehead at that time the Anzac myth was born, and "by the first anniversary it glowed with holiness" (Inglis 84). While seen in the ensuing national narrative as the laconic outback male "cattle drover," who is able to survive in the desert landscape of the outback through sheer determination, subduing the environment and native inhabitants, so too the resolute "diggers" survived the horrors of the Gallipoli campaign in the First World War. The eventual failure of the campaign and subsequent historical research revealing the glaring errors in the narrative has done nothing to dim its mythic extent, as the story has been converted into a heroic struggle "whose failure was appropriated to outside forces" (Beaumont 52).

However, as revealed in the current literary output there is a schizophrenic shift occurring in national psyche in which this "male landscape desert myth" is moving to one associated with the sea, and back again to some kind of liminal zone. As reflected in its more recent literary canon, the Australian sea and its beaches were recently seen as "deliverance to many, from the inland and from an imperial otherworld" (Scutter 53). Still, as Scutter continues:

> ... living by the sea is to indulge in hedonism and escapism, to dwell in Neverland, to refuse to grow up. The concluding movement away from the coast parallels the movement away from childhood and towards what is perceived as grown-up engagement with the imperatives of culture and civilization [54].

Is it any wonder then that Hywood contends, "We are a nation undecided—or at least lacking a consensus—? about some fundamental values." Although clinging to the old male-dominated narrative, there are obviously gaps appearing in the new symbolic codes. It would appear that there is recognition that the nostalgia of the primary narrative is not providing direction or a genuine familiarity in a changing world or sense of cultural fulfillment.

For many researchers it is generally accepted that mythic analysis provides the facets for a genuine understanding of national myth and that its literary "construction as deferred narrative and repetition" (Bhabha 101) does not always code the public psyche or the development of "national identity" as complete image or metaphors. In literary narrative, more often than not are actually "inversions" of the popular image, where the metaphoric element has "turned the image inside out" so as to provide a more complete understanding (Warner 137). However, it is in poetry that this meta-narrative focus and its "inside out image" are more completely reframed. If narrative tells the clearest truth about the conscious layers of humanity and the truth a culture holds at a particular time, then it is poetry that provides the clearest revelation of the "unconscious lies" that a culture clings to as it changes.

This is especially true in the poetry of Chris Mansell, who tells the feminine aspect of the Australian myth through the eyes of what can only be called the "transformative feminine." The lesser half of the Australian male motif, the subordinate wife of the "laconic, pioneer bushman-soldier" has often taken on the role of a quiet, intelligent, bored and subjugated partner in Australian narrative, something akin to the "monstrous feminine" in zombie mode. Mansell repudiates this trope completely, casting the feminine aspect as an act of "communal recovery" (Doty 120). Either consciously or unconsciously, she attempts to counteract "the all pervasive masculine processes of nationalism" (G. Turner 134) or "masculine lies embedded in the positioning of woman in the Australian national myth." She achieves through the use of single "nodes of myth," or critical single "constituent parts that charter, or found social self understanding and hence world view" (Doty 68). While these mythic nodes can be formed in many ways, they are often generated in the "liminal space," that period of "wilderness," "othering" or "in between time" in which an individual or group are unaware of who they are. Thus her poetry represents the current national condition as well revealing a mode of representing and revealing genuine identity. Kristeva contends that this liminal space and the lacunae markers represent the place and naming of the "abject," that "which disturbs identity, system, order. What does not respect borders, positions, rules" (4). While in a socio-psychological place akin to death or "deep in the belly of the whale" experience, it is also on the other hand a place of opportunity, out of which an individual or collective may begin to build "myths, metaphors, symbols, rituals and philosophic systems" (Deardorff 13).

Mansell's Poetic Map of the Feminine in The Good Soldier

In her poem *The Good Soldier*, Mansell initially links the typical Australian meta-narratives of the "outback soldier" and the "outback" with the national Anzac narrative, which supposedly reflects "the whole social history of Australia" (Ross 21). Through a careful weaving of mythic elements, she maps out the 'taken for granted' psyche of the Australian male as being the mythic desert hunter, but lost in a land where "distance is slung out" and "where the dirt is dead." In this metaphoric space of desolation, the mythic narrative reverts to those forms, which are always coded as a culture where the notion of the hero has become lost and replaced by ritual. Mansell clearly indicates that the substance and historical truth has been replaced by an inferior symbolism. However, Mansell's male figure wanders through "another's place," as "a stranger" and "not being able to remember home." Through the process of picturing, imagining and revisiting this central frame, this process of poetic delineation adds to the perception of crisis but also reveals that its signification is being carefully managed within the culture by the symbolic forms generated by the ongoing "harsh land and drought" (Hoorn 12) male narrative that still impacts on Australian literature. That is, the polar opposite of the key metaphor has been marginalized while in reality it offers an answer to central tenets of the overall discourse. When viewed through the lens of mythic analysis, this bipolar signification process has several keystone aspects. Firstly, the male motif in Mansell's poem bears a striking resemblance to the male being swallowed by the "mythic mouth" (O'Flaherty 268) or the "monstrous leviathan" (Campbell 83). Both of these monstrous symbols in narrative represent the total transformation and dissolution of self and culture. As Schildrick contends, this process signifies the "collapse of boundaries between self and other," which "constitutes an undecidable absent presence at the heart of human beings" (81). Thus, the poetic narrative exophorically speaks of the need for the feminine narrative of genuine care and empathy to enter and supersede the Australian narrative to provide the counterbalance "to the male passing itself off as nature" (Millett, ch. 2), or pretending to be linked to the natural setting.

The second aspect speaking as both explicit motif and subtext in Mansell's poem is the notion of the hunter male being totally "outside" of the sense of place and self but still possessing an echo of what should have been his clearest memory: "putting his hand on the ground / he'll feel it beating." Nonetheless, he can't remember home.

As Deardorrf believes, this separation is the perhaps the "ultimate wound," "the soul gap where we are split, where we are broken ... the cross roads of identity" (112, 216). While this marker has distinctly dystropic terms for the Australian context, it once again speaks of the need for wholeness. However, the shades of meaning bought forth in this mythic modality is one of choice and one of revisiting which fork of the crossroads tells the purest form of this national epistemological-ontological connection. While the "soldier-digger" lies at the heart of the Australian myth, there are social commentators who have begun to challenge the veracity of this narrative. Lake for example clearly labels these war heroes as carrying forward the racist and imperial ideals of "Mother England." Her socio-historical analysis came to the conclusion that in reality Gallipoli "had come to serve as White Australia's creation myth" (Lake 18). It seems that the feminine academic voice needs to be sounded much clearer and much louder.

Thirdly, embedded in *The Good Soldier* the unnamed and homeless male briefly "sees the luscious curl of intimacy, the uncommon life." This brief sexual reference reflects the "other" of woman's bodies as found in the majority of narrative texts. This particular poem represents a clear example of Steward's contention that this ongoing narrative "discourse by and about men, is a discourse that is articulated masculinity as and through its own marginalizations" (Steward 2). It would appear that Mansell is suggesting that retaining power in a culture is ultimately through fantasy whereby male anxieties are represented and inscribed onto woman's bodies. While in narrative this typically represent the exclusion of woman from the upper echelons of mythic and symbolic order, Mansell uses this notion as an inverted allegorization suggesting that the feminine cannot be suppressed. In this poem this single reference also appears in the very center of the poem, separating a chiastic framework in which the very mythic essence of the feminine, again framed as birth and rebirth, is at the heart of this poem and the heart of the Australian consciousness. The concept of fertility within the male gaze of this poem reveals for the "lone hunter" a visual context that in narrative "is both a desirous and fearful" (Aguirre 195). In this instance though, its positioning and context in the flow of the poem views the feminine and reproduction as a solution, a reunification to the sterility of the entire Australian milieu. The womb is often representative of the need of cosmic or ideological change (Oliver), which this poem suggests is to be longed for, but also dreaded as it reveals an uneasy but necessary solution for this ambivalent feeling of being lost within the uncontrollable.

Mansell's Poetic Topography of the Feminine in Where Edges Are

Unlike the poem discussed in the first section, in which the feminine is embedded as exophoric points of reference, the notion of the feminine in *Where Edges Are* is expressed as explicit and nested topographical contours. Set mostly in the same Australian "desert pastoraphilia" (Hoorn 195) where "[h]er skin is blistering," and there is "crick of grass underfoot" this poem utilizes the second person feminine pronoun "she" in tandem with a series of liminal-mythic frames of "nature and spirit as shaping tools" (V. Turner 581).

The first of these "shaping tools" is the reference to the "dark halls of town" marking the ongoing decline of Australian rural towns. In Eliade's mythic concept within *The Two and the One*, these are the places that used to form a distinct threshold between the essence of being alive, and in the Australian context, the ever-encroaching desert: Once ordinary places where the "pioneer spirited" bush dwellers undertook the elements of everyday life that became socio-emotionally fused into important stages of existence and meaning. As with all humanity, in inscribing these sites with the rituals of everyday life, the home and community worldview become imbued with emotional awe and a sense of identity. Thus these ordinary places become sacred. However, as stated, changing economics have forced a decline in outback and rural towns, which in many ways has also caused a shift and questioning of what makes up the Australian narrative. Mansell shifts this question to the feminine, describing this mythic designation as "effulgent." Thus the feminine shines in the darkness, relocating the national sensibility to one of compassion and emotional engagement. In turn Mansell sets up the possible relinquishing of the post-colonial sense of ownership and domination of the land, and according to this poet, the nation as a whole is "hearing." As revisited several times in this poem the unnamed and unknown populace are "hearing" the "heavy paces" of change, which is a possible allusion to the process of reconciliation process with the indigenous population. With the former prime minister only recently making a public apology for the wrongs done to these peoples the process of abandoning the former myth of dominating the land to one of living with land as is indeed laden with "heavy paces," and slow paces.

Related to this concept of the indigenous view of the land is Mansell's use of the warrigal metaphor within the "hearing breathing process." A wild dog, commonly called in the Anglicized version the dingo, the mythic qualities of this beast are seen by many indigenous communities as being at once of a free-ranging creature who is a protector of the people and on the other hand a trickster. It is a trans-textual essence of bloodshed and destruction as well as peace and safety. The British colonial attitude or colonization view was that it was a pest, another form of fauna that needed to be eradicated, as were the indigenous people. Both are symbolic of that which is unwanted and unloved by the dominant culture (Woodward 91), simply property to be euthanized for the greater good of the colonies or the wealth of the pastoral paradigm. In this model there was no concept of identity with the land beyond the ability to consecrate it by measuring and dividing it up.

In an interesting shift, Mansell ends this poem with reference to the soldier learning down and connecting physically with the land, and through language use that is clearly a "whisper in the mind and shy hope in the heart" (Thornhill 173). 'Whispering and hoping' represents the first call to change in regard to the need to shift dominant and domineering paradigms. As Botting explains, this whispering call represents the "disturbing return of pasts upon present" (1). Mansell then shift's the readers gaze to a focus on water as a place of growth within a metaphorical context of dryness and death, this image also mythically represents the actual issue when crossing the boundaries between time, space, ideology and culture. While water has always represented chaos and the disorder social re-birth brings, Eliade (*Patterns* 212) suggests that understanding and defining borders through the mythic symbolism of water is related more to the concept of eternity, potentiality of all things or the primordial source of creation. That is, it gives birth to all things but can never be re-created. Eliade further continues that water also metaphorically links the chaos of birth, life and death, in that at death the body is dissolved becoming the potential seedbed for new life. In this instance Mansell uses this mythic reference to water through two allegorical images to reinforce the pain that change causes. Each of these is symbolic reference to the rupture, blood and boundaries. The woman returns to that which gives birth and rebirth but must break through the surface of the water. The skin of her "naked feet" then has the potential to be also ruptured through the "sharp edges" of the oyster beds. Mansell appears to be reinforcing the physical and emotional pain that arises from shifts in understanding, as well as poetically sketching the "double bounded" isolation of liminality that the male-dominated myth has generated in the Australian narrative. All of these facets in this last line also "tell the more to the story" regarding the social distance created by "stories" that won't work and continue to blind a national worldview to the realities of their jaundiced and confining frameworks.

Reframing the National Narrative: An Imperative of Mythic Proportions

The brief mythic analysis of two of Chris Mansell's poems clearly suggests that the current Australian national narrative is one riddled with fault lines. As has apparently been the case since time immemorial, a culture's national mythic narrative and "the process of nationalism at is most definitive is unsurprisingly masculine" (G. Turner 193). Arising out of a false set of historical narratives in tandem with political expectations of the time, and the socio-cultural need for a national narrative celebrating heroism, an airbrushing away of the actuality of the nature of the Anzac heroes has simply created a narrative with no definitive grounding. The symbols and metaphors on which the Anzac narrative rests need revisiting so that a genuine cultural pathway and understanding can be recalibrated. However, Mansell's poems indicate the reinscribing of the temporal, spatial and narrative place for women within the Australian story.

With the Anzac legend celebrating its centenary in less than five years and the story underpinning its identity in transition, redefining the symbols on which the notion of what it means to be Australian is an imperative. "As a story, transition becomes a narration of impermanence and decline, but also of transformation and rebirth, being ultimately about a search, an open Odyssean story" (Capone 172).

Works Cited

Beaumont, Joan. *Australia's War 1914–1918*. Sydney: Allen & Unwin, 1995.
Bhabha, Homi K. "A Quest of Survival: Nations and Psychic States." Ed. James Donald. *Psychoanalysis and Cultural Theory: Threshold*. Basingstoke: MacMillan, 1991. 89–103.
Botting, Fred. *Gothic*. New York: Routledge, 1996.
Campbell, Joseph. *The Hero with a Thousand Faces*. Princeton: Princeton University Press, 2004.
Capone, Giovanna. "Shirley Hazzard: Transit and the Bay of Noon." *Australian Literary Studies*. 13.2 (1987): 172–183.
Day, David. *Australian Identities*. Melbourne: Australian Scholarly Publishing, 1998.
Deardorrf, Daniel. *The Other Within: The Genius of Deformity in Myth, Culture and Psyche*. Ashland: Whitecloud, 2008.
Doty, William. *Mythography: The Study of Myths and Rituals*. Tuscaloosa: University of Alabama Press, 1989.
Eliade, Mircae. *Patterns in Comparative Religion*. Lincoln: Bison Books, 1996.
_____. *The Two and the One*. London: Harvill Press, 1965.
Hoorn, Jeanette. *Australian Pastoral: The Making of a White Landscape*. Freemantle: Freemantle Press, 2007.
Huggan, Graham. *Australian Literature: Postcolonialism, Racism, Transnationalism*. Sydney: Oxford University Press, 2007.

Inglis, Kenneth. *Sacred Places: War Memorials in the Australian Landscape.* Melbourne: University Press, 2005.
Lake, Marilyn. "Introduction: What Have You Done for Your Country?" *The Militarisation of Australian History.* Ed. Marilyn Lake and Henry Reynolds. Sydney: University of New South Wales Press, 2010. 1–24.
Millett, Kate. "Theory of Sexual Politics." St. Albans: Granada Publishing, 1969. Web. June 10, 2007. http://www.marxists.org/subject/women/authors/millett-kate/theory.htm
O'Flaherty, Wendy. *Woman, Androgynes and Other Mythical Beasts.* Chicago: University of Chicago Press, 1980.
Oliver, Kelly. *Reading Kreisteva: Unravelling the Double-bind.* Bloomington: Indiana University Press, 1993.
Ross, Jane, *The Myth of the Digger: The Australian Soldier in Two World Wars.* Marrickville: Hale & Iremonger, 1985.
Scutter, Heather. *Displaced Fictions.* Melbourne: Melbourne University Press, 1999.
Shildrick, Margrit. "The Body Which Is Not One: Reflections on Conjoined Twins." *Body Modifications.* Ed. Mike Featherstone. London: SAGE, 2000. 77–92.
Turner, Graeme. "Nationalising the Author: The Celebrity of Peter Turner." *Australian Literary Studies,* 16.2 (1993): 131–139.
Turner, Victor. "Myth and Symbol." Ed. David Sill. *International Encyclopedia of the Social Sciences.* New York: MacMillan, 1968. 576–582.
Woodward, Wendy. "Dog Stars and Dog Souls: The Lives of Dogs in *Triof* by Marlene van Niekerk and *Disgrace* by J Coertzee." *Journal of Literary Studies* 17 (2001): 90–110.

Sister of Life, Sister of Death
Fluid Roles in Catherynne M. Valente's The Descent of Inanna

VALERIE ESTELLE FRANKEL

Inanna, later known as Ishtar, Astarte, Ma, Anahita, Asherah, and more, was worshipped continuously from 3500 to 500 BCE in Sumer, Babylon, and other areas of the Ancient Near East (Gadon 115). Her epic poem, "Inanna's Descent to the Nether World," became the one of the world's first recorded love stories, illuminating the relationship between sex and death and the meaning of sacrifice. "The Descent of Inanna" by Catherine M. Valente retells this epic closely, but twists aspects to reveal the emotional story of reconciliation underneath.

In the original epic, Inanna, goddess of life and fertility, is consumed by a need for her sister, grieving in the underworld. Further, the underworld itself calls to her. As the epic tells, "From the great heaven Inana set her mind on the great below" (Inana's Descent, 1). The epic of Ishtar's descent, a later retelling, is nearly identical to this one. However, Ishtar descends to rescue her lover, Tammuz, from death. Inanna, in a purer form of the tale, travels seeking the lost side of herself.

The Inanna descending in Valente's version is a heavenly goddess but imperfect, flawed as her mortal readers with welts and scars from living in the sun. She remains beautiful and enticing, a goddess of nature and fertility with life-filled epithets: Lemon-planting Inanna, Fleece-carding Inanna, Calf-birthing Inanna.

As she approaches the underworld, Valente's darkness is not cast as evil but enticing, scented with spices and pungent meat on the edge of decay. When Inanna enters, she is "infant with tectonic skull" (16) but also a nursing woman, with mushrooms suckling at her body. In the liminal gateway, she is babe and mother, goddess and supplicant as she bends to the earth and crawls through the mud. This dichotomy of goddess and supplicant continues, as she is named "Waif-Queen of Runaways" (49), and her stately crown is described as choked with leaves and fruit peels. Crickets in her crown sing a dirge, signifying her departure from the world of life and her intimate demise.

Famously, Inanna's seven majestic treasures must be left behind at each of hell's seven gates, forcing her to enter the underworld shorn down to her essence. In Valente's poem, Inanna first journeys on a seven-part quest to seven temples and retrieves her belongings. She draws each of her treasures from dust-coated reliquaries and old wells—the treasures are ancient, well-preserved, sacred even, but rarely worn. Day-to-day, then Inanna does not garb herself as a queen, leaving her symbols of state out of sight. However, the descent into death requires ceremony, pomp, preparation. Valente's list of Inanna's adornments mirrors the original text, reproduced below:

> She put a turban, headgear for the open country, on her head. She took a wig for her forehead. She hung small lapis-lazuli beads around her neck. She placed twin egg-shaped beads on her breast. She covered her body with a *pala* dress, the garment of ladyship. She placed mascara which is called "Let a man come, let him come" on her eyes. She pulled the pectoral which is called "Come, man, come" over her breast. She placed a golden ring on her hand. She held the lapis-lazuli measuring rod and measuring line in her hand ["Inana's Descent" 18–25].

However, like herself, the reality is far less impressive than the high reputation in Valente's version. Inanna's necklace and breastplate are "awkward and severe" (112) when she finally dons them. They leave red marks on her skin, as the weights and fetters they are.

She also confesses to her closest friend that she is trembling beneath her regalia: She is going into the "dark," the "other," and she is afraid (125–127). Elinor W. Gadon comments in *The Once and Future Goddess*: "We first meet Inanna as a woman fearful, anxious about her awakening sensuality and her future responsibilities as queen of the land. As the story unfolds, she discovers her feminine powers, her strength as a leader, her spirituality, and ultimately her wisdom" (122). Inanna had a personality similar to Aphrodite's, and indeed, the Greek goddess of love and pleasure is said to derive from her. Valente's gatekeeper mockingly calls her "Inanna whose-legs-lie-open" (279), and tells her she has no place in the underworld.

Inanna demands to see her sister, to mourn with her as she grieves, and the Gatekeeper laughs at her excuses. It is his job to cast off the superficialities. Scholars disagree on Inanna's motivations on entering the realm of death, suggesting she's questing for power, or perhaps spiritual enlightenment. There's no evidence of deep feelings for her sister. Whatever the reason Inanna tells herself, there's something in the Underworld she lacks, something she needs.

At last, Inanna ventures the true reason, as much as she has admitted to herself. As mistress of life, the realm of death is another part of her realm: "An apple fermented is no less fruit" (313). Valente's interpretation, that Inanna is rightfully ruler of the Underworld, is intriguing. Though Inanna lays claim to what she's never explored, it is indeed a part of her, as the realm of dreams and the unconscious waits in every person, tapped or not.

At this insight, Inanna is allowed to enter. Ereshkigal waits within, "steeped in all the beauty / dark things possess" (388–389): It is Inanna, stripped of all her excuses, who is losing beauty at the gates of death. In mythology, Ereshkigal may actually predate Inanna, as she appears in some of the oldest writings discovered in Sumer. "Kigal" means Great Earth, casting her as an ancient earth mother (Stone 249). If so, Inanna is the shallow, untried maiden, questing to find her source. In one legend, the warrior Nergal disrespects Ereshkigal and she forces him to descend through the seven gates into hell and bow before her throne (Stone 249–250). Inanna's consort Dumuzid is feasting and celebrating without her as she descends. To deal with him and to become a true wise goddess, Inanna must learn from her sister.

Ereshkigal gives permission for Inanna to enter, adding that she must leave her adornments at the gates "else she will unbolt my chest and slither into me / like the rose that strangles the wheat" (434–435). The metaphors are telling: Inanna is the pretty, useless, thorny rose compared with her sister, the sturdy, life-giving wheat. Inanna cannot be allowed to destroy the underworld with her feminine perfumed sweetness. If she enters robed in all her sweet perfumes and glittering ornaments, she will set herself above her sister, enter her, become her. Of course, in Valente's tale such a thing happens anyway.

Though the gatekeeper of the original Inanna epic acts apparently of his own accord—the rules of death are considered inflexible—the Ishtar version echoes this exchange. Ereshkigal thunders:

> What has moved her heart [seat of the intellect] what has stirred
>   her liver [seat of the emotions]?
> Ho there, does this one wish to dwell with me?
> To eat clay as food, to drink dust as wine?
> I weep for the men who have left their wives.
> I weep for the wives torn from the embrace of their husbands;
> For the little ones cut off before their time.
> Go, gatekeeper, open thy gate for her,
> Deal with her according to the ancient decree ["Descent of Ishtar" 31–38].

Ereshkigal is expressing the pain and conflict inside Inanna—Inanna displays herself as proud and queenly, unaffected by doubt, but her sister mourns for those who suffer. Inanna, living only for outward appearance, must discover what dwells underneath.

As with the original myth, Valente's Inanna protests the loss of each badge of office. Without them, the land of the dead will touch her unguarded skin. The gatekeeper responds to each protest dismissively calling her a stranger unfamiliar with their customs. Indeed, she is a stranger, a foreigner unused to the customs of death, and this must be emphasized seven times as she descends, discarding a layer of herself at each step. Her epithets appear often here, emphasizing her connection with the world of life, suggesting she is abandoning them as well. They are meaningless titles, echoes of her stolen talents and queenship, but not who she is underneath.

In another myth, Inanna made the father god Enki terribly drunk. As they feasted together, she tricked him out of ninety-four *Me*'s, divine decrees or talents. These included useful skills: the craft of the carpenter, the craft of the coppersmith, the craft of the scribe, the craft of the smith, the craft of the leather-worker, the craft of the fuller, the craft of the builder, the craft of the reed-worker ("Inana and Enki" Segment D 10–13) and also more spiritual ones: heroism, power, wickedness, righteousness ("Inana and Enki" Segment D 1–5). In the morning, Enki realized he had given up all the skills of the world, together with his crown, his throne and scepter. He had been the god of the waterways and fertility, but Inanna had bested him at persuasion and taken the powers of birth and growth, which she meant to share with those below. Enki pursued Inanna and sent monsters to chase her, but she had already ridden the Boat of Heaven and returned home with her treasures.

Inanna's divinity has relied on her father's tools, the beautiful adornments both physical and spiritual that she stole. Now as she descends into death, she goes to find the dark earth mother, the older, more primal power. She discards her pretty jewels, and with them, the hard-won skills of heaven—eloquence, joy, sorrow. In the underworld there are no clever disguises or enticing skills. There is only what remains below.

> The Dark Goddess forces us to look at ourselves with utter, naked honesty. For many of us, this is very frightening—to see ourselves stripped of our illusions and false pretensions. Like Inanna, who had to discard an article of clothing or an ornament at each gate of the underworld, when we go down into the darkness we must cast away all that is not true about ourselves and our lives [George 230].

Nonetheless, in Valente's retelling, Inanna feels relieved as she loses each weighty article, Naked and free, she steps into the underworld. Her final protest is, as always, the most heartfelt: "*Without my tools / who will know me?*" She feels quite bereft, adding plaintively, "*I will not know myself*" (637–639). She has made herself a splendid goddess through the seven *Me* she wears and the many more she stole for humanity. But she has no idea who she is without their artificial grandeur. Indeed, in the underworld her name and the epithets she loved have vanished. When a pillar, speaking with Ereshkigal's voice and heralding their forthcoming meeting calls her "the lime-tree's mother" (670), Inanna is no longer sure. She protests:

> the name, dropped into me,
> sounds no splash of water [682–683].

The pillar challenges Inanna, accusing her of trespassing and stealing, adding, "You are the dark sister, and I am the light" (688). What is this? Inanna is traditionally the daylight sister, Ereshkigal, mistress of the underworld. Is Inanna the dark sister because she's intruding on a ruling queen, subservient in the other's domain? Because she's lost her majesty and stripped to a shadow? Or is this conversation, filled with specifics but no names, meant to emphasize that the two sisters are one, ever-shifting who is of light and who of dark?

Their quests they describe, of traveling to find the night, taking the seven treasures, could actually be attributed to either: Ereshkigal was once a daylight queen of happiness, possessing ornaments like those Inanna had. Valente describes them as the opposite of Inanna's: A black hematite necklace, robe of aloe and asphodel, ointment of hartsblood and galena, breastplate of beaten silver that cries *"Stay off from me, stay"* (730). These are the talismans of darkness, of isolation and pain, rather than Innana's of queenship and enticement.

> Though the shadow-self has hidden positive qualities, she shrouds them in loss and rage that the heroine of light must battle through to absorb. The shadow loathes the heroine, who has all the youth, beauty, and advantages of the upper world. Thus her rejection of this lighter self.
> At the same time, understanding Ereshkigal and her lessons is vital for the shallow maiden. While she consists primarily of the magical and regenerative crone, the shadow also contains aspects of mother and maiden.... As the patriarchy came to fear these qualities, women were persuaded to abandon them. Thus, heroines descend into the darkness, seeking to reintegrate [Frankel 120–121].

After this moment of reconciliation, Ereshkigal rejects her sister. She has not shared her sister's suffering in the underworld, has not learned the character-building lessons. The judges descend, echoing Ereshkigal's rejection like her unsatisfied impulses. They name Inanna at last, crying, *"Naked we know you. / Naked we see your name"* (762–763). Ereshkigal knocks her dead, with great ambivalence, letting out a great wail of mingled guilt and triumph.

The original epic is less clear on her feelings. In fact, Inanna and Ereshkigal never speak to each other and are robbed of the critical confrontation both seek: Ereshkigal is passive, barely a player in this sisterly battle.

> After she [Inanna] had crouched down and had her clothes removed, they were carried away. Then she made her sister Erec-ki-gala rise from her throne, and instead she sat on her throne. The Anuna, the seven judges, rendered their decision against her. They looked at her—it was the look of death. They spoke to her—it was the speech of anger. They shouted at her—it was the shout of heavy guilt. The afflicted woman was turned into a corpse. And the corpse was hung on a hook ["Inana's Descent" 166–172].

The dark goddess's mouthpieces kill her; the light goddess's clay figures restore her to life. The sisters ultimately never speak.

In the Ishtar version, Ereshkigal voices her rage, though a conversation isn't seen:

> Now when Ishtar had gone down into the land of no return,
> Ereshkigal saw her and was angered at her presence.
> Ishtar, without reflection, threw herself at her [in a rage].
> Ereshkigal opened her mouth and spoke,
> To Namtar, her messenger, she addressed herself:
> "Go Namtar, imprison her in my palace.
> Send against her sixty diseases, to punish Ishtar"
> ["Descent of Ishtar" 63–69].

Upon reaching the underworld, Inanna, frivolous life goddess, thinks she has mastered death. She orders her sister to surrender the throne. Ereshkigal, however, knows Inanna has not yet suffered enough, not known the pain and ordeal of actual death. With a look, she transfers all the misery of death onto her sister. Inanna sinks down dead.

Following this episode, Inanna hangs dead on a hook and Ereshkigal lies moaning on the floor, in the pains of labor. As Reis notes:

> Ereshkigal, once a mighty and powerful Goddess, was assigned by the new ruling gods to the dry, dark realm of the dead as her domain. She suffers there. She eats clay and drinks dirty water, she moans, she smites her thighs and sets up great lamentations. In the myth, she is portrayed as a woman in labor—a dry labor with no birth [26].

Her pains certainly resemble birth pains, explained by most commentators as the impossibility of giving birth in the Underworld. However, Valente sees this labor following a different path: Ereshkigal realizes *"Her name is writing itself on the walls of my womb, / Inannainannainanna."* By killing her, the death goddess has absorbed her. She adds, *"I am become the cannibal-queen, / chewing my way out of my own flesh"* (1012–1030). Inanna, now dead, has become a part of Ereshkigal, the love and guilt she's taken into herself by rejected the light-filled, loving side of her personality. By killing Inanna, Ereshkigal is pregnant with her. Just as Inanna must die to learn the dark side of her nature, Ereshkigal must give birth to discover the life-giver within. Further, she must literally birth the life-giver, allowing new life to flourish in the underworld at last.

She calls on the creeping golems sent from the world above and they sympathize with her, as in the original epic. Then she calls on them to do far more and help her birth the awful force within. After the labor, the golems revive Inanna's corpse. "Love wielding Inanna," (1131) who perhaps now wields love for her sister and herself, awakes, adorned by her seven pieces of regalia.

The poem concludes just there, halfway through the original epic. Through her act of birth, Ereshkigal has become Inanna, goddess of life.

Through dying, Inanna has become her sister. Each understands the other, each is a queen of her own realm, crowned and adorned. Here the poem ends, with the reconciliation and acceptance that are central to Valente's poem, rather than with Inanna's quest for someone to take her place and die for her, and the childish actions of her consort. This refocuses the story on the two sisters: while there are other characters, all are supporting players, servants who are aspects of one goddess or the other.

Having met their other self, loved and been loved, died and been born, Inanna and Ereshkigal need nothing more from their epic. The two sisters are one, both well and crowned after their twin descents through the mysteries of death and birth.

WORKS CITED

"Descent of the Goddess Ishtar into the Lower World." *The Civilization of Babylonia and Assyria: Its Remains, Language, History, Religion, Commerce, Law, Art, and Literature.* Ed. Morris Jastrow. United Kingdom: J.B. Lippincott Company, 1915. Web. http://www.sacred-texts.com/ane/ishtar.htm.

Frankel, Valerie Estelle. *From Girl to Goddess: The Heroine's Journey through Myth and Legend.* Jefferson, NC: McFarland, 2010. Print.

Gadon, Elinor W. *The Once and Future Goddess.* San Francisco: Harper & Row, 1989. Print.

George, Demetra. *Mysteries of the Dark Moon: The Healing Power of the Dark Goddess.* New York: HarperCollins, 1992. Print.

"Inana and Enki." Ed. and Trans. J.A. Black. Translation 1.3.1. *The Electronic Text Corpus of Sumerian Literature.* The ETCSL Project. Oxford: Oxford University, 2006. Web. http://www-etcsl.orient.ox.ac.uk.

"Inana's Descent to the Nether World." Ed. and Trans. J.A. Black, G. Cunningham, E. Fluckiger-Hawker, E. Robson, and G. Zólyomi. Translation 1.4.1. *The Electronic Text Corpus of Sumerian Literature.* The ETCSL Project. Oxford: Oxford University, 2006. Web. http://www-etcsl.orient.ox.ac.uk.

Reis, Patricia. "The Dark Goddess." *Woman of Power* 1.8 (Winter 1988): 24–27, 82. Print.

Stone, Merlin. *Ancient Mirrors of Womanhood.* Boston: Beacon Press, 1990. Print.

Valente, Catherynne M. *The Descent of Inanna.* USA: Papaveria Press, 2006. Ebook. http://www.catherynnemvalente.com/store/ebooks.

PART III:
WITHIN THE CLASSROOM

Female Icons in Popular Culture
A Semiotic Approach to Teaching

ELIZABETH JOHNSTON

[I came to explore] the wreck and not the story of the wreck
the thing itself and not the myth.
—Adrienne Rich, "Diving into the Wreck," 1973

Medusa, Little Red Riding Hood, The Little Mermaid, Eve, the Virgin Mary, Pocahontas, Mona Lisa, Queen Elizabeth, Madonna, Marilyn Monroe, Rosa Parks, Barbie, Wonder Woman, Martha Stewart, Oprah. Most likely, if you live in the Western world, you know the names listed above; chances are, you would recognize their faces in paintings or photographs, although a number of these women lived and died long before you were born. What gives these women their staying power? *Female Icons in Literature and Popular Culture*, a course I designed in 2007 for Monroe Community College in Rochester, NY, uses the study of these female icons to try and answer this question, and others. Originally created as the capstone course for a gender studies certificate in the Honors Program, the course integrates a number of interdisciplinary approaches to studying gender constructions in western culture. The primary, although certainly not the only, goal of this course is to examine how myths of gender permeate all aspects of culture, reinforcing gender stereotypes and limiting the possibilities for representations of femininity outside the accepted social "norms." Through careful, critical analysis of the visual and textual iconographies of a variety of female icons, we examine how myths of gender recycle themselves in different guises across cultural and historical space. This course offers students an interdisciplinary approach to gender studies and the humanities by asking the following epistemological questions: how does examining significant historical events that occurred alongside a particular woman's rise to iconic or mythological status also help us to better understand what she might represent for her culture?; how can studying different modes of representation, such as an icon's appearance in paintings, poetry, and song, alongside each other complicate our understanding of her "meaning" to her culture?; further, how does her "meaning" shift over time or within different sub-cultures, and why? The essay which follows is a sort-of "start-up" manual for replicating this course elsewhere. An appendix of suggested readings is likewise attached.

Background and Rationale

It might be useful to understand how the course was born. I received my Ph.D. at West Virginia University, specializing in Eighteenth Century British Literature with a focus on gender studies; in 2003, after two years of teaching at Indiana University of Pennsylvania as a visiting professor, life events brought me to Monroe Community College, in Rochester, NY, as an adjunct instructor. MCC has a population of thirty thousand some students, forty percent of them students of choice. We also have a robust English department with over eighty full-time and part-time faculty members and a variety of course offerings, including Detective Fiction, the Graphic Novel, and the Literature of the Holocaust. Innovative courses are encouraged to attract the interests of our very diverse student body.

I was hired tenure-track in 2004 and started teaching *Women in Literature* for both the English department and the Honors College soon thereafter. I opted to use the *Norton Anthology of Literature by Women*, eds. Sandra Gilbert and Susan Gubar, for the course textbook. As I designed the course syllabus, I noticed the textbook's inclusion of a number of poems about individual mythical women. I decided to organize my syllabus thematically and included a section on "Myths of Femininity," devoting one week to three different icons, one per day. So, for example, we spent a day on Medusa and discussed poems by May Sarton ("The Muse as Medusa") and Sylvia Plath ("Medusa").[1] I also brought in a videotape (these were the days before I was a YouTube user!) of *Clash of the Titans*,[2] to provide students a visual image of the legendary monster to jumpstart class discussion. On another day, we looked at *The Little Red Riding Hood Project*, an online collection of Little Red Riding Hood stories from the Seventeenth Century forward, and discussed Angela Carter's "The Company of Wolves." The next semester, I devoted two weeks to mythic women. By the third semester, we were moving into a month of study. And students ate it up. In their course evaluations, a number of them expressed desire to expand the study beyond a month. I knew I was onto something. Students were recognizing the relevance of these icons to their lived experiences; the poems, plays, and fiction we were discussing were enabling them to discuss feminism and feminist theory in a way that was not only exciting for them, but that was changing the way they viewed the world. The standard resistance to feminist theory ("I'm not a feminist, but...") had all but been dissolved by visible, tangible, and inarguable evidences of patriarchal ideology's stranglehold on society. It was at that point that I went to the Honors director and suggested a new fifteen-week long study entitled *Female Icons in Popular Culture*.

I wrote up a proposal for *HMN 295: Female Icons in Popular Culture*, a special topics Honors course that would employ an interdisciplinary and semiotic approach to the study of female icons and which would include analysis of relevant written, visual, and musical texts. I proposed the course as a seminar, limited to eighteen participants to encourage deeper discussion. The proposal was accepted and the course was put on the schedule for the following semester. It immediately filled. As it turned out, teaching it as an interdisciplinary Humanities course, rather than a traditional solely text-based literature course made the course richer and more meaningful for students.

Navigating the Practical

First, I did what all good professors do: I googled "female icons" and "syllabus." Imagine my dismay when nothing came up. After further investigation, I found a similar course of study in Canada—but it was for graduate students, and no detailed syllabus was provided. Moreover, although I could find book collections for individual female icons, I couldn't find a text that examined several female icons simultaneously.[3] It quickly became apparent to me that I would need to start from scratch.

I started with a list of objectives. By course end, students should be able to demonstrate that they understand the following concepts:

- icons as ideological constructs (to separate who they are from what they represent as myths)
- gender, race, and class as constructs rooted in culturally and historically specific ideologies
- semiotic theory as it applies to the study of written and visual texts
- how the study of female icons is directly related to their other courses
- how to make real-world connections between what they study in my course and their lives outside

Accomplishing this set of objectives meant choosing the icons for study very deliberately and very explicitly clarifying what it means to be a "female icon." I chose three determining factors based on how scholars in the field have defined iconicity.[4]

First, the icon must lay claim to *longevity*; she must have been famous for a long period of time—usually beyond death. Secondly, an icon must be *ubiquitous*; she must be recognized everywhere, not just in specific subcultures. For example, everyone knows the Virgin Mary, even if they are not Catholic. The same is not true of other religious icons, like Joan of Arc or Mary Magdalene. Students might know the name of Virginia Woolf, but they are unlikely to be able to tell you anything about her unless they are English majors; Jane Austen, however, has permeated popular culture, thanks in part to the film industry and books like *Pride and Prejudice and Zombies*. While Katharine Hepburn and Ava Gardner are film icons, most students today, unless avid watchers of the Turner Classic Movie channel won't know who they are. But they all know Marilyn Monroe.

Finally, the icon must possess the element of *distinction*; she must be associated with a specific set of values/ideas so that when her name is said, students can immediately draw up a list of concepts associated with her. The icon must stand out from the celebrities which surround her as embodying a set of values associated with a specific time period in history. Students will associate Madonna, for example, with female sexuality, rebelliousness, materialism, consumerism, the excesses of the 1980s, and gay culture, among other ideas. In particular Madonna, with her cone-shaped bras and corsets and her gender-bending dancers was able to call attention to femininity as performativity. Britney Spears, on the other hand, is a celebrity but is difficult to distinguish from her imitation of Madonna. Likewise, it is difficult to determine now whether Lady Gaga will be able to carve out for herself a series of meanings separate from those already claimed by Madge.

Having established my criteria for iconicity, the next question was what icons we would study. I knew I wanted to move historically; this way, they could establish a sense of how ideals of femininity and gender roles have changed (and failed to change) over time. Particular icons depend on the earlier prominence of icons who they, in turn, recall. For example, Queen Elizabeth purposefully called upon images associated with the Virgin Mary and the goddess Diana; Princess Di, in turn, recalled for her admirers Cinderella, Queen Elizabeth I, and the Goddess Diana; Madonna strategically played on allusions to the Virgin Mary and Marilyn Monroe in her own image-making. It is important to talk about the earliest icons of femininity in order to understand these icons as part of a conversation about gender and power; in turn, they often discover that what is "said" about femininity really hasn't changed that much over the centuries despite the successes of the Virginia Slims, "We've Come a Long Way, Baby" campaign (an advertising icon in its own right). I also wanted to be able to discuss the impact of race on constructions of gender and vice versa. So many popular female icons express Western ideals of beauty. The non-white icons who are wildly popular tend to represent not only femininity but their particular ethnicities as a whole. I knew this would be interesting for students to discuss and might raise their awareness of how monolithic versions of femininity in mainstream media actually are. Asked to think of a Native American female icon, only Pocahontas would come to mind. Although Sacajawea is a historical icon, few students know who she is or what role she played in American history. Likewise, students asked to imagine an African-American icon are likely going to come up with only two names: Rosa Parks and Oprah. Unfortunately, they will not be able to say much about Parks other than her role in the Civil Rights movement. They will know a lot about Oprah, however, whether they've ever watched her show. Asian-American or Hispanic-American icons are non-existent in the popular imagination. These absences are also an important part of the course discussions.

Finally, I wanted to be able to choose icons who represented different kinds of popular desires and anxieties. What does a popular *religious* icon look like? What does a popular *sex* icon look like? What does a *fairytale* icon look like? What does a popular *political* icon look like? How are these icons different because of the roles they assume for the popular imagination? How are they the same by virtue of being women and being imagined as "essentially" feminine?

For each icon, I created a course booklet and corresponding PowerPoint lecture. Each week, students receive a set of readings that help them better understand the time period and significant cultural/political events, as well as the ideological context surrounding the icon; biographical/autobiographical material that purports to be "true" (biographies, documentaries); creative textual representations of the icon (poetry, drama, fiction, film, song); visual representations of the icon (film, sculpture, paintings); scholarly interpretations of the icon; and more global essays on gender, race, and class construction.

So, for example, in the booklet about Medusa—a powerful female whose meaning is later reinterpreted by patriarchal Greek and Roman cultures and thus provides a useful baseline for how figures of feminine strength are often rewritten—they receive the following: anthropological studies of Medusa imagery: essays by feminist anthropologists offering evidence of the existence of an early Goddess Culture which might have worshipped gorgon-like goddesses; Greek and Roman "histories" which provide various versions of her story, such as Homer's *Iliad* and Ovid's *Metamorphosis*; literary interpretations of the Medusa myth, as in Percy Shelly's "On the Medusa of Leonardo Da Vinci in the Florentine Gallery" (which I teach alongside the painting), as well as feminist poetry such as May Sarton's "The Muse as Medusa," and

"Medusa" poems by Sylvia Plath, Louise Bogan, and Patricia Smith; artistic renderings of Medusa by Sixteenth and Seventeenth Century artists, including Caravaggio's *Head of Medusa* and Bernini's *Bust of Medusa*, as well as links to images of her in films like *Clash of the Titans* and *Percy Jackson and the Olympians: The Lightening Thief*; advertisements relying on direct references to Medusa, as in Versace's Medusa campaign; and scholarly interpretations by critics from the Renaissance forward, including Sigmund Freud's theories of castration theory in "Medusa's Head" and Helene Cixous's feminist response to Freud, *Laugh of the Medusa*.[5]

Likewise, in studying Eve, they read Sumerian accounts of the creation which include an early version of the Garden of Eden and man's banishment from it; excerpts from Genesis which offer not one, but *two* conflicting accounts of Eve's creation; excerpts from *The Malleus Malificarum*, a Fifteenth Century German text on witchcraft which influenced Cotton Mather in the Salem witch trials and which blames the problem of witchcraft on Eve's failure to resist Satan's temptation; excerpts about Eve's temptation from Milton's Seventeenth Century *Paradise Lost*, perhaps the most damning account of Eve in Western modernity; proto-feminist poetry like Seventeenth Century poet Amelia Lanyard's *Eve's Apology*, feminist short fiction like Ursula Le Guin's "She Unnames Them," and feminist music, as in Ani Difranco's gritty "Adam and Eve" lyrics.

Alongside these texts, they examine depictions of Eve by Michelangelo's "The Fall" fresco on the Sistine Chapel and William Blake's illustrations of Eve's temptation in Milton's *Paradise Lost*, and we compare this to contemporary ads which allude to the Eve story.[6]

Next, I provide students information about Ruth Handler's creation of Barbie and subsequent adoption by Mattel; we also discuss changes to Barbie's image in response to the second-wave of feminism (for example, Barbie's "I Can Be" line which features Barbie in non-traditional female roles like doctor, veterinarian, astronaut, and president, as well as changes to the doll's physical measurements to make her more "realistic"). I give students essays specific to Barbie scholarship, such as Kami Cunningham's, "Barbie Doll Culture and the American Waistland," as well as feminist scholarship on beauty, such as excerpts from Naomi Wolf's *The Beauty Myth*. Students read poems like Marge Piercy's "Barbie Doll," as well as excerpts from fiction, such as Sandra Cisneros' "Barbie-Q" from *The House on Mango Street* and Julia Alvarez, *How the Garcia Girls Lost Their Accents*. We analyze both the lyrics to and video of Aqua's "Barbie Girl." Additionally, students examine revisionist art, such as images of Pregnant Barbie, White Trash Barbie, and Breast Cancer Barbie.[7] I am fortunate to live in the same city as the Strong National Museum of Play, so I often take my students to its extensive Barbie exhibit. The "Human Barbie" Ukrainian sensation, Valerie Yuklanova, a young model who has used plastic surgery and make-up to make herself look like Barbie, has been an interesting addition of late.

Aunt Jemima is one of my favorite icons to teach. I provide various book chapters on her history, such as a chapter entitled "Aunt Jemima: The Most Battered Woman in History" from *Slave in a Box*. We discuss her brand creation in 1889 and the various women who have played her (Nancy Green, Anne Robinson), the marketing strategy employed by various owners of the brand, as well as discussion of stereotypes and how she fits into the mammy archetype. The literature on Aunt Jemima is scarce,[8] but a play called "Remembering Aunt Jemima: A Menstrual Show," which features characters like Dorothy Dandridge, Sojourner Truth, Anita Hill, and Pecola from Toni Morrison's *The Bluest Eye* as Aunt Jemima's daughters, is an excellent text for study. Artistic images of Aunt Jemima are, on the other hand, plentiful. In addition to spending time poring over early pancake ads, students analyze revisionist art inspired by the Civil Rights movement, including Jeff Donaldson's "Aunt Jemima and the Pillsbury Doughboy" (1963), Murry DePillar's "Aunt Jemima" (1968), and Betye Saar's "The Liberation of Aunt Jemima" (1971).[9]

Pocahontas, because she was both a living person and an icon, is no less a construction, since the only access we have to her biography is provided by the white colonists who knew and exploited her. Thus, we read John Smith's narrative of Pocahontas, *The Generall Historie of Virginia, New-England, and the Summer Isles (1624)* with a skeptical eye and alongside various scholars of race theory who discuss the Indian princess stereotype in myth and history. Students read Nineteenth Century poems, like Lydia Howard Sigourney's "Pocahontas," and plays, like James Nelson Barker's *The Indian Princess; or, La Belle Sauvage* (1808) and George Washington Custis's *Pocahontas; or, The Settlers of Virginia, A National Drama* (1830). They analyze Nineteenth Century paintings such as John Gadsby Chapman's *Baptism of Pocahontas* (1837) and Henry Bruekner's *Marriage of Pocahontas* (1855), and compare these to films in the Twentieth Century depicting Pocahontas. A documentary entitled *Mickey Mouse Monopoly* provides a brief, but fascinating, overview of some of the problems with Disney films about Pocahontas.[10] We consider how race consciousness has shaped (or failed to shape) narratives about her iconicity. A useful website which compiles documents and videos is *The History Channel*'s site on Pocahontas.[11]

Evaluation/Assessment

Assessment of student outcomes is accomplished through their completion of various types of essays and a final project. Written assignments for the course include a formal summary of feminist critical scholarship of a specific icon, a traditional literary analysis of a creative written text about the icon (a poem, short story, play, song, or novel), and a semiotic analysis of a visual text (artwork, sculpture, film). The first assignment, a summarizing overview, requires that they can articulate, in brief, a particular icon's changing meaning over time. Students are asked to synthesize critical scholarship on the icon as well as rely on the creative works discussed in class to draw a central conclusion about one aspect of the icon's meaning over time. The second assignment demonstrates their ability to articulate how a single written text produces meaning about an icon, and to identify where that meaning is situated within the discourse surrounding that icon. This assignment is a traditional literary analysis and depends on the students exercising close, critical reading and interpretive skills. The final essay asks students to explain how artwork can be read as a text, producing meaning through image rather than words, but also existing in a dialogue with other representations of the icon. Like the literary analysis, the visual analysis asks them to slow down and pay attention to details in a single text and to explain how it produces meaning.

So, for example, a student might for the first assignment, the summary, provide both an overview of how Little Red Riding Hood's representation has changed from her appearance in Charles Perrault's Seventeenth century moral tale[12] up through the animated film, *Hoodwinked*. The student should be able to identify three to four significant points in time in which her representation shifted, and be able to account for that shift by considering the cultural context within which those shifts occur. In the second assignment, the student might provide a literary analysis of "In the Company of Wolves," by Angela Carter, identifying what is new or unusual about Little Red's characterization, and then contextualizing the production of this meaning within its specific historic and cultural moment (for example, by considering how second-wave feminism might have influenced Carter's rendition). In the third assignment, the student might choose Tex Avery's 1943 *Red Hot Riding Hood*,[13] and assess the sexualization of Little Red's image in the context of what they know about gender roles in the first half of the twentieth century.

Students also do a final group presentation wherein they choose an icon not discussed in class. Students present for twenty to thirty minutes, providing an overview of the icon's history and biography (if a real person), and identifying seminal scholarship about the icon, creative versions of her story, and visual images, including representations of her on television, in films, in advertisements, and in the art world. Students must be able to defend the woman's status as an icon (i.e., prove she meets the course definition of iconicity) and also be able to establish a coherent narrative about her shifting meaning over time and across cultures. Students provide a PowerPoint and create a booklet of their own, complete with a bibliography. Students have chosen interesting icons; perhaps the most interesting have been Jenna Jameson and Ru Paul.

An Introduction to Semiotics

What this course asks students to do is, obviously, very sophisticated. Thus, some time should be spent discussing how to prepare students for this kind of sustained and nuanced analysis. Because, at MCC, students are required only to take College Composition before entering the course, I cannot trust that students have any foundation in literary study, sociology, or history, much less in feminism (although, since the course is optional, students usually have an interest in the latter; students enrolled in my *Women in Literature* course often follow me to the Honors *Icons* course). Having taught this course for six years now, I do recommend that anyone creating a similar course establish prerequisites that include both college composition and some sort of humanities course that requires them to do close study of texts (either in literature or art or music). A history course is useful, as well. Students often come to class lacking a sense of history; things we take for granted about what students know about the past need to be reconsidered. At MCC the course is a 200-level (sophomore) Honors course; it could easily be taught as an upper-division non-honors course, as well.

If taught as an interdisciplinary course (in other words, not as a course for students already versed in cultural studies), the class should begin with an overview of what it means to study popular culture. It's important for students to understand *why* they are taking this course and why the study of culture is valuable. Terms specific to the study of popular culture should be reviewed (providing a glossary is useful). I begin the course by trying to get students to think about what they're studying in this class as part of a larger context. I ask them why an English teacher might be teaching a course in cultural studies. Initially, students don't understand the connection. I provide them some brief history about the pedagogical shift in English departments to value literature as a cultural artifact rather than just for its aesthetic qualities. Marxist theory frames the discussion as I explain how studying literature can help us to understand how ideology is circulated and sustained, as well as sometimes contested. I then discuss the origins of Cultural Studies and the valuing of other kinds of artifacts as objects of study. I discuss with them the pioneering work of Raymond Williams in Cultural Studies. I explain to them that critics now analyze various aspects of popular culture, from television sitcoms, to Harlequin romances, to rap music, to fashion trends, as reflections of what our culture values, desires, fears, etc. I explain that if we want to understand how ideas about gender roles are created, sustained, and/or challenged, then we need to look at mass culture, where representations of gender are, everyday, produced and circulated.

I also spend the first week introducing them to semiotic theory; this nudges them into recognizing female icons as symbols or "signs" signifying particular values. I briefly lecture on Ferdinand De Saussure's semiotic theory, the study of the ways in which signs (like letters or words) make meaning. I use a PowerPoint lecture to walk them through how De Saussure used a picture of a tree and the word "tree" to explain the difference between the "signifier" and the "signified." I remind them that there is nothing which connects intrinsically the sound of the word to the image, and yet we learn, as we learn language, to associate the two. This association, eventually, becomes inseparable for the speaker. As De Saussure explained, we cannot speak or hear the word "tree" without imagining the image of a tree.

I next show them the famous painting by Renee Maggrite of a pipe, under which is the words "This is not a pipe." This example, pulled from the work of Michel Foucault, helps to remind students that a drawing of a pipe *is not* actually a pipe, but a representation of a pipe.[14] This image, in particular, really seems to "click" for the students. Again, what I am trying to do is to get students to slowly separate the signifier from the signified, to recognize the two as distinct. Many of them have never before considered this concept.

Next, I show students the universal icon for women we see on restrooms. I then remind students, like the representation of the pipe, this is not a woman. In fact, she doesn't look like any human woman; still, we recognize what this symbol means without even thinking about it because the concept and the sign have been naturalized for us. What we wear is entirely behavioral, but the icon/sign naturalizes gender roles so that being a woman means wearing dresses, and being a man means not wearing dresses. Every time we read the signs on a restroom to determine which door to enter, we are attesting to the universality of this myth as well as confirming this myth as "truth."

We then talk about how power informs representation. I like to use an example borrowed from Terry Eagleton in *Literary Theory: An Introduction*. In Lewis Carroll's *Alice Through the Looking Glass*, Humpty Dumpty and Alice argue over the meaning of words, Alice objects to Humpty's making up and misusing of words. Humpty explains, quite assuredly, that he can make a word mean whatever he wants it to mean; after all, he explains, whoever is "Master" gets to decide. I then introduce them to Roland Barthes's analysis of literature and popular culture as systems of signs reproducing ideology, or what he termed "myth." Barthes extends De Saussure's theories to consider how an image can signify a set of values and, in particular, bourgeois ideology. Barthes refers to a photo of a Black boy saluting a French flag. The first level of signification, he says, was what de Saussure had described: the signifier (the photo) represents the signified (a Black boy saluting a flag). However, Barthes goes further and identifies a second level of signification: the set of values (French patriotism) called up by or associated with the concept of the boy saluting the flag.

Barthes is concerned with how the values which he says are embodied in the image work to inculcate viewers into mainstream ideology, therefore rendering them subjects of the state. Daniel Chandler in *Semiotics for Beginners* (a useful website to which to direct curious students) explains that the "function" of myth, according to Barthes, is "to make dominant cultural and historical values, attitudes and beliefs seem entirely 'natural,' 'normal,' self-evident, timeless, obvious 'common-sense'–and thus objective and 'true' reflections of 'the way things are'.... The power of such myths is that they 'go without saying' and so appear not to need to be deciphered, interpreted or demystified."

Thus, I begin to move students in the direction of discussing semiotics in terms of power dynamics. I explain that Barthes has been criticized as understanding the myths circulated by popular culture as primarily serving the interest of those in power. Instead, there may be multiple ways of reading meaning, as meaning resides largely in the reader/interpreter of the text. Thus, a sign can contain simultaneous, contradictory meanings within itself—some supporting dominant ideology and others contesting it.

Pedagogical Challenges

One immediate challenge of teaching this course is that students initially may not recognize what hard work it is to study popular culture and may sign up for the course because it sounds like "fun" (we find the same issue with students who sign up for "Children's Literature," assuming that the course will entail reading rather than study of literature for children). Prerequisites may prevent these issues, as well as a clear course description in the college catalog and promotional materials for the course.

Another challenge is that students may bring to the class their identities as fans, and/or may relate to the icons as too sacred to interpret (this is especially true of religious icons, like the Virgin Mary). Thus, there may be some initial resistance from students to approach their understanding of the icon objectively and as informed by their own cultural interpellation. They may be resistant to "breaking open" the image, to reading the icon as a construction rather than a "truth."

Students also may respond so personally and emotionally to certain issues raised by examining the icon that they are unable to read her within an academic context. This has occurred in interpretations of Medusa which center on her rape by Poseidon, and students may need to be warned ahead of time of potential triggers. However, I've also had an entire seminar break into tears in discussion of Marilyn Monroe; Monroe, whose vulnerability is part and parcel of her iconicity, elicits from students the desire to protect her.

Thus, I found myself in the awkward and frustrating position of defending the course's examination of her as an icon against claims that she should finally be "left in peace." A patient and focused professor can handle these obstacles in ways that provide sensitivity to students while also pushing them to move beyond their own prejudices.

A challenge (though also a boon) for the instructor of this course is the ubiquity of material about these icons. New versions or readings enter the popular imagination daily. Staying "tapped in" to popular culture is especially important. Anyone teaching this course should expect to update frequently and substantially the materials used for the course. Last minute changes to my teaching plans routinely occur because some new interpretation of an icon appears on my radar: I open up a magazine to see a picture of Martha Stewart dressed like Medusa for Halloween, or I'm watching television and a trailer comes advertising a new Queen Elizabeth movie, or a student passes me in the hall on the way to class flaunting a bright pink Barbie tattoo on her arm. Expect, too, that students will become completely enthralled with finding representations of these ubiquitous icons; my inbox is generally flooded for the entire semester with links to images and articles my students have happened across and found relevant to the course study. I remind my students when they are surprised that I may not have seen a particular television show starring Little Red Riding Hood or a read a new fictionalized account of Pocahontas that I am not an "expert" on any particular icon. Instead, I am a semiotician—as I expect them to become—trained to read signs within their semiotic contexts, and to transfer these skills to the interpretation of all the other kinds of signs which surround us in our daily lives.

The other challenge you may encounter teaching this course is time management. Students often lament that we have only fifteen weeks for study, complaining that three hours is not enough time to spend on any one icon. They are, of course, right. I have found it most manageable for both my students and myself to devote one hour of a class to an icon's biography and feminist scholarship about her, one hour to written creative texts about her, and one hour to visual texts. Sometimes this means giving students more to study than we have time to discuss in class. It is all-too easy to spend an entire class period or more analyzing a particular poem when I've assigned five. In other cases, I may assign readings in groups. So, for example, I may give one group of students one essay to read and another group of students another essay to read. I may have the students report back next class, providing brief summaries to their classmates about what they read. To better manage time, I've learned to have students watch any movies or film clips outside of class, although I do provide extracurricular opportunities for them to watch these together if they prefer (a Netflix account is very useful since many of films are available through instant streaming). Occasionally, we watch significant scenes in class together, especially as I'm preparing them for their visual analysis essay. An example of this would be watching a five minute clip from *Elizabeth* wherein Elizabeth "becomes" the Virgin Queen. Another way in which I've found ways to use time in the class more productively is to have them apply critical scholarship to the creative texts and images. For example, if I've assigned more critical scholarship than we can cover thoroughly in the first hour, we may in the next hour break up into groups and practice applying key passages to interpretations of designated poems. As much as possible, I try to let my students determine the direction of the class. If I've given them a poem, a short story, and a play to read, but they want to spend the entire class period on the play, then I go where they want to go. I use PowerPoints to provide key information I want them to consider and, if we don't have enough time to cover it all in class, I provide it for them electronically to view at their convenience.

Outside Activities

Another element that makes the course successful is that I work to make sure that the students can make links between their studies in my class and the community around them. One of the benefits of teaching a course in popular culture is that there is almost always some new film, television show, song, or other media construction from which to draw. For the past few years, a new film featuring a female icon has come to theaters and I've been able to secure funds for my students to attend together. Thus far, I've taken my classes to see *Agora, Amelia Earhart, Queen Victoria, Marilyn, Little Red Riding Hood,* and *Elizabeth: The Golden Age.* When possible, we've met after the films to discuss them over coffee. I've also held film viewings on campus, sometimes coordinating events with other courses or clubs. For example, one semester the Student Organization of Women Leaders, a club I was advising, ran a fall film-festival, featuring viewing followed by discussion of three different Little Red Riding Hood films: *In the Company of Wolves, Freeway,* and *Hoodwinked.* I strongly encourage supplementing the course with films and have suggested a number at the end of this article. One way to encourage students to attend is provide extra-credit. Alternately, I've made seeing films mandatory, requiring written responses to the films as part of their course grades. This is especially important with an icon like Marilyn Monroe; though students know her, they do not know her films. Having them watch a film like *The Seven Year Itch* is certainly helpful, especially read alongside her diary entries and comments to her interviewers.

I have also been fortunate to find relevant plays to which to take my classes. The MCC theater department has produced *Elizabeth Rex* and *The*

Vagina Monologues, both of which I've taken students to. Likewise, I took students to see a local performance of Jane Austen's *Pride and Prejudice.*

If there are area museums you can visit, these also add depth to the course. We live about an hour's drive from Seneca Falls, so although we didn't study Elizabeth Cady Stanton, our discussion of early feminism was deepened by a trip to Seneca Falls National Women's Hall of Fame and to Stanton's house. I've also taken students to the Susan B Anthony house and, as noted above, the Barbie exhibit at Strong Museum.

If you live in a big city or teach at a large enough school, no doubt you'll be able to coordinate your course with speaking events. I've had the luck of taking students to see Gloria Steinem and Barbara Ehrenreich speak (I even have a group photo of my students with Steinem).

Because I'm part of the Greater Rochester Consortium of Women's Studies Faculty, I've also been able to provide my students with networking opportunities with gender studies students from other colleges. If you teach in a city large enough to host several colleges, it's worthwhile to identify faculty at other schools teaching in the Humanities and Gender Studies fields; they may be hosting events to which you can bring your students. If you teach at a two-year school, as I do, this opportunity to network for students is especially exciting. I've had students from my course meet faculty members at four-year schools who later became their advisors when they transferred.

Student Accomplishments and Feedback

One of the best parts about teaching this course is that its unique focus means that others are often eager to hear about it; thus, students are provided with plentiful opportunities to show off their own scholarship. Students have proposed and had accepted panels associated with their work in my class at four MCC Scholars Day events. Each year, students from these panels won awards for "best paper," receiving substantial monetary scholarships. Annually, students have submitted and won the English Department Awards contest for best philosophical essay and best literary analysis. One student wrote a poem from Ophelia's perspective and it won first place in the poetry category. In 2012, students from the 2011 course presented a panel at the Seneca Falls Dialogue conference which brought together gender studies faculty and students from across the region. In 2012 and, again in 2013, students' papers from the course were accepted for inclusion on panels at the Northeast Regional Honors Conference. A 2012 student presented an abstract of her work on Little Red Riding Hood at the SUNY State Legislature Poster Session in Albany. Further, students tend to pursue majors and/or minors in gender or women's studies after taking this course. In fact, two former students have since used themes from the course for their senior theses at the schools where they transferred.

Student feedback about the course has been extremely positive, and I've included some responses below in the hopes that it might encourage other faculty to develop a similar course for students at their respective schools. After the Fall 2012 course concluded, students were anonymously surveyed. Of those surveyed, 100 percent said they felt the course challenged them, while student opinion of Honors courses overall was lower, at 66 percent. One hundred percent said it encouraged them to think critically than much more than their non–Honors courses, compared to 53 percent for all other Honors courses. All students said they would strongly recommend the course to others and agreed that the course helped them to analyze the strengths and weaknesses of what they read and hear more than their non–Honors courses. Students were also given the option to provide written feedback. What follows are some of their comments:

- This course has helped me take considerably more responsibility for my views. Instead of asking me to work in a detached theoretical framework, it allowed the opportunity for discussion on topics that were relevant enough to my life that I had actual investment in the arguments I made. Coupled with the information given in class and the availability of the professor for private discussion and e-mail exchanges, it fostered an environment of acceptance while also requiring careful defense of positions.
- I found the selection of particular female icons to be relavant [sic] and often relatable to each other and to current popular culture. Each of the required readings were focused [sic] in a way that made the topic more accessible [sic]. I really enjoyed the in class discussions and found that I always left class feeling like I had learned something and that I wanted to know more about the female icons being studied.
- This course is one of my favorites. The discussion was the best aspect of the class because everyone had such thought-evoking opinions.
- I really enjoyed the women that we studied. I thought there was well constructed discussion and Professor Johnston allowed us to stray off the original topic as long as it pertained to the icon we were talking about. That gave us the opportunity to talk more in depth.

In close, I want to reference a poem with which I began this essay and with which I routinely begin this course. "Diving into the Wreck," by Adrienne Rich, relies on an extended metaphor of a diver exploring an underwater wreck. The final stanza describes Rich explaining that women carry exploration gear and also a book of myths "in which / our names do not appear." I open the class with this poem because I believe that this is what the course does—it dives into the wreck of women's history, the wreck that is women's representation in myth, history, literature, and popular culture. As semioticians, my students and I "find our way back," exploring along the way how and why the images of women have evolved, and asking what the implications of these stories in "the book of myths" are for us, both men and women. We find ways to re-write these myths to allow for a diversity of stories about gender, to find narratives with which we can identify and call our own, to give name to what it means to be women in history and in the world today.

Notes

1. In Gilbert and Gubar, *Norton Anthology of Literature by Women*.
2. *Clash of the Titans*. Dir. Desmond Davis. Perf. Laurence Olivier, Harry Hamlin, Claire Bloom. Warner Bros, 1981. DVD. I now contrast this with the most recent remake: Dir. Louis Leterrier. Perf. Sam Worthington, Liam Neeson, Ralph Fiennes. Warner Bros, 2010. DVD. Note: clips of Perseus's slaying of Medusa in both movies are now available on Youtube for side-by-side comparison. For the 1981 version, see Istuit. "Clash of the Titans—Medusa battle (original) 1981." *Youtube*. Youtube. 22 Sept. 2011. Web. 7 Feb. 2013. For the 2010, see Cinefantastique. "Medusa: Clash of the Titans." *Youtube*. Youtube. 31 Mar. 2010. Web. 7 Feb. 2013.
3. In 2012, after I presented a conference paper about this course, Littleman and Rowe contacted me about writing such a book; I am currently in the proposal process.
4. See Dennis Hall and Susan Hall, *American Icons*; Jim Cullen, *Popular Culture in American History*.
5. See Maria Gimbutas and Joseph Campbell, *The Language of the Goddess*.
6. Ads using Eve are plentiful and can be found by doing an image search in Google. Ones of particular interest include an ad for Kellogg's All-Bran Fruit, a Dior ad for "Hypnotic Perfume," a 1971 ad for Eve Filter Cigarettes, and a 2003 Playstation 2 advertisement. I also sometimes show my students a magazine advertisement for the series *Caprica*, featuring a young brunette ready to bite into a red apple.
7. Again, Google image searches are especially useful here.
8. Literature about mammies, however, is not, and I sometimes use excerpt from Nineteenth Century novels to supplement our discussions. The popularity of the book-turned-movie, *The Help*, has recently provided a useful starting point for discussion of the mammy archetype.
9. A Google image search is useful here, as well.
10. Also available in clips on Youtube.
11. I have also, in the past, included Princess Di, Ophelia, Lolita, Wonder Woman, Buffy the Vampire Slayer, and Cleopatra.
12. Available on *The Little Red Riding Hood Project website* and in Catherine Orenstein's *Little Red Riding Hood Uncloaked*.
13. Also available on Youtube.
14. See Michel Foucault, *This is Not a Pipe*.

Recommended Resources

Many of the following are collections from which I've pulled essays and images for the course.

Allen, Paula Gunn. *Pocahontas: Medicine Woman, Spy, Entrepreneur, Diplomat*. New York: Harper Collins, 2003. Print.
Aqua. "Barbie Girl." Dirs. Peder Pedersen and Peter Stenbæk. Universal, 1997. Music Video.
Barbie Nation: An Unauthorized Tour. Dir. Susan Stern. Perf. Ruth Handler. PBS, 1998. DVD.
Caputi, Jane. *Goddesses and Monsters: Women, Myth, Power, and Popular Culture*. Madison: University of Wisconsin Press, 2004. Print.
Chandler, Daniel. *Semiotics for Beginners*. Aberystwyth University. 11 Oct. 2011. Web. 7 Feb. 2013.
The Company of Wolves. Dir. Neil Jordan. Perfs. Sarah Patterson, Angela Lansbury. Shepperton Studios, 1995. DVD.
Dame, Enid, ed. *Which Lilith? Feminist Writers Recreate the World's First Woman*. New York: Rowman and Littlefield, 1998. Print.
Dobson, Michael, and Nicola J. Watson. *England's Elizabeth: An Afterlife in Fame and Fantasy*. Oxford: Oxford University Press, 2002. Print.
Elizabeth. Dir. Shekhar Kupar. Perfs. Cate Blanchett, Geoffrey Rush. Polygram, 1999. DVD.
Ford, Elizabeth, and Deborah C. Mitchell. *Royal Portraits in Hollywood: Filming the Lives of the Queens*. Lexington: University Press Kentucky, 2009. Print.
Garber, Marjorie, and Nancy Vickers, eds. *The Medusa Reader*. New York: Routledge, 2003. Print.
Huffman, A.J, and April Salzano *B*. Daytona Beach: AJ Huffman, 2013. Print.
Lofton, Kathryn. *Oprah: The Gospel of an Icon*. Berkeley: University of California Press, 2011.
McDonough, Yona Zeldis. *All the Available Light: A Marilyn Monroe Reader*. New York: Touchstone, 2002. Print.
_____. Dirs. Chyng Sun and Miguel Picker. Media Education Foundation, 2001. DVD.
Mickey Mouse Monopoly. The Barbie Chronicles: A Living Doll Turns Forty. New York: Touchstone, 1999. Print.
Orenstein, Catherine. *Little Red Riding Hood Uncloaked*. New York: Basic Books, 2002. Print.
Peabody, Richard, and Lucinda Ebersole, eds. *Mondo Barbie*. New York: St. Martins, 1993.Print.
_____, and _____. *Mondo Marilyn. An Anthology of Fiction and Poetry*. New York: St. Martins, 1995. Print.
Peck, Janice. *The Age of Oprah: Cultural Icon for the Neoliberal Era*. New York: Paradigm, 2008. Print.
Queen Elizabeth I of England. Ed. Annina Jokinen. *Luminarium: An Anthology of English Literature*. Luminarium Encyclopedia Project. 3 June 1996. Web. 7 Feb. 2013.
Rogers, Mary F. *Barbie Culture*. Thousand Oaks: Sage, 1999. Print.
Sexton, Adam. *Desperately Seeking Madonna: In Search of the Meaning of the World's Most Famous Woman*. New York: Dell, 1993. Print.
Tilton, Robert. *Pocahontas: The Evolution of an American Narrative*. New York: Cambridge, 1994. Print.
Walker, Julia. *The Elizabeth Icon, 1603–2003*. New York: Palgrave, 2004. Print.
Wilke, Stephen R. *Medusa: Solving the Mystery of the Gorgon*. Oxford: Oxford University Press, 2000. Print.
Yoe, Craig. *The Art of Barbie*. Chapel Hill: Algonquin, 1999. Print.

Part III: Within the Classroom

WORKS CITED

Alvarez, Julia. *How the Garcia Girls Lost Their Accents.* Chapel Hill: Algonquin, 1991. Print.
Aqua. "Barbie Girl." *Single.* Universal, 1997. CD.
Barthes, Roland. *Mythologies.* New York: McMillan, 1972. Print.
Blake, William. *Eve Tempted by the Serpent.* London: The Victoria and Albert Musem, 1699–1700.
Bogan, Louise. "Medusa." *The Norton Anthology of Literature by Women.* Eds. Susan Gilbert and Sandra Gubar. New York: Norton, 2007. Print.
Caravaggio, Michelangelo Merisi da. *Medusa.* Uffizi, Florence: Virtual Uffizi: The Complete Catalogue, 1597. Web. 7 Feb 2013.
Carter, Angela. "The Company of Wolves." *The Norton Anthology of Literature by Women.* Eds. Susan Gilbert and Sandra Gubar. New York: Norton, 2007. 2326–2337. Print.
Chandler, Daniel. *Semiotics for Beginners.* Aberystwyth University. 11 Oct. 2011. Web. 7 Feb. 2013.
Cisneros, Sandra. *The House on Mango Street.* New York: Vintage, 1991. Print.
Clarke, Breena, and Glenda Dickerson. "Re-membering Aunt Jemima: A Menstrual Show." Kathy A. Perkins and Roberta Uno. *Contemporary Plays by Women of Color: An Anthology.* Psychology Press, 1996. Print.
Cullen, Jim. *Popular Culture in American History.* Oxford: Blackwell, 2001. Print.
Cunningham, Kami. "Barbie Doll Culture and the American Waistland." *Symbolic Interaction* 16.1 (1993): 79–83. Print.
Difranco, Ani. "Adam and Eve." *Lyrics007.* 7 Oct. 2012. Web. 7 Feb. 2013.
Eagleton, Terry. *Literary Theory: An Introduction.* Minneapolis: University of Minnesota Press, 1983. Print.
Foucault, Michel. *This is Not a Pipe.* Berkeley: University of California Press, 1983. Print.
Gilbert, Sandra, and Susan Gubar. *The Norton Anthology of Literature by Women.* New York: Norton, 2007. Print.
Gimbutas, Marija, and Joseph Campbell. *The Language of the Goddess.* New York: Thames and Hudson, 2001. Print.
Hall, Dennis, and Susan Grove. *American Icons.* Westport: Greenhaven, 2006. Print.
Hoodwinked. Dirs. Cory Edwards, Tom Edwards, and Cory Leech. Perfs. Anne Hathaway, Glenn Close, James Belushi. BAC, 2006.
Kramer, Heinrich, and James Sprenger. *The Malleus Malificarum.* 1487. *The Malleus Malificarum of Heinrich Kramer and James Sprenger.* Trans. Christopher S. MacKay. Windhaven Network. 1992–2013. Web. 7 Feb 2013.
Lanyer, Amelia. "Eve's Apology in Defense of Women." *Selected Poems of Amelia Lanyer.* 1998. Web. 7 Feb 2013.
Le Guin, Ursula. "She Unnames Them." *The Norton Anthology of Literature by Women.* Eds. Sandra Gilbert and Susan Gubar. New York: Norton. Print.
Manring, Maurice M. *Slave in a Box: The Strange Career of Aunt Jemima.* Richmond: University Press of Virginia, 1991. Print.
Medusa's Head. Uffizi, Florence, ca. 1600. *Virtual Uffizi: The Complete Catalogue.* Web. 7 Feb 2013.
Michaelangelo, Buonarrotti. "The Fall of Man and the Expulsion from the Garden." Sistine Chapel: Vatican, 1508–1512.
Mickey Mouse Monopoly. Dirs. Chyng Sun and Miguel Picker. Media Education Foundation, 2001. DVD.

Milton, John. *Paradise Lost*. Project Gutenberg. 1991. Web. 7 Feb 2013.
Percy Jackson and the Olympians: The Lightning Thief. Dir. Chris Columbus., Perf. Logan Lerman, Kevin McKidd, Steve Coogan. Fox, 2010. DVD.
Piercy, Marge. "Barbie Doll." Poemhunter.com. Poemhunter, n.d. Web. 9 Feb 2013.
Plath, Sylvia. "Medusa." *The Norton Anthology of Literature by Women*. Eds. Sandra Gilbert and Susan Gubar. New York: Norton, 2007. Print.
Red Hot Riding Hood. Dir. Tex Avery. Metro Goldwin-Meyer, 1943. DVD.
Rich, Adrienne. "Diving into the Wreck." 1973. *Poets. Org*, Academy of American Poets. 23 May 2009. Web. 7 Feb. 2013.
Salda, Michael N., ed. *Little Red Riding Hood Project*. de Grummond Children's Literature Research Collection. University of Southern Minnesota. Dec. 1995. Web. 25 Jan 2013.
Sarton, May. "The Muse as Medusa." *The Norton Anthology of Literature by Women, 3rd ed*. Eds. Sandra Gilbert and Susan Gubar. New York: Norton, 2007. 505. Print.
Smith, Patricia. "Medusa." *Poets.Org*. Academy of American Poets, 1997–2013. Web. 7 Feb 2013.
Wolf, Naomi. *The Beauty Myth: How Images of Beauty Are Used Against Women*. New York: Harper Collins, 1991. Print.

La Llorona and La Malinche in Re-Vision
Chicana Poets Countering Traditions and Claiming Voice

LEIGH C. JOHNSON

"What do you already know about La Llorona?" I asked by way of introducing Sandra Cisneros's story "Woman Hollering Creek" to my students in an Introduction to Chicana/o Literature class at the University of New Mexico. "She lives in the creek behind my house!" one of my students called out. Others laughed, good-naturedly commenting that she lived near their homes too. Now teaching at a university near Washington, D.C., I find that my students have very little context for the legend of La Llorona, the Weeping Woman, unless they have specific cultural knowledge of her story.

The myths and archetypes present in Chicana literature are varied and fascinating. Stories about the legendary La Llorona and the historical person, Malintzin Tenepal, turned mythic La Malinche, originated around the time of the Spanish Conquest of Mexico. Despite being based on tales that are 500 years old, the interpretations of myths about these women are in constant flux, largely as a result of Chicana poets and literary scholars reconfiguring the persistent misogyny the myths held into powerful statements of Chicana agency. However, as these myths enter the public consciousness beyond the limitations of Chicana literary production, there is some danger that cultural appropriation may occur and the myths could be used to resincribe some of the political and social inequality the Chicana poets have worked to mitigate. Domingo Renee Perez argues in "The Politics of Taking: La Llorona in the Cultural Mainstream" that as nonnatives appropriate La Llorona, they "sever La Llorona from her cultural community or primitivize the members of her parent culture" and "promote the ideas that Mexican@s and Chican@s are primitive, superstitious, and dominated" (155). Perez illustrates this argument through an examination of the television show *Supernatural* and Tony Hillerman's *The Wailing Wind* (2002). Taking her point seriously, I argue that it is urgent to educate students of myriad racial and cultural backgrounds regarding these myths and their reformations by Chicana poets and literary scholars, so that students may recognize and question appropriations of La Llorona or La Malinche that support racist or stereotypical views.

This essay examines contemporary Chicana poets' representations of some of the most prominent mythic figures of women at the time of Spanish Conquest. These myths are still important because they shape the ways Chicanas are represented in literature. By rewriting these myths, Chicana poets are revising mythology for their own purposes. La Malinche is the native woman who married Hernán Cortéz, translated for him and gave birth to two children who become ancestors of the Mexican people. La Llorona is a woman who marries a man above her station. When he leaves her, the legend goes, she drowns their children. Later she haunts bodies of water, especially rivers, looking for other children to drown. This essay addresses some of the ways that women overcome the challenge of re-visioning commonly understood myths as well as examines how women feminize "traditionally male mythological perspectives." This essay argues that poetry by Carmen Tafolla, Cordelia Candelaria, Alicia Gaspar de Alba, Angela de Hoyos, Victoria Moreno, and others takes potentially damaging myths about women and revises them to find their creative potential. By suggesting that the myths hold a kind of repressed feminist power, the poets are able to create entirely new images of women through their revisions.

While the three archetypes available to women in Mexican cultural symbols are La Virgen, La Malinche, and La Llorona, revisions of these myths remain popular for Chicana/o scholars, artists, performers, and writers. However, La Llorona may be the most difficult to reinvent, "due in part to the infanticide of the tale, which is horrifically tragic and not usually seen as an act of agency by storytellers" (Perez, *There Was a Woman* 44). The folk story of La Llorona (the Crying Woman) has many incarnations. In *Infinite Divisions: An Anthology of Chicana Literature*, Tey Diana Rebolledo and Eliana S. Rivero have collected an impressive number of poems that address the La Llorona and La Malinche archetypes. They remark, "La Llorona is also symbolic of Chicano culture, whose children are lost because of their assimilation into the dominant culture, or because of violence and prejudice. Associated with water, drownings, and the mysterious forces of night, La Llorona comes to represent the unpredictability of nature" (194). By linking natural forces to cultural forces, Chicana poets can adapt the myth of La Llorona to poems addressing loss as a result of political or social violence against women and children.

Cordelia Candelaria's poem, "Go 'Way from My Window, La Llorona

(1)" draws on the myth of La Llorona to describe the feelings of childhood terror her image evokes, and then the speaker attempts to resolve the dilemma she faces by banishing La Llorona from her mind. Debra Blake's study of working-class and semiprofessional Chicanas reveals that women recount their first memories of the La Llorona myth as children hearing frightening stories of other children abducted and drowned by a ghost-like figure. Blake argues that this creates self-regulating behavior, in which "La Llorona's surveillance takes the form of a 'faceless gaze,' invisible and omnipresent [...] Not only does La Llorona possess the power to discipline; her legend implies that she has the power to punish" (148). Candelaria's poem is an attempt to reject the discipline and punish aspect of the La Llorona legend. Instead, she describes having her childhood scared away (lines 9–10). As a stand-in for the parents' gaze, La Llorona sees wayward children; however in this poem, the speaker rejects her parents' abusive marriage and domestic violence to reveal at the end, the judgment La Llorona's children pass upon her, linking their "clear-eyed" stare to the disdain the speaker has for her own parents (line 29). This poem is easily accessible and allows for studying the effects of the La Llorona myth on childhood.

Using the La Llorona myth in poetry allows writers to revise her voice—from weeping and crying to speaking some kind of truth. Alicia Gaspar de Alba explains her approach:

> My voice is also a fronteriza voice. Had I not grown up in an environment so deeply infused with magic and superstition and history. Had I not been able to understand all those horrifying cuentos about La Llorona, and that mythical, mystical Wailing Woman of the Mexican and Chicano culture who appears in my writing as everything from ghost to guardian angel, and who is my primary symbol of individuation. [...] I can't even imagine what kind of writer I'd be, or if I'd be a writer at all [viii].

In this way, Gaspar de Alba suggests that La Llorona becomes part of her writer's consciousness, and to deal with the haunting, she must not only keep La Llorona in her awareness but she must also find a way to let her rest. Gaspar de Alba's poem, "Kyrie Eleison for La Llorona" grafts a pagan-turned-Christian religious connotation to the La Llorona myth. Kyrie Eleison is a pre–Christian Greek expression (Lord have mercy) later incorporated into the Christian liturgy (Fortescue). In its first section, the speaker laments that La Llorona has never had anyone show compassion for her; by the third and final section, the speaker has linked environmental harm, sweatshop labor, atomic destruction, and homophobia to the lack of compassion people have for La Llorona's plight. The final line, "Lord, have mercy" calls back to the Kyrie Eleison of the title to suggest a possibility for reconciling La Llorona's fate through conflation of a Christian and pagan intersection. By privileging the pre–Christian words, Gaspar de Alba's reimagining of the La Llorona myth supports Perez's argument that "European motifs were assimilated into or grafted onto Native stories about the gritona, the shouting woman," and furthermore, "would allow the Indigenous peoples of Mexico through the figure of La Llorona to account for and even explain the effects of European contact and conquest" (*There Was a Woman* 18). With a contemporary setting, the poem uses the La Llorona myth to explain current social injustices. As a cultural insider, Gaspar de Alba uses the figure to problematize her voice and speak back to her family and community. Still, she also recognizes that as Chicana literature has grown more popular, it is exposed to the outside world of "airports and shopping malls across the country" but remains rooted in the "landscape of La Llorona" a place "crafted of Spanish and English, river and desert, sunlight and mountain, blood and bones and black sounds" (ix). The origins and nuances of the La Llorona legend provide essential foundations to avoiding the misinterpretation of her symbolism as Chicana literature (and consequently, archetypes) becomes more mainstream.

The fear of damaging cultural appropriation may seem extreme, especially with regard to a figure whose image has been appropriated and re-appropriated for everything from warnings to children against arroyos with a potential to flood, to men who are cheating on their wives, to women who might transgress gender roles, to the bigger narrative of colonial struggle and loss. However, Blake points out, Chicana writers overwhelmingly "reinvent La Llorona as an active agent, a woman of discord who ruptures the status quo and creates change" (184). This interpretation of writers' ability to harness La Llorona's image to create agency and invoke a kind of power in performance necessarily depends on seeing her as woman of a specific cultural construct. Divorcing her mestiza identity from her actions diminishes her power to comment on colonialism and complex gender relationships in the Chicano/a community. For instance, Perez describes how recent popular culture iterations of La Llorona have diminished her "cultural potency" by presenting her as white, changing her name, or erasing other key elements from the legend ("Politics" 166). Especially significant is that the venues, television and popular genre novels (vampire and mystery) are written by cultural outsiders *for* cultural outsiders, thereby ensuring that the story of La Llorona can be used without the cultural baggage Chicana writers must navigate. More recently, the NBC series *Grimm* told the story of La Llorona attempting to drown three children. The resolution is vague because while she escapes the police, she does not succeed in drowning the children. It is good that as the legend gets more attention, there is potential for new interest in Chicana poetry, but there needs to be a conscious effort on the part of professors and critics to ensure that students know the larger cultural context. The legend in all its complexity deserves wider cultural knowledge to circumvent the potential for new La Llorona stories to undermine the agency Chicana writers have tried to inscribe through their poetry.

While Chicana poets have often published in venues of literary importance, it is important to mention that poetry is not limited to books, magazines, and podcasts. Albuquerque slam poets Reed Bobroff and Olivia Gatewood wrote and performed "No Longer a Myth (La Llorona)," for the Brave New Voices 2010 HBO series. The performance offers both poets on stage speaking the poem as they interpret the legend of La Llorona. They follow the traditional storyline that she was desirable until her husband cheated on her, at which point she drowned the children. Then Bobroff and Gatewood transfer the story to a modern setting wherein La Llorona takes children who are in the throes of addiction. Their parents do not hear her cries as she steals them. The haunting poem speaks especially to the crisis of heroin addiction in Albuquerque high schools. The video is available on You Tube and the text of the poem is on HBO's website. Their interpretation particularly echoes Victoria Moreno's 1977 poem, "La Llorona, Crying Lady of the Creekbeds, 483 Years Old, and Aging" that flips the idea of a woman drowning her children and instead suggests that social policies unfriendly to poor women, women of color, and their children are in fact what "took away" her children. These poems enhance a cultural understanding of the social, political, economic, and gendered injustice that led to the legend of La Llorona in the first place five hundred years ago.

Reinventions of La Llorona seem to depend on her continued potential for transgression and danger. Alternatively, revisions of La Malinche (sometimes called La Chingada) depend on retelling the circumstances of her relationship with Cortez, the fate of her children, and her place as the mother of a mestiza race. Almost all the poets are, on some level, responding to Octavio Paz's 1950 essay *The Labyrinth of Solitude* which claimed:

> If the *Chingada* is the representation of the violated Mother, it is appropriate to associate her with the conquest, which was also a violation, not only in the historical sense but also in the very flesh of the Indian women. The symbol of this violation is Doña Malinche, the mistress of Cortez. It is true that she gave herself voluntarily to the conquistador, but he forgot her as soon as her usefulness was over [...] And as a small boy will not forgive his mother if she abandons him to search for his father, the Mexican people have not forgiven La Malinche for her betrayal [86].

Clearly, Paz's comments are significant in their woman-blaming. Chicana poets have had to contend with this image of Malinche in order to subvert the argument that women are responsible for the selling out of indigenous peoples to the Europeans. Emma Pérez makes a persuasive statement about Paz's position showing that by sympathizing with the colonizer father, Paz makes Malinche the "dreaded phallic mother who will devour him, castrate him, usurp him of his own phallus / power [...] the driving force behind a form of patriarchal Chicano nationalism that repudiates feminism" (107). Most of the widely read, taught, and studied poems about Malinche have been written since the Chicano Movement, when Chicana feminists sought gain awareness of issues impacting women that had been marginalized by the some activists. Their poems retain Malinche's power without sacrificing her particular personal tragedy in a way that does not always survive La Llorona revisions.

Carmen Tafolla's 1978 poem "La Malinche" remains the most popularly studied and widely read example of Chicana poets revising this story. Her poem is a clear example of the criteria Rebolledo and Rivero establish for Chicana resistance to the patriarchal abhorrence of Malinche as traitor. The poem sees Malinche as "a victim of her family and historical circumstances" declaring Malinche's family responsible for selling her out to protect her brother (Rebolledo and Rivero 193, 198). Tafolla's poem participates in a "resuscitation of La Malinche as part of the process of acknowledged *mestizaje*" and "the symbolic mother of a new race" by fashioning Malinche as a seer who believes her child is part of a new world that Cortéz and Europeans cannot understand (193, 199). Rebolledo and Rivero discuss the importance of translation, code switching, and interpretation with regard to writing about Malinche (193). By making Malinche talk, when her voice is not part of the historic record, Tafolla reclaims her voice—a mode of exchange—as a tool for Chicana agency. Finally, Rebolledo and Rivero argue that Chicana writers see La Malinche as a survivor—a woman who "cast her lot with the Spaniards in order to ensure survival of her race and a woman who lives on in every Chicana today" (193). Perhaps this is the most important element the revisions of Malinche reveal—the fact that she can say, as Tafolla does, "I was not a traitor to myself" (line 57). The ability to reject patriarchal constructs of Malinche through poetry enables what Blake calls countermemory, a way to combine "linear history and orally transmitted popular history to reconstitute history" (23). Creating countermemory productively challenges cultural memories that are racist, misogynist, or homophobic.

Occasionally the folklore surrounding La Llorona is conflated with that surrounding the real life Malinche. She had a son with Cortéz before she married his deputy and had a daughter. Luis León describes the conflation as, "Some have said La Llorona is actually a synecdoche for La Malinche, who purges the soul of the New World, as well as her own soul, of colonial excess by destroying the patrimony of Cortéz: the first mixed-race children, or *mestizos*" (14). Perez observes that the conflation "arises primarily from the fictionalized fate of Malinche's children" (*There Was a Woman* 30). While Malinche does not murder her children to keep them safe from Cortéz, she loses her children to "assimilation" and to "history" (31). La Llorona's lament precedes Malinche, and the conflation of the two figures makes them seem less redeemable than they are separately. By denying the conflation of their identities, there is more room for scholars to create revisions of the legends.

There are two pitfalls to avoid (or at least be aware of) with studying or teaching Malinche. Unsurprisingly and discussed above, sometimes La Llorona and La Malinche are conflated as cultural symbols; alternatively, Malinche may be confused with other Native women who helped colonizers. American students who encounter Malinche for the first time may be tempted to relate her story to Pocahontas's. Even without the Disney treatment, Malinche's story is more difficult to whitewash. As Kristina Downs deftly argues:

> Because La Malinche was a folk tradition that was created in group, by a culture that included strong elements of the indigenous heritage she came from, her assistance of the colonizers condemns her. The tradition surrounding Pocahontas was created by a society [that] functioned almost completely in the European tradition [...and made] her into a virginal mother figure for the United States [412].

However, what Downs does not say, and some Chicana critics do point out is that La Malinche's tribal identification was not Aztec. Her people had some interest in seeing the Aztecs out of power, so her image was also created by a rival tribal group. Angela de Hoyos's poem "La Malinche a Cortez y Vice Versa/La Malinche to Cortez and Vice Versa" constructs a dialogue in which Malinche speaks to Cortez and he talks back, but she has the last word that highlights her insider knowledge of her culture and his. The dialogue is appropriate, because Malinche translated for Cortez, and their relationship depended on her ability to communicate. Compared to Paula Gunn Allen's poem "Pocahontas," it is remarkably similar in theme. Allen's poem has Pocahontas watching over her English husband, commenting that her people have found Europeans' weakness for tobacco and that as a cultural translator, she possesses intimate knowledge (of the future, even) that he does not. Examining the similarities in these myths and poems can be a useful way to introduce students to issues in ethnic folklore.

There are many more examples of Chicana poets revising these myths than I have been able to discuss here. I hope to have given a broad enough overview of the stakes involved in both resurrection of these myths as powerful symbols of Chicana agency as well as the dangers inherent in popular culture stripping these myths of their cultural relevance. Even in my current role as a professor of early American and multicultural literature (i.e., not solely Chicana/o studies), I find it appropriate to introduce the archetypes of La Llorona, La Malinche, and La Virgen. By integrating these myths as culturally rich symbols into broader discussion of literature and folklore, it is possible to imagine, as Mary Louise Pratt argues, that these revisions can "correct the linear postulates of orthodox ethnonationalism" that relegate women to the margins of the ethnic subject's struggle for equality (862). Rather, by reading these poems as re-visionary, we are able to grasp the potential for counter-narratives to dominant national myths to build agency and potency.

WORKS CITED

Blake, Debra J. *Chicana Sexuality and Gender: Cultural Refiguring in Literature, Oral History, and Art.* Durham: Duke University Press, 2008.
Bobroff, Reed, and Olivia Gatewood. "No Longer a Myth (La Llorona)." *Brave New Voices.* HBO.com. 2010. Web.
Candelaria, Cordelia. "Go 'Way from My Window, La Llorona (1)." Rebolledo and Rivero 215–16.
Carbonell, Ana María. "From Llorona to Gritona: Coatlicue in Feminist Tales by Viramontes and Cisneros." *MELUS* 24.2 (1999): 53–74.
de Hoyos, Angela. "La Malinche a Cortez y Vice Versa / La Malinche to Cortez and Vice Versa." Rebolledo and Rivero 200–02.
Downs, Kristina. "Mirrored Archetypes: The Contrasting Cultural Roles of La Malinche and Pocahontas." *Western Folklore* 67.4 (2008): 397–414.
Fortescue, Adrian. "Kyrie Eleison." *The Catholic Encyclopedia.* Vol. 8. New York: Robert Appleton Company, 1910. Newadvent.org. Web.
Gaspar de Alba, Alicia. *La Llorona on the Longfellow Bridge: Poetry y otras movidas 1985–2001.* Houston: Arte Público Press, 2003.
León, Luis D. *La Llorona's Children: Religion, Life, and Death in the U.S.-Mexican Borderlands.* Berkeley: University of California Press, 2004.
Moreno, Victoria. "La Llorona, Crying Lady of the Creekbeds, 483 Years Old, and Aging." *The Third Woman: Minority Women Writers of the United States.* Ed. Dexter Fisher. Boston: Houghton Mifflin Company, 1980. 319–20.
Paz, Octavio. *The Labyrinth of Solitude and Other Writings.* Trans. Lysander Kemp, Yara Milos, and Rachel Phillips Belash. New York: Grove Press. 1985.
Perez, Domino Renee. "The Politics of Taking: La Llorona in the Cultural Mainstream." *The Journal of Popular Culture* 45.1 (2012): 153–72.
_____. *There Was a Woman: La Llorona from Folklore to Popular Culture.* Austin: University of Texas Press, 2008.
Pérez, Emma. *The Decolonial Imaginary: Writing Chicanas into History.* Bloomington: Indiana University Press, 1999.
Pratt, Mary Louise. "'Yo Soy La Malinche': Chicana Writers and the Poetics of Ethnonationalism." *Callaloo* 16.4 (1993): 859–73.
Rebellodo, Tey Diana, and Eliana S. Rivero, eds. *Infinite Divisions: An Anthology of Chicana Literature.* Tucson: University of Arizona Press, 1993.
Tafolla, Carmen. "La Malinche." In *Infinite Divisions,* eds., Rebolledo and Rivero 198–99.

Ancient Voices
Bringing the Greeks to Life for Students K–12

Kate Hovey

D.H. Lawrence called mythology "an attempt to narrate a whole human experience, of which the purpose is too deep, going too deep in the blood and soul, for mental explanation or description" (Lawrence and Mara Kalnins 49). With budget constraints, rigid curriculum requirements and assessment tests assailing them at every level, how can teachers effectively engage students in this complex, vital subject? One approach has proven to be adaptable in a variety of classroom settings: doing it the way the Greeks did thousands of years ago, using dramatic poetry and the ancient art of the mask.

Though no early examples have survived to modern times, the familiar Greco-Roman comic/tragic mask design with its distinctive, gaping mouth has remained a potent theatrical symbol throughout the ages. Ancient textual and pictorial evidence indicate that masks worn on the Greek stage were cumbersome, helmet-like devices made to fit over the actors' heads, often resting on their shoulders. But authenticity was never the focus or aim of the mask project presented here. Rather, the idea began as an attempt to replicate quickly and inexpensively the large copper and leather hand-held masks used in school performances.

My work as a mask maker, poet and visiting author in the schools affords me the opportunity to share ideas with educators across the country, testing in their classrooms the projects and methods presented in this essay. The results confirm what the Greeks knew long ago: a mask is a playful yet deceptively powerful, transformative tool, giving voice to the heights and unspeakable depths of human experience—the wellspring, as Lawrence says, of all myth.

Versatility is a major hallmark of this hand-held mask design. It can be used in a wide range of classroom projects, from storytelling activities and simple plays in the lower grades to Readers Theater productions and the creation and performance of dramatic poetry, monologues and dialogues. The mask's larger-than-life scale adds visual impact to every project, enhancing student performance while providing a more nuanced experience of early Greek oral traditions.

Storytellers have played a key role in the transmission of Greek mythology since before the Bronze Age, and what better place to keep this ancient tradition alive than in the elementary school library and K–4 classroom? As the teacher or librarian narrates, small groups of students act out the stories. The mask provides an imaginative link to the storytelling process, allowing for a deeper understanding of the myths presented. Introverted children often find it comforting to "hide" behind the mask, which paradoxically encourages greater freedom of expression. Students of this nature who are typically reticent to participate also respond well to performing in a Greek-like chorus, reciting lines in unison with others at appropriate points during the narration. For new readers, bits of dialogue may be added. Short scripts attached directly to the backs of these large masks relieve the pressures of memorization. The addition of costumes further enhances the project; an authentic Greek *chiton* can be easily fashioned from two cloth rectangles pinned together at the shoulders and belted with simple cording.

Originally geared for older students, the mask instructions appearing at the conclusion of this essay can be adapted for lower grades by making one simple change: instead of constructing the mask with the described raised facial features, younger students can draw faces directly onto the poster board using crayons and colored markers. In fact, most older students use a combination of raised and drawn features. No hard and fast rules apply; individual creativity and imaginative use of materials are important aspects of the project. Additional assistance and supervision when cutting out and shaping the masks will be required, but the bulk of remaining tasks—adding construction paper hair, pre-cut crowns, symbols, helmets and other embellishments—are well within the youngest student's skill set.

Readers Theater offers students and teachers a break from the time-honored classroom tradition of silent reading and a powerful, innovative way to bring the characters of myth to life. Unlike a play, a Readers Theater performance requires neither sets nor elaborate staging, no props or costumes and no memorization. Essentially a reading exercise, students recite directly from a book or prepared script. It is still a performance, however, requiring varying degrees of individual and group preparation, the central idea being to build fluency by reading the same piece over and over.

In the upper grades, Readers Theater becomes the perfect vehicle for launching an exploration of both classical and contemporary dramatic poetry. Because students take the poems home and practice reading them aloud, they develop an ear for poetic language, its music, rhythms and cadences. A great part of the enjoyment of poetry is hearing it read aloud, and the Greeks knew this—Greek poets gave birth to the spoken word performance and accompanied most of their poetry with the lyre. Excerpts from classical poems and plays, Homeric hymns and epics make terrific RT performance pieces, reacquainting high school students with mythological characters and themes while introducing them to Greece's immortal poets. Myth-based persona poems by contemporary poets encourage students to view the gods, goddesses and heroes of old through a distinctly modern lens, and poetry anthologies such as *Orpheus and Company* and *After Ovid* contain a wealth of performance-ready material from which to choose.

Persona is the Latin word for "mask." Though masks are not typically used in Readers Theater, these large hand-held versions work especially well in RT-style performances of persona poems and other forms of dramatic poetry. On a practical level, a poem can be printed out and attached to the back of the mask, thereby facilitating the dramatic reading. On a deeper level, the mask can act as a kind of portal or numinous link to the past, evoking the ancient drama and Greek oral tradition. Something happens when a student speaks through the mask; the performance becomes more than a mere recitation. Indeed, the mask-making project itself serves to enrich these performances, as throughout the process students acquire greater knowledge and understanding of the characters their masks represent.

Persona poems, both classical and contemporary, provide inspiring examples for students to follow in their exploration of the characters of Greek myth. The impulse to "put yourself in her shoes"—to transport oneself into another's life, explore an alien psyche and see the world through entirely different eyes—is ancient in origin, and the mask has traditionally been the vehicle of choice through which this transformation occurs. When the ancients put on the mask of a god, goddess, hero or creature, they believed they were transformed by the power of the mask into whatever it represented. Putting on the mask was an act of extraordinary empathy and imagination; putting on the mask in a poem gives students that same opportunity, empowering them to fully inhabit these characters and experience the timeworn world of myth in a profoundly new way.

When I work with students on a persona poem project, I usually start with a timed idea-generating exercise. Students are asked to divide a page of notebook paper in half vertically, creating two columns. The left column is labeled "Facts and Observations" and the right, "Dreaming." Starting with the left side, students are instructed to write down everything they know about the mythological characters they have chosen—only the verifiable facts and observations drawn from written sources and ancient art—within five to seven minutes, keeping in mind the following:

Facts and Observations:
Things to Consider

1. What does your character look like (physical traits and distinguishing features, special clothing)?
2. What symbols and emblems belong to your character?
3. Who is related to your character (parents, siblings, husband/wife, daughters/sons)?
4. What stories/mythological facts are important to your character?

On the "Dreaming" side, students are instructed to write down any thoughts that arise about their chosen characters—no editing allowed—within seven to ten minutes. At the beginning of this stream-of-consciousness portion of the exercise, students are invited to close their eyes and imagine themselves as their characters, keeping in mind the following:

Dreaming into Your Character:
Things to Consider

1. Engaging the senses: What do you (as your character) see, taste, touch, smell, hear?
2. Environment: What impressions do you have of the immediate surroundings? The larger world?
3. Insights: What do you feel, think, dream about? What is your greatest joy or pleasure? Greatest fear?
4. Focusing on a particular event or the high or low point of a day in your character's life, what do you (as your character) believe about the situation? What does the situation reveal about you?

These prompts remain on the whiteboard or screen throughout the exercise, which concludes with a brief Q & A and discussion of the writing process. Students craft their poems by weaving together words and images from both sides of the exercise sheet. Before beginning, they are shown several contemporary persona poems representing different approaches or strategies. From the enigmatic, riddle-like approach of Donald Justice's "The Thin Man" to the straightforward, declarative statement of the copper wire in Carl Sandburg's "Under a Telephone Pole" and the invitation implicit in Walter de la Mare's "Snowflake"—these and countless other highly inventive examples offer students a solid toehold on that treacherous slope all poets face: where to begin.

"Some images, in the course of many generations of men, become symbols, embedded in the soul and ready to start alive when touched, carried on in human consciousness for centuries" (Lawrence and Kalnins 49). D. H. Lawrence's words certainly ring true in the realm of Greek myth. The potent, enduring symbols of which he speaks abound in these stories, arising from that deep, very human desire to penetrate the mysteries of creation, to answer perplexing moral questions and explain the altogether terrifying and sublime phenomena of the natural world. While constructing their masks, students cannot help but become steeped in these ancient symbols, and the result of this immersion process is often reflected in the poems they create. Indeed, symbols are as essential to the art of the mask as figurative and symbolic language is to poetry. Like a poem, a mask is intended for an audience; symbols incorporated into the mask's design help the audience identify the character it represents.

"Many ages of accumulated experience still throb within a symbol. And we throb in response," says Lawrence (Lawrence and Kalnins 49). I am reminded of this every time I watch students cutting and shaping Apollo's sun, Artemis's moon or Zeus's thunderbolt.

The word "symbol" derives from the ancient Greek *symbolon*, a kind of token that was either torn or broken in two and eventually reunited with its missing half, thereby ensuring the safe delivery of a message. Together, poem and mask act as a *symbolon* in this project. Two halves of a whole, they complete each other, uniting to deliver one timeless, dramatic message.

Resource Guide

Readers Theater Scripts
Grades 5–12

1. Suzanne Barchers, *From Atalanta to Zeus: Readers Theatre from Greek Mythology* (Libraries Unlimited, 2001).
2. Gwen Bowers, *Read Aloud Plays: The Iliad, the Odyssey and the Aeneid* (Scholastic Teaching Resources, 2007).
3. Carol Pugliano-Martin, *Greek Myth Plays: 10 Readers Theater Scripts Based on Favorite Greek Myths That Students Can Read and Reread to Develop Their Fluency* (Scholastic Teaching Resources, 2008).

Greek Myth-Related Poetry Anthologies
Grades 9–12

Use poems from these collections in Readers Theater productions and as examples to jumpstart dramatic poetry projects.

1. Deborah Denicola, editor, *Orpheus and Company: Contemporary Poems on Greek Mythology* (University Press of New England, 1999).

2. Michael Hofmann and James Lasdun, editors, *After Ovid: New Metamorphoses* (Farrar, Straus and Giroux, 1995).
3. Nina Kossman, editor, *Gods and Mortals: Modern Poems on Classical Myths* (Oxford University Press, 2001).

Persona Poem Project
Grades 5–12

Poems cited by the author in "Voice of the Mask" workshops:

1. Donald Justice, "The Thin Man," from *Collected Poems* (Knopf, 2004), 88.
2. Carl Sandburg, "Under a Telephone Pole," from *The Complete Poems of Carl Sandburg* (Houghton Mifflin Harcourt, 2003), 70.
3. Anthony Hecht, "Giant Tortoise," from *A Bestiary: Lithographs by Aubrey Schwartz and Poems by Anthony Hecht* (Plantin Press, 1962).
4. Thom Gunn, "Tamer and Hawk," from *Selected Poems* (Farrar, Straus and Giroux, 2007), 4.
5. Michael Hannon, "What the Rose Said, What the Crow Said and What the Cicada Said," from *Changing Light: A Collection of Myths, Poems, Prayers*, edited by J. Ruth Gendler (Harper Collins, 1991).
6. Walter de la Mare, "Snowflake," from *The 20th Century Children's Poetry Treasury*, edited by Jack Pretlutsky (Knopf Books for Young Readers, 1999), 10.
7. Homer, "Song of the Sirens," from *The Odyssey*, translated by Richmond Lattimore (Perennial Classics, 1999), Book XII, lines 184–191.
8. Margaret Atwood, "Siren Song," from *Collected Poems II* (Houghton Mifflin, 1987).
9. Louise Gluck, "Siren," from *Meadowlands* (Ecco, 1997).
10. H.D., "Oread," from *Collected Poems* (New Directions, 1986), 55.

The mask-making project detailed below fulfills several important classroom criteria: affordability, widespread availability of materials, versatility and ease of construction.

Inexpensive poster board, the mask's main component, can be found at the nearest drug store in a wide variety of colors. Though any color may be used, a special dual-sided gold and silver board available at most craft and office supply stores is a favorite for this project. Students enjoy working with this lustrous material, which resembles the metallic finish of the original performance masks. Though it costs more than conventional poster board, it is still highly affordable and practical for classroom use. The current price for a standard 22" × 28" sheet is .99 cents; each sheet cut in half makes two 14" × 22" masks, keeping the cost for the entire project well below $1.00 per student.

Hand-Held Mask Project

Materials and Tools

1. Poster board, dual metallic finish (gold/silver), standard size (22" × 28") cut in half to make two 14" × 22" masks (extra for helmets, crowns, etc.)
2. Colored construction paper (extra black, brown, yellow and red)
3. White craft glue and glue sticks
4. Scissors
5. Hand-held staplers
6. Cardboard rods from clothes hangers
7. Transparent tape
8. Pencils
9. Colored markers or crayons (extra black and brown)
10. Rulers
11. Super #77 spray adhesive (for optional backing, can be used instead of white glue.)

Using Guidelines

With pencil and ruler, lightly draw guidelines on poster board, dividing into four equal quadrants (see A). Sketch features over guidelines, placing eyes, nose and mouth along the vertical and horizontal lines as shown in B. Make sure to draw lightly, as these lines will be erased later.

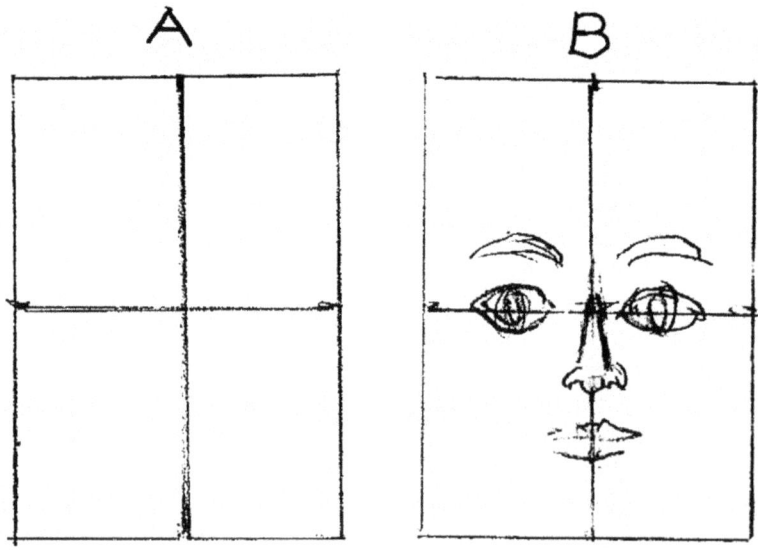

The Nose

To make the nose, cut a rectangular piece of poster board about ½ inch longer than the nose in your sketch, then fold piece in half lengthwise. Practice making noses with plain paper first, until you are happy with the results. The nose is basically a triangle; the broader the nose, the wider the base of your triangle. Determine the length of your triangle's base, then cut (away from the fold) in a straight line from the base to the top of the triangle (see C). Refine shape of nose to suggest nostrils as shown in D. Run a bead of glue along sides of nose and attach over sketched nose on poster board, taking care not to flatten it by pressing too hard.

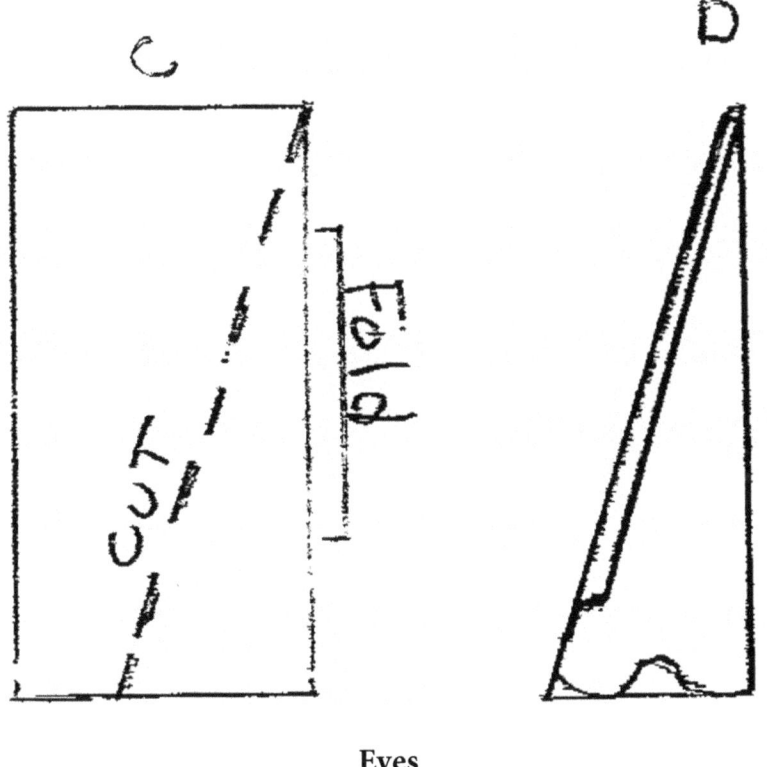

Eyes

Eyes are made in layers, beginning with the white eyeball. Eyeballs are basically ovals with pointed ends; they can be narrow or wide, depending on how you want them to look. Eyes made from narrow ovals, for example, suggest slyness or suspicion; wide ones may give the face a look of surprise or innocence. Cut two eyeballs from a folded piece of white construction paper and glue over sketched eyes on poster board. To make the iris, fold a piece of colored construction paper in half and cut two circles—they should be slightly smaller in diameter than the height of the eyeball.

Glue each iris to the center of the eyeball. To make the pupil, cut out two smaller circles from a piece of folded black construction paper and glue to center of each iris. Alternatively, the iris and pupil can be drawn on the eyeball with colored crayons or markers.

Eyes can be finished in a number of ways. They could be outlined in dark crayon or marker to suggest lashes, or individual lashes could be drawn on. Lashes may also be fringe-cut from construction paper and glued to top and bottom of eyes. To give the eyes added detail and dimension, eyelids can be made.

Eyelids: An Optional Detail (but worth the extra effort)

To make eyelids, cut identical half-circles from a folded piece of posterboard or colored construction paper (the diameter of the half-circle should be a little longer than the eyeball.) To give the eyelid a more natural appearance, cut a soft arc in the half-circle's straight edge—the higher the arc, the more open the eye appears (see E). If desired, glue a fringe of lashes cut from construction paper to the underside of the bottom edge of eyelid. When glue is set, curl fringe up and over eyelid (lashes may be trimmed and feathered to look more natural.) Gently curl each eyelid between thumb and index finger, then apply bead of glue to curved edge and set above eye, holding in place until glue sets.

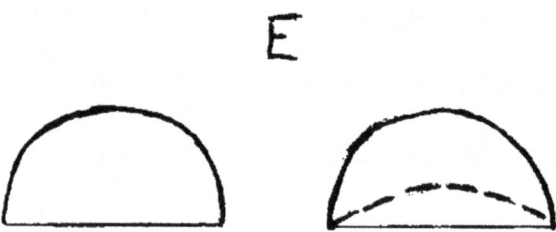

Eyebrows and Ridges

To make eyebrows, cut identical shapes from folded piece of poster board. Score each eyebrow as shown in F and bend along scored line. Scoring is a great way to give three-dimensional qualities to a flat piece of paper. This is done by drawing a line across the paper with the point of the scissors. The line should be visibly incised, but the scissors should never cut all the way through the paper. Apply glue to edges of eyebrows and set in place. When dry, eyebrows can be colored in with marker or crayon. Color only the upper half, above the scored line—the lower half, below the scored line, represents the brow ridge and should remain the same color as the face.

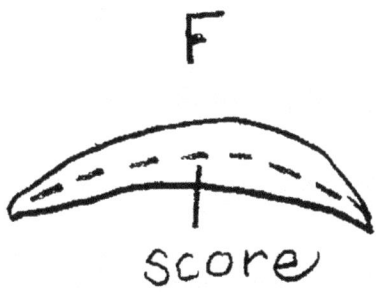

The Mouth

To make the mouth, cut upper and lower lips from poster board or construction paper. Score the upper and lower lips as shown in G and bend along scored line (make cuts in upper lip as shown before bending.) If the mouth is to appear slightly open, draw a thick line with a black marker where the interior of the mouth will show and glue the lips in place above and below this line, overlapping it slightly. Make teeth from white construction paper, if desired. Glue teeth in place first, and then glue lips in desired position over teeth. When gluing lower lip, take care not to flatten the scored edge by pressing down too hard.

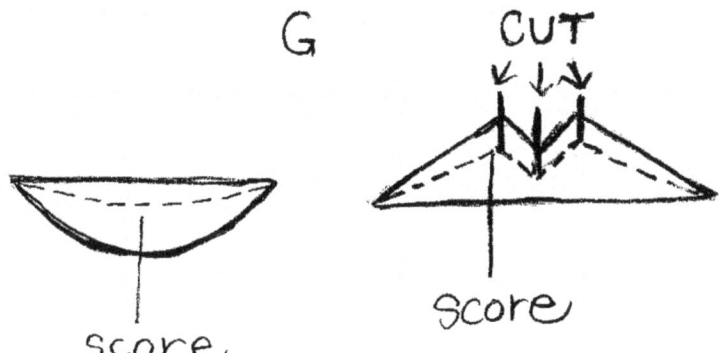

Shaping the Face

The chin is formed by cutting an inch-long slit at the bottom of the poster board along the vertical guideline. Overlap the two sections and staple together (see H). Use scissors to cut away the square edges of the poster board, creating the jaw line. If a more angular, masculine chin is desired, cut two inch-long slits equidistant from the vertical guideline but not wider apart than the corners of the mouth. Overlap the sections and staple together, using scissors to shape the jaw line. To shape the forehead and add rigidity to the mask, cut two inch-long slits at the top of the poster board about 4½ inches on either side of the vertical guideline (see I). Overlap the sections and staple

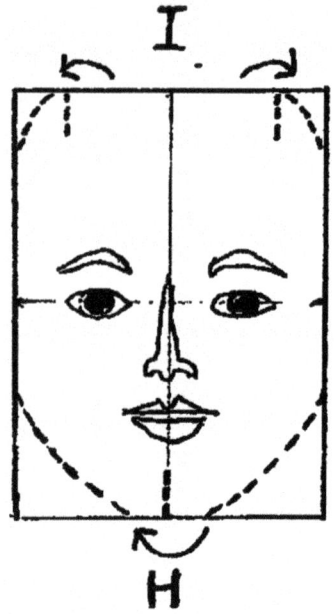

together. Round the corners of the poster board with scissors and shape the head as desired.

Hair

There are a variety of ways to make hair out of construction paper. Layers of fringed paper can be glued along the hairline and curled over a pencil, then trimmed and feathered to create the desired style. Long curls can be made by cutting individual strips, curling around a pencil and gluing to the back of the mask along the hairline. Instead of paper, try using yarn or string; cut pieces of rope and unravel the strands. One student made frizzy gray hair using tufts of steel wool—brilliant! Indulge your creativity—the possibilities are endless.

Symbols and Emblems

The Olympian gods and goddesses were associated with a number of symbols and emblems. On poster board, design a headdress or crown using symbols appropriate to the god or goddess your mask represents. Cut out designs, score, bend and attach as desired. Again, creativity is the key; symbols can be displayed as tattoos, on earrings—even the iris of the eye can be used as a design space for lightning bolts, musical notes, flames, etc.

Finishing Touches

To complete the mask, attach the cardboard rod from a clothes hanger to the back with masking tape (see K). Brush glue on large sheet of black construction paper and apply to the back of the mask, covering it

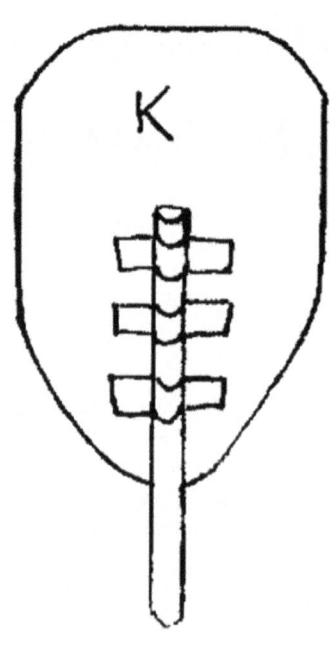

entirely and concealing the rod and tape. This gives the mask a neat, finished appearance.

WORKS CITED

Lawrence, D. H. and Mara Kalnins. *Apocalypse and the Writings on Revelation*. Cambridge: Cambridge University Press, 1980.

Taking Pomegranates from Strangers
Contemporary Female Poets on Persephone

SARAH R. WAKEFIELD

Leda, Europa, Medusa, Philomela, Daphne, Persephone: the motif of rape is thickly woven into classical mythology. When we teach Greco-Roman myths, we may gloss such stories as explanations for the laurel tree or the seasonal cycle, as in the case of Kore, the maiden who becomes Persephone/Proserpine, Queen of the Dead. Presenting her instead as a rape survivor can be a balancing act in a class of young adults, since statistics suggest that many of the women have experienced sexual violence.

"The Sexual Victimization of College Women," a widely cited (and criticized) 2000 report from the U.S. Department of Justice, draws conclusions from interviews with over 4,000 women. 1 out of 36 respondents experienced a rape or attempted rape just during the previous seven months; from this figure, the researchers estimated that over a typical five-year college career, as many as 20 to 25 percent of female students are raped (Fisher, Cullen, and Turner 10). Almost half of the participants (48.8 percent) whose experiences met the legal definition of rape did not see themselves as victims of a crime, however. If we trust these statistics, this is vital information for teachers to have: a college class with twenty female students could include four survivors, two of whom do not believe they were raped.

Compounding the delicate situation is the teaching of mythology in many American classrooms. High school students often read William Butler Yeats's poem "Leda and the Swan," about Zeus's rape of the mortal queen, an event that one critic terms "an unusual sexual intercourse" and "what *looks like* a ruthless rape" (Terrinoni, my italics). Students may have been taught that the poem is *really* about the dialectic rise and fall of civilizations or about Britain's long domination of Ireland. In other words, "rape" in Greek mythology *really* is consensual sex, which actually is a metaphor for colonization.

For several reasons, therefore, young women may be reluctant to discuss Persephone. Yet English professor Elizabeth Breau argues that sexual violence can and should be

> a valid arena of intellectual endeavor.... Discussions of sexual violence in the college classroom introduce students from high-risk populations to a rigorous multidisciplinary critical apparatus that is designed to prevent them from abusing or being abused and to encourage those who have been (or are being) victimized to seek the help they need.

When we present the myth of Persephone/Proserpine as a story of rape with multiple versions of events, we frame a critical exercise that goes beyond a perfunctory "was she or wasn't she?" discussion. Starting with Greek and Roman versions of the myth, students examine discourses surrounding the abduction, move into critical theories regarding gender and power, and finally analyze five twentieth-century poems to debate contemporary attitudes towards sexual assault.

Discussion of Two Versions of the Persephone Myth

Experts date the earliest version of Kore's story, the Homeric *Hymn to Demeter*, at 650 BCE. To summarize, Zeus permits Hades to take his daughter Kore to the underworld as his bride; no one consults the girl's mother, the goddess Demeter. The king of the gods places an irresistible narcissus flower in Kore's path to lure her away from the other virgins picking flowers that day—Narcissus is the beautiful hunter who disdained his admirers and was cursed to fall in love with his own reflection. The god of the dead "snatched the unwilling maid into his golden chariot / and led her off lamenting" (Foley 19–20). By modern definition, this is a rape. Once Demeter realizes her daughter has been abducted, she goes mad with grief, even when the sun god Helios urges the goddess to accept her powerful new son-in-law. Demeter refuses to nourish the earth, and as humanity slowly starves, Zeus sends Hermes to fetch Kore, now Persephone, Queen of the Dead. Hades releases his bride but also sneaks a pomegranate seed into her mouth, ensuring her return to the Underworld for part of every year. The Homeric *Hymn* ends with praise of the Eleusinian Mysteries, encouraging the audience to partake in Demeter's secret rites.

Ovid's Roman version of the myth in Book V of *Metamorphoses* (8 CE) starts with a significant plot wrinkle. Rather than a patriarchal bargain between

Jupiter (Zeus) and Dis (Hades), a power-hungry matriarch sets the drama in motion. Venus complains to her son Cupid,

> Why not extend your mother's kingdom and your own? ... I am scorned in heaven, and Love's power diminishes with mine. Don't you see how Pallas, and the huntress Diana, forsake me? And Ceres's daughter too, Proserpine, will be a virgin if we allow it, since she hopes to be like them. But you, if you delight in our shared kingdom, can mate the goddess to her uncle [Kline V: 332–384].

Under the influence of Cupid's arrow, Dis instantly falls in love with Proserpine, whose reaction is coded sexually: "The frightened goddess cries out to her mother, to her friends, most of all to her mother, with piteous mouth. Since she had torn her dress at the opening, the flowers she had collected fell from her loosened tunic, and even their scattering caused her virgin tears." In an even more pointed translation, Horace Gregory refers to "the brief loss of spent virginity" (151). Similar to the Homeric *Hymn to Demeter*, *Metamorphoses* presents an unwilling girl, and in another parallel, the new Queen fails to embrace her new life. When Proserpine learns she will see Ceres again, "The aspect of her face and mind alters in a moment. Now the goddess's looks are glad that even Dis could see were sad, a moment ago" (Kline V: 533–571).

Students can read the Homeric *Hymn to Demeter* and then Ovid's version, or selected excerpts surrounding the girl's rape and the woman's return, looking for differences in plot, characterization, and connotation. For a more interdisciplinary approach, instructors can integrate artwork available online, particularly Bernini's exceptionally realistic sculpture *Pluto and Proserpina*. Simone Pignoni's "The Rape of Proserpine" shows a menacing Hades, Dante Gabriel Rossetti's "Proserpine" a pensive queen, and Frederick Leighton's luminous painting "The Return of Persephone" the joyous reunion of mother and daughter.

Critical Theories About the Myth

In my experiences teaching the Persephone myth, at this point, students still prefer to see her story as an explanation for the changing seasons. To move them to a more critical examination, we can introduce gender theory, both in the classical era and modern criticism, using quotes from two scholars.

First, Tamara Agha-Jaffar notes in her study of the Homeric *Hymn*, since daughters were property of their fathers, "if placed within its cultural context, Hades' abduction and rape of the young girl lies well within the acceptable patriarchal norms of his society" (142). She further argues that the rape "inculcate[s] in Persephone—and by extension, all women—the notion that their proper role consists of submission to male hegemony" (144). Instructors may want students to push past an easy "that's just how things were back then" response to more challenging questions. How are norms established? Who decides what is acceptable? Here, another quote from Agha-Jaffar might be useful: "What Zeus and his male counterparts in ancient Greece perceived as a perfectly reasonable way of marrying off one's daughter could be interpreted by women in a totally different way: as a violation and an abomination" (15). If Persephone's rape is a violation, can women protest patriarchal norms like Demeter/Ceres does, using their own powers to bring the world to a screeching halt?

In a similar exploration of gendered power, critic Kathie Carlson sees the myth as a struggle between Demeter and Hades, with Kore as a tool to win mastery. She splits readings into two main categories:

Matriarchal Accent	Patriarchal Accent
• hero = Demeter, defiant mother who bends the gods to her will	• hero = Hades, transformative lover who helps a naïve Kore become a woman
• enemy = Hades, violent rapist	• enemy = Demeter, possessive mother
• resolution = female triumph, with the additional power of death (the Crone) added to a strong mother-daughter bond	• resolution = male triumph, with Demeter subdued and Persephone given real power as Hades' Queen

Carlson points out that patriarchal-accented explanations often portray Persephone as a willing participant, either in the initial assault or the consumption of the pomegranate seed. She concludes:

> My own sense is that these interpretations see through a contemporary patriarchal filter that has informed and infused long-standing collective views of relationships between women, including and perhaps especially framing our views on the relationship of mother and daughter [15].

Between Agha-Jaffar and Carlson, we have ample fruit to spark student-led discussions and writing prompts. Looking back to the original myths, what is the mother-daughter bond like? Who seems triumphant in each version, and what textual support can students offer? In Ovid's version, how does Venus's speech about expanding her power affect our understanding of matriarchal vs. patriarchal accents? In one myth, Kore calls for her father and in the other, her mother—is this an indication of where the real power lies? Which accent do students find more plausible and why? Are we, the enlightened readers of the twenty-first century, more reactionary than the ancients?

We can teach contemporary Persephone poems with two focal questions: first, how do the poems affect our understanding of the myths, and second, is Carlson correct that the patriarchal accent dominates in the twentieth century? It seems simple, but in the process of applying this binary opposition to the poems, students likely will struggle to choose, finding evidence for both accents in the same work, if not the same line. Instructors can model a deconstructive approach, not as a cop-out but a shift from an either/or mindset to what feminist critic Rachel Blau DuPlessis calls "a both / and vision born of shifts, contraries, negations, contradictions" (6).

Close Reading of Five Poems

Students receive two sets of carefully paired poems plus a final piece, many available online through the Academy of American Poets. The first pair includes Rita Dove's "Persephone, Falling," a cautionary tale about strangers, and Louise Glück's "A Myth of Innocence," which explores Persephone's motives. For the Formalists, Dove's poem echoes the structure of a Petrarchan sonnet with plenty of literary devices like synecdoche, enjambment, and anaphora. In fourteen lines it also shows how easily a woman's reputation falters. The poem baldly proclaims that Persephone wanders away from her friends and thus the god Hades "claimed his due" (6). Lured by the strange beauty of the narcissus flower, which places us with the Homeric *Hymn*, the girl becomes a sexual cautionary tale. Readers are urged to avoid eye contact with strangers and stay close to a group because otherwise, tragedy comes too readily. Most women have heard a variation on these warnings, but if girls wander off, are rapists merely claiming their due? Is this evidence of a patriarchal accent?

In "The Myth of Innocence" by Louise Glück, rather than finding a narcissus flower, Persephone suffers from the subtle self-absorption of a teenager who thinks herself worldly. When the girl goes to the fateful field, she often looks at her reflection in a pond just like Narcissus. Feeling "daughterliness still clinging to her" (6), she chafes under the watchful eye of everything in nature, controlled by her mother. While Persephone stands there, longing to be alone, the handsome Hades appears, representing an escape, a way to be more than Demeter's daughter. Glück's Persephone tells herself that she wants to go with the god, rather than being forced; the speaker, however, comments on her naiveté. This poem, like Dove's, blames a girl's desire to do or be something different. But Glück's speaker suggests that Persephone only *thinks* she knows what she is asking for, a child daring to let the dark god hug her while her uncle, the sun god, watches. How does this affect the patriarchal accent of the poem? Is it rape if she goes willingly but doesn't understand the long-term consequences?

With the second set of poems, students may anticipate a matriarchal accent, but literature as well as critical interpretations "see through a contemporary patriarchal filter" (Carlson 15). In "A Myth of Devotion" by Louise

Glück, we see Hades' perspective, without mention of Cupid's arrow, Zeus's consent, or mystical flowers. He plans the abduction for years, convincing himself that his niece will be sexually responsive due to her "appetite" for different flavors and scents (20). Believing himself a transformative (and welcome) lover, patriarchal Hades is stymied by the horror and dread of a terrified girl who sees him through matriarchally-accented eyes, as a rapist. Therefore Hades changes tactics to achieve dominance: he informs his niece that she is dead. This poem ties back nicely to Agha-Jaffar's observation that what gods see as acceptable, goddesses and women perceive "as a violation and an abomination."

What if Persephone knows what a future with Hades holds and wants that life? What if she finally gets a chance to speak for herself? This is the case in Rachel Zucker's "Letter [Persephone to Demeter]," part of her 2003 collection *Eating in the Underworld*. Like "The Myth of Innocence" by Glück, this poem shows Persephone unhappy in her mother's realm, represented by yellow, earth tones, and lack of inertia. Persephone longs for different primary colors, for reds and blues and action, "furious, sexual" (9), but Hades' Underworld, with all its contrast to the world above, represents a new prison where dead things move. It even seems to resist language, as the girl tries to describe "the sea in a place which has no blue and is not the sea" (11). In addition to an opportunity to talk about deconstruction and definition via oppositions, the overwhelming negation suggests that Persephone has not found what she hoped. Perhaps the most telling words of the entire poem are its first wistful two: "At home." Persephone sees Demeter's earth, not her husband's fiercely red kingdom, as her home. Whether she left this home willingly or not, it is still patriarchal. Students sometimes expect that female poets must be feminists, all about girl power, but these two pairs of poems skew heavily toward Carlson's patriarchal accent. What would a poem in the matriarchal accent look like? An interesting activity could be to ask students to write one.

A final selection, "Persephone the Wanderer," calls into question everything students have done to this point, for Glück's speaker jeers at those who analyze the myth. Persephone, "pawed over by scholars" (13), suffers continued violation through close reading. How do students feel about being in this position, especially if they have written their own interpretive poems? Are we imposing our 21st-century ideas about date rape and female sexuality onto a myth? To guide students into making broader connections, is this so far removed from our justice system? Rape victims often report feeling as if they are the ones on trial, as they repeat their story to doctors, detectives, judges and juries trying to determine the girl's reactions, especially those that might indicate consent.

The speaker then instructs us on the proper reading of the myth, with emphasis on the god and goddess rather than Persephone, who "is just meat"

(85). The crudeness of the descriptor aside, the poem again alleges that we ask the wrong questions. Is our focus on Persephone misplaced, when we should be looking more at the rivalry between Ceres/Demeter and Dis/Hades? Why *is* the earth goddess so opposed to the powerful King of the Underworld as a son-in-law?

For Kore/Proserpine/Persephone, whether she is a victim or collaborator, in the end she belongs to someone. The young woman goes from husband to mother, never alone but somehow isolated. Glück's "Persephone the Wanderer" explodes the previous exercise with its ambivalence about the maiden's experience and about attempts to pin it down. The poem's closing lines turn a question back on the reader, asking, "What will you do / when it is your turn in the field with the god?" (98–99)—not "if" but "when." This allows students to reflect not only on how much their own feelings have colored their readings of the myth and poems but also how widespread sexual violence is.

Matriarchal or patriarchal. Earth or underworld. It seems like an either/or situation, but in these poems intimate, boundaries blur. Persephone can both consent and refuse; she can love (and hate) both her husband and her mother. Helping our students appreciate such complexities shows them how very relevant Greco-Roman mythology remains today while fostering critical thinking. Who knows? Maybe students will create a new accent that links Persephone to neither mother nor lover—a version where the powerful queen visits her mother on holidays (if she can get away from pressing obligations in the Underworld, where she reigns alone).

Works Cited

Agha-Jaffar, Tamara. *Demeter and Persephone: Lessons from a Myth*. Jefferson, NC: McFarland, 2002. Print.
Breau, Elizabeth. "Teaching Rape and Incest." *Thirdspace: A Journal of Feminist Theory & Culture* 3.1 (2003). Web. 9 Nov. 2015.
Carlson, Kathie. *Life's Daughter/Death's Bride: Inner Transformations through the Goddess Demeter/Persephone*. Boston & London: Shambhala, 1997. Print.
Dove, Rita. "Persephone, Falling." *Mother Love*. New York: W. W. Norton & Company, Inc., 1995. 9. Print.
DuPlessis, Rachel Blau. *The Pink Guitar: Writing as Feminist Practice*. New York: Routledge, 1990. Print.
Fisher, Bonnie S., Francis T. Cullen, and Michael G. Turner. "The Sexual Victimization of College Women." *National Institute of Justice* (Dec. 2000). Web. 10 Nov. 2015.
Foley, Helene. *The Homeric Hymn to Demeter: Translation, Commentary, and Interpretative Essays*. Princeton: Princeton University Press, 1993. Print.
Glück, Louise. *Averno*. New York: Farrar, Straus and Giroux, LLC, 2006. Print.
Gregory, Horace, trans. *The Metamorphoses*. New York: Mentor Books, 1958. Print.
Kline, Anthony S. *The Metamorphoses: Book V*. Web. 9 Nov. 2015 http://ovid.lib.virginia.edu/trans/Metamorph5.htm.
Terrinoni, Enrico. "Literary Contexts in Poetry: William Butler Yeats' 'Leda & the

Swan.'" *Understanding Literature: Literary Contexts in Poetry and Short Stories.* Great Neck Publishing, 2006. EBSCOHost Literary Reference Center. Web. 9 Nov. 2015.

Zucker, Rachel. "Letter [Persephone to Demeter]." *Eating in the Underworld.* Middleton, CT: Wesleyan University Press, 2003. 9–10. Print.

PART IV: ANCESTRY, THE PERSONAL
AND SELF-WRITING WOMEN

Family Lore, Suffragist Ancestors and the Scrapbook of a 19th Century Poetess; or, How to Find a Topic for the Dissertation

LAURA MADELINE WISEMAN

Family Mythology 101

Iowa, December 2003

It's the holidays. You're home for a visit from grad school, a fistful of days during which you spend a half-hour here, a half-day there, a night somewhere else. You travel in a borrowed truck on two-lane highways powdered with a hard, cold snow that lifts like dust from beneath the tires of cars ahead of you and blows in a fine, white, haze at asphalt level under a pale sky. This is Iowa, where you come from, where your people have come from for over a hundred years, though you don't know that yet. What you know is you're freezing. You turn on the seat warmer in the truck and drink mugs of convenience store coffee—stale, bitter, and only a little worse than the Folgers offered to you at your arrival destinations. You're freezing because for months you've been living in the desert, in the mirage of heat and glare, where you study, hike sprawling canyons of saguaros and teddy bear cacti, and have lost a few pounds, somehow, back to what you weighed when you were a long distance runner in high school, an almost necessary shedding of flesh, an offering, even, to the endless blue skies, the monsoon storms, the sand, the dry river beds, and the delicious, wavering heat.

As you drive in Iowa, the temperatures skittering in the teens and plunging to subzero with wind-chill, your teeth chatter and your chest quakes with cold. You turn up the truck's heater and place your palms on the vents.

At your paternal grandparents, after the Hy-Vee bakery sweets, Folgers coffee previously made that morning and re-warmed in the microwave now, after talk and chat, after a *hello!* from your aunt who lives just next door and who offers you a plastic wrapped paper plate of homemade cookies dusted in red and green granulated sugar, and after treats for the pets who scramble along the linoleum, collars jangling and leases dragging, after all this your father says, *You should look up your ancestor, Matilda Fletcher.*

Why he says this, you don't know, but offer a *Who?* as you scratch his dog, a white mutt speckled with black spots. She opens her mouth in a wide dog grin. Her wet, pink tongue lolls to one side as you attend to the ears, neck, and chest.

Matilda spoke at Chautauquas while her stepchildren sang and danced.

Oh, you say, returning to the scruff, as the dog leans her heavy flank against your legs.

Back and forth they go around the kitchen table—your father, grandfather, and grandmother—piecing together the family myth, the legend, the known lore of Matilda, all of which amounts to little more than, *She spoke at Chautauquas while her stepchildren sang and danced,* and a teeny bit more about her second husband, your great-great-great-grandfather.

Contact my cousin, your father finally says. *She's got Matilda's scrapbook. She should send it to you.*

> *Myth:* She spoke at chautaques whiles her stepchildren sang and danced.[1]
> *Fact:* She spoke at a chautaque.[2]
> *Fact:* She had three stepchildren.[3]
> *Fact:* She was a poetess.[4]

Myth: The Poetic Dissertation Topic

Arizona, 2003–2006, & Nebraska, January 2009

Upon your return to the desert, you do email the distant relative, your father's cousin, and ask if she will send you Matilda's scrapbook, to which she replies with a clear, but firm *No*. A few years later, you ask again and get the same *No*, but as before she offers this: *You are welcome to come here and see it.* Here, as in Illinois, as in very far from Gila monsters and cactus wrens. You wonder if the scrapbook even exists or if it is an ephemeral object, a chimera, a ghost, a myth based in a reality that once was.

What then, makes you curious again a few years later, after you've moved, started a Ph.D. program, and are thinking that at some point you're going to have to come up with a topic for the dissertation? You don't email her this time on a mild Nebraska winter afternoon, a mug of tea at your desk, and two cats curled into a swirl of silver and brown tabby behind you on the dark, shaggy carpet. This time you enter Matilda's name into a search engine and press the return key on your laptop. What you find astonishes you, because you find Matilda everywhere—articles in the *New York Times,* her patent application to the U.S. government for an improvement in portable trunks, poems in *The Los Angeles Times,* and a brief biography on Matilda that appeared in Susan B. Anthony's and Elizabeth Cady Stanton's *The History of Woman Suffrage,* acknowledging Matilda's suffrage work, and noting that she was a lecturer from Iowa "worthy of mention," who was married to an impoverished school teacher.

All you can think is, really? Your ancestor was a suffragist? She was a poet? Really? Why did you not know this?

Here's where things get complicated for you. You research Matilda by spending long hours on the computer examining digitized scans of news articles about or by her. You request materials from interlibrary loan and when they arrive, you climb the shadowy stairs to the dimly lit digital area and place reels of film on a reader to painstakingly examine each lit image of text—poems, lectures, and out-of-print books. You visit the historical state libraries, museums, local town libraries, and places where Matilda spoke, trying to piece together her life, trying to find fact from what is so much myth. There are many hours on the road. Green and then brown fields of corn and soybean falling away from the interstate and highways like blocks of neat text framing where you're going. Every mile or so, a hawk lifts its wings from a rotted tree branch—gnarled, grey and forgotten by property lines—to fly. Red-winged blackbirds balance on mile markers and barbed wire fences. Katydids and cicadas drone. All this, mind you, while you read, write, and defend your comprehensive exams. You propose to write a creative dissertation on Matilda in the form of poems. Your chair approves your topic choice. Your chair retires. You find a new chair—when, let's say you've written and polished the dissertation and you're in draft twenty-seven or so. You rewrite the dissertation, polish, reorder, revise, polish, rethink, and rewrite it some more.

Wait. Pause the narrative. You must mention the ghost.

You have few, if any ghost stories. The ones you do have all derive from middle school slumber parties—Ouija boards, ghoulish attempts to spook your friends, and *light as a feather, stiff as a board.* However, here's a ghostly truth: the moment you decide to enter Matilda's name into a search engine (January 2009) is one hundred years to the month she died (January 1909). A coincidence?

Ahem, continue the story, please.

Then, this relative, this keeper of Matilda's scrapbook sends you, after so many years of asking, a disk with high resolution photographs of every page of the scrapbook. Oh wow, you think and then, somehow, misplace a couple of weeks examining her poems and prose, knowing that this is good stuff. You take the disk to the copy center and have the whole thing enlarged, printed in color, and bound so you can read it closely, write on it, take notes a little while longer.

But there's a problem. The months are ticking by and you have to turn in your dissertation on Matilda. You have to defend it. You have to graduate. You want to include Matilda's scrapbook in the dissertation, but there's no time. You do, then, what any researcher does at moments like this when presented with new information and a deadline approaching. You save it for later. You defend, you pass, and you graduate, while Matilda patiently waits.

Myth: Once you find a dissertation topic, the research is easy. Facts crawl into your lap like a litter of kittens—happy, playful, loving. The interlibrary loan office opens its arms to you because you know all the right questions to ask, the correct files to seek, the perfect demeanor that says, *I know what I'm doing.* The well-paid and well-staffed librarians in historical and local libraries mentor you, teach you, show you without grumble or frustration exactly what you've come to find, though you're not even sure, half the time, what you want. Your clan offers, without even asking, every item they've ever collected on Matilda and will spend hours and hours with you on the phone and in their kitchens because their only job in life is to ensure you receive your Ph.D.[5]

Fact: The scrapbook exists.[6]

Fact: Susan B. Anthony and Elizabeth Cady Stanton attended Matilda's lecture (Letter to the Editor June 1871).

Fact: Matilda's first husband was an impoverished school teacher.[7]

Fact: No one will write this dissertation for you.[8]

Meanwhile, While Dissertating, You Fear
Nebraska, 2010–2011

Because you've decided to save the scrapbook for later, you can't help but worry you'll misplace the bound photographs of Matilda's scrapbook in the meantime. You don't call your relatives and fret. No emails to your chair. No, you suffer in silence, your interior stage lit with gaslights that flicker and pulse with horrors. You worry you'll step off a train to meet someone with a strong bear hug and just as you finish your *hello!* and have lifted your suitcase, the train begins to rumble, to pull back from the station, to shudder and hiss and gain speed. *Oh no!* You realize you've left Matilda on the train. She's right there on the table between four seats. The flicker of lights glints across her plastic cover as she heads for a nostalgia trip to New York City. Never mind that you can't seem to find many trains in the Midwest, let alone ride them, this is what you fear.

Or maybe you check your bag, but the airport loses it and Matilda is inside. You stand there with the grouchy, militant, prison-guard-like American airport personnel, who always take your water bottles, who ignore you if you ask a question, and who forever seem to want to pat you down, swab you hands with a chemical to see if you've got bomb dust there, and run their blue latex gloves through the dresses, long sleeve tee-shirts, and bras of your carry-on. Searching for what, you don't know. The personnel woman barks, *Ma'am. Ma'am,* and then something about how you're to return to the airport in a few days to claim your temporarily lost bag, but you can't listen. Your brow furrows because all you can think is Matilda, safe inside your suitcase, is about to go over Niagara Falls in a bucket. The water sparkles. The spray and sun rainbow. She'll never survive the drop.

Or Matilda stamped and ticketed has just arrived in Canada on the pebbly beach of Lake Superior. The post-thunderstorm waves crash and toss up bobbers and twists of big box plastic shopping bags. You think, won't someone move her please? You fear the water's cold, blue tongue.

Or your suitcase with Matilda inside is tucked under someone's arm as they climb Grays Peak in a bear suit. It's a long climb, but it can be done in a day. Problem is, suddenly a real brown bear appears and the bear suit person drops Matilda, runs the switchbacks, and finds a few spots to slide down the snowfields, down, down, down to the parking lot of SUVs. The real bear reaches for Matilda. Why, you wonder? Maybe she hopes Matilda will be as sweet as honey, as plentiful as wild berries, as life altering as an empty mountain and so lumbers off to share Matilda with the cubs in the den.

Or maybe not.

But still, you double-check where Matilda is when you return from each of your travels. She's always there on the shelf. She awaits the reach of your hand. But you don't reach, you wait and wait and wait for later.

Myth: You have a suitcase inside of which Matilda could fit.[9]

Fact: Matilda spoke in New York City ("By Wire from Gotham"), saw Niagara Falls,[10] and climbed Grays Peak.[11]

Post-Ph.D.: No Limbo, No Myths, but the Thing Itself

Illinois, Summer 2011

Later arrives in the form of a coincidence. You're in Illinois, July through mid-August, six sultry weeks when you get up most mornings before seven to walk through residential neighborhoods carved into woods teeming with yellow swallowtails, gold finches, and grey squirrels. A fat orange tomcat stalks the bushes around a one-hundred-foot blue spruce on your route. Deer cross the road ahead of you or graze the lawns specked with pink clover heads, ears frozen at your approach. Large, iridescent dragonflies swing across the open dollies of queen anne's lace that line the ditches. The cicadas sing their percussive rattles, a shifting current of noise through which you walk.

At a party on a porch before a field where swallows zigzag and swoop, someone asks you about your dissertation, which makes you begin to wonder about the scrapbook and Matilda, about your father's cousin who lives in Illinois, somewhere. The next day you look up her address and enter it into Google maps to find that she is twenty minutes away. You wonder, given that you are here, would she let you see the scrapbook? You call and ask.

Sure, she says.

That night you think on family legends, on myth.

A few years before, you grandmother gave you two handwritten accounts of family lore composed by your great-aunt. The first, written in cursive on unlined paper, described your family line the came from England in the 1700s and settled peaceably in the South for generations. However, your great-aunt writes, "their neighbors made life unpleasant for the family" because they were "vocal in their opposition to the Southern plan to secede from the union." The second handwritten account described Matilda,

> In the McKinley campaign, Matilda Fletcher Wiseman took her stepchildren with her. They posed as child prodigies, singing campaign and Civil War songs. First they had to audition before Theodore Roosevelt at campaign headquarters in Detroit. He was then the Police Commissioner of New York City and helped arrange the great rallies where Matilda spoke. Great torchlight processions preceded the speeches, which were held in circus tents.

You asked several relatives where to find this information, where you might corroborate a myth with fact, but no one seemed to know. This, then, must be yet another myth. You go to bed wondering, as you've wondered many times, if anything is a fact at all.

In the morning you drive the twenty minutes to your father's cousin's home. She is shorter than you expect, friendly, and has the round, wide eyes of a girl, dark, open, and curious. You know you met her once, though you have no memory of this, at your great-grandmother's ninetieth birthday. She's there in pictures in the wide, round, tinted glasses of the 1980s. And so are you, a girl with blonde, sun-bleached hair, a smattering of freckles across your nose and cheeks, and an impish grin of a child who's paused long enough for the photo, but who will disappear any second to run off and play.

You talk for an hour and a half, during which time she shows you one wonderful family heirloom after another—a family tree scrapbooked in pretty paper and protected by plastic sleeves, a wedding gift of English china, and a trove of family photographs dating back to the mid-1800s. After all this, you feel a little breathless and a little like you'd really prefer it if you could enter whatever closet she stores this stuff in and live there for a while, but instead you explain what you'd like to do, saying, *Can I borrow Matilda's scrapbook while I'm in Illinois?*

Her answer: *Yes.*

    Myth: See all of the above quotation on Matilda from the letter by your great-aunt. (Wiseman, Family papers)
    Fact: Matilda stumped for a presidential candidate. (Wiseman, Family papers 2)
    Fact: Matilda walked in a torchlight process.[12]

On the Subjects of Ghosts

Iowa, Summer 2009 & Illinois, Summer 2011

About six months into your research, you visit the Woodlawn Cemetery in Des Moines. The plot map, handwritten by your father and photocopied for you, shows four gravesites, though only one is readable, Matilda's. One is a small, worn nub. Two are unmarked. Beyond Matilda's plot, are other descendants in your clan laid out under the pin oaks, among the peonies and tiger lilies, inside the up and down slopes and rises of Des Moines' oldest cemetery.

As you stand there at Matilda's grave, you expect oddly, something mysterious to happen—Matilda's ghost to appear from nowhere and whisper some poetic secret in ghost tongue before she shimmers and fades from sight. Or maybe a clue will be etched below her name and you'll know which train to take, what town to debark in, and how many paces to step before you find the X that marks the spot. Or maybe as your hand brushes the dusty, sap speckled stone, you expect some surge of mystical energy will pass through the granite to you and you'll know the truth that's plagued people for millennia—the secrets to the heart of a man, how to tear off the mask of your frenemies, or what you can do to know the evil genius of love. No source of the Nile here. No trees falling in the forest. No cave of shadows and light. As the grackles squawk and the sparrows peck along the cobbles, you snap a few photos, feel a little bored and disappointed, and then you get in the car and drive.

However, it is when you borrow Matilda's scrapbook—the actual thing, not the photographs, but the thing itself—that you feel haunted. First, when your father's cousin opens the box to show it to you, you say, *Oh, wow,* because you imagined a small handheld journal with cramped handwriting and teeny-tiny newsprint text, not what size it is with the dimensions of a coffee table book.

Second, when you bring it back to where you work in Illinois, you leave it in its box for days unable to do any more than peek inside and then suddenly feel a need to go in the other room, brew a fresh cup of tea, or go for a walk, while the scrapbook waits.

When you do get it out, you're paranoid you'll spill said ever present cup of tea or your bold rollerball ink will bloom the pages in black flowers as your pen has pollinated your shirts and sweaters, your notepaper and your books, your hands and your bags—an ink that won't launder unless caught immediately while the ink still bleeds. Or you fear to leave the scrapbook open, lest the sunlight from the windows fades the script or printed poems.

And when you get up for a drink of water in the middle of the night, glasses-less and half-blind, you're sure your desk chair is not your desk chair, but instead Matilda in her black alpaca dress. She reaches for you and pulls you into her arms. And what do you do? Your only choice is to go.

Notes

1. So claimed by those in your clan. Maybe she did. Maybe they did. Maybe it's impossible to know.

2. According to a scrapbook clipping from the *Tribune and Republican,* Matilda is reported as saying her lecture on presidential candidate Ulysses S. Grant will be some "musings from a philosopher of Chappaqua."

3. Many places like the *Chicago Daily Tribune* announced Matilda and your great-great-great-grandfather's marriage in the evening of January 21, 1886, in Des Moines, Iowa, with the Rev. D. Webb officiating. *He* was the pastor of Grace Methodist Episcopal Church in Des Moines and a widower, losing both his first wife and fourth child in 1883. Matilda was a widow of eleven years. *She* became stepmother to one girl and two boys—ages ten, eight, and six. They lived in Des Moines, in a house in Sherman Hill. The house is gone. In its place is an apartment complex that overlooks a medical center and a busy crossroad with four lanes, and is within hearing distance of the oceanic purr of traffic on I-235.

4. Countless newspapers and contemporaries call Matilda a poetess and/or poet, mention her lectures that were often given in the form of poems, or note her that her lecturers had a poetical quality. See for example, the endorsements at the end of *The Trial* (Wiseman, 187). In her most recently published poem "The Heart of a Man," the first line reads, "The heart of man. It is a toy."

5. Research happens in chunks, illogical, incomplete, non-linear, out of order, chaos. Take, for example a 1888 piece from the *Chicago Daily Tribune,* "Miss Matilda Fletcher, the lecture[r h]as [a] new subject—"The Happy Couple." [It is] perhaps needless to remark that the lectu[re] does not refer to Cleveland and Thurman." Missing and unreadable words aside, unfortunately, this brief mention tells you only that Miss (was she single then? or was the reporter unaware?) Matilda Fletcher was giving

the new (what was the old?) lecture "The Happy Couple" sometime (when?), somewhere (in Chicago? near Chicago? or elsewhere? at what location in the city? a church? a hall?) and on some topic (couple as in marriage? marital happiness?) unrelated to Cleveland and Thurman (not politics then? or on politics, but on the opposing side?). Less often, you found more thorough accounts like one from *The Yankton Press*. That article offers a bit more to go on, noting when she'll lecture (March 1873, though not what day or time), where she'll be (South Dakota, though not what town and not what hall or church), what her fees are (sixty to one hundred dollars), what lectures she can present (at the very least "Men and their Whims"), where she hails from (Council Bluffs, Iowa), who might hire her to speak (Young Men's Club), what audience members will pay (fifty cents), what her reputation is (highest commendations from the press and people). It can also be inferred that she's likely her own tour manager (the newspaper received a letter from her).

    6. You have seen the scrapbook, held it, opened it, read it. Indeed, it is in your father's cousin's private collection. She's asked to remain unnamed.

    7. Matilda notes that she married her school teacher (*The Trial*, Wiseman 12). The 1869–1870 Council Bluffs Directory lists Matilda's first husband as the teacher and principal of Court Street School.

    8. Actually, your father's axiom is *I can't do it for you*, meaning all things in life, dissertation included.

    9. You do have plenty of places that could fit the photographed scrapbook, but yearn to own the trunk she patented and designed herself.

    10. From the scrapbook, Matilda's letter to the editor that describes her trip to Niagara Falls in the winter of 1869–1870.

    11. Many newspapers described her July 1871 climb to Grays Peak, including the *Daily Central City Register*. Matilda, however, did not wear a bear suit.

    12. Two newspapers in Matilda's scrapbook discuss a torchlit procession escorting Matilda to the lecture hall. For example, the Monmouth, Illinois, *Atlas* describes the evening parade as composing of forty young ladies in "uniform—white dresses, blue capes, pink hats" who each carried "a transparency, inscribed with the names of Grant and Wilson" under two hundred lamps.

WORKS CITED

"By Wire from Gotham. Special Dispatch to *The Post*." *The Washington Post*. 5 June 1878. 1.

Fletcher, Matilda. "The Heart of a Man." *The Los Angeles Times* (Los Angeles, CA). 2 Sept 1889.

_____. "Improvement in portable trunks." Patent number 158,056. 22 Dec 1874.

Mahany, J.G., Agent and Correspondent. "Clear Creek County Excursion to Gray's Peak." *Daily Central City Register* (Central City, CO). Issue 292, col C. 8 July 1871.

"Matilda Fletcher." *The Yankton Press*. Issue 30, Col C. 26 Feb. 1873.

"Matilda Fletcher A Wife." *Chicago Daily Tribune* (1872–1963). 22 Jan 1886. ProQuest Historical Newspaper Chicago Tribune (1849–1986). 6.

Other 6—No Title. *Chicago Daily Tribune* (1872–1963). 22 Dec 1888. ProQuest Historical Newspaper Chicago Tribune (1849–1986). 4.

Wiseman, Matilda Fletcher. *Scrapbook*. Personal Family Collection. Morton, IL.

_____. *The Trial and Imprisonment Geo. W. Felts: A Deaf Old Soldier Robbed of His Rights*. Rockford, IL, 1907.

Works Cited from Matilda Fletcher's Scrapbook

Note to reader: Unless noted for a given newspaper article, letter to the editor, or any of the other miscellany included in Matilda's Scrapbook, publication source and date were unreadable, never included, not paginated, and/or presently lost.

Atlas (Monmouth, IL).
Fletcher, Matilda. Letter to the Editor.
Fletcher, Matilda. Letter to the Editor. 23 June 1871.
Tribune and Republican (Omaha, NE). 25 July 1872.

Creating Light
Myth-making of Lucille Clifton

GLENIS REDMOND

    The transatlantic slave trade intertwines with and entangles the lineages of most African Americans. The vital branches of our family trees have been severed by the violence and inhumane treatment of human trafficking. True, most families' histories—whether black, brown, or white—branch into difficult stories. But African Americans' ancestral trees are fraught not only with the usual complexities, but also gnarled and devoured by the blight of slavery, all too often rendering our stories and histories untraceable. In genealogical terms, this inaccessibility means, "hitting the wall." Many of our genealogical searches end in that murky place in history where slave ships left the shores of Africa and sailed into the infamous voyage, the Middle Passage. Here our historical trails become as cold, unreadable and mysterious as the Atlantic Ocean. Much of who we are as African Americans are cannot be retrieved because of that forced voyage. Enslaved, our African ancestors were robbed of all of their material possessions. They came to a new country with only their ravaged bodies and souls. What remained of their spirit was tried and broken with the use of cruel implements—shackles, manacles, collars, gags, racks, whips, and more—all designed to break the spirit. Many of the enslaved Africans could not stand the rigor of inhumanity: they died or chose to kill themselves. Those who lived were the ones who had the will, luck, grace and strength to survive. They subsisted on the bits and ends of food, clothing, and shelter.
    Ripped from the homelands and brought to a foreign land with an unfamiliar climate and unknown history, the Africans carried their traditions from Africa in their minds and their hearts' memories. Accordingly, the oral tradition became even more important to the Africans now Americans. Through their retelling and remembering we have, centuries later, a patched together history. Making story, song, art, and poetry a necessity: revolutionary acts insuring

that culture would not be forsaken and forgotten. Artistic expression became a healing balm to counteract the everyday struggles and strife of slavery, during which much was taken and much was lost. Though the oral tradition was embedded in all African countries, it became the only avenue of expression for the majority of slaves who could not read or write. Furthermore, mandates and laws were passed making it illegal for African Americans to read or write. Therefore, once Africans were enslaved in America, the travesty was cemented. Education was not an option. They could not write/right their way to freedom.

We cannot mop this mess up—nor can we escape the fact that we come from a stolen people. Averting our gaze does not strengthen or ameliorate the past. As poet Audre Lorde wrote from her book *The Cancer Journals,* "Your silence will not protect you." It is here the poet's role becomes integral, giving voice to that which was stolen—giving voice to those who were intentionally silenced.

Lucille Clifton's work amplifies what is necessary, as she becomes the mouthpiece for her own personal history, as well as the African American collective. Her poems and prose stare unashamedly and unapologetically at the past. In her memoir *Generations,* her pen becomes a tool that she uses to grapple with history. She demonstrates that it is possible to tend to the ripped places of family lineage utilizing fact, myth, and the power of the imagination.

In this memoir Clifton pioneers new territory as she reckons with her ancestry poetically. Her greatest strength is her ability to take the existing facts and render them with her enlightened imagination. Turning her gaze both outward and inward, she crafts poems and prose that read as autobiographical documentation. What she brings back from her internal depths feeds the whole. Richard Rohr, a writer and a Franciscan friar, speaks to the immediacy and the necessity of work such as Clifton's: "If we don't learn to mythologize our lives, inevitably we will pathologize them."

Lucille Clifton does tremendous work stitching together a torn lineage as she addresses how history exacted its toll on her family, the Sayles, the family name also recorded ironically as Sales. She sheds light on America's shadowed cancerous history. Without averting her gaze, with a brave eye and hand, she does poetic battle. In her slender, but palpable memoir, she reckons with many injustices such as her father's illiteracy:

> My Daddy wrote me a letter my first week there (Howard), and my Daddy could only write his name. But he got this letter together and it said "Dear Lucilleman, I miss you so much but you are there getting what we want you to have be a good girl signed your daddy." I cried and cried because it was the greatest letter I ever read or read about in my whole life [*Generations: A Memoir* 69].

In both word and wing, Clifton's verse is full blown with sorrow and celebration. Out there on the limb, she shapeshifts into Sankofa, the mythical bird that turns its head back to the past in order to remember its history.

At the beginning of *Generations*, Clifton orients the reader. The book opens with a biblical passage that sets the tone, a psychological building block, and a powerful premise on which she and her family stand: "Lo, mine eye hath seen all this, mine ear hath heard and understood it. What ye know, the same do I know also; I am not inferior unto you." (Job 13:1–22)

Clifton aligns her life and her family's life with Job's trials and tribulation—so as readers we might already conclude this journey is fraught with illness and strife. Yet Job's voice asserts an omnipresent understanding of his destiny. In the first verse, the mode is one of acceptance and awareness, and Job does not internalize his external conditions.

In the second verse, Clifton instructs us how to read *Generations*. As Job asserts confidence, Clifton summons and draws this same power and strength to the circumstances in which she and her family were born. Thus, as readers we have a context for Clifton's emboldened psychology. She is ever-present and poised, as she voices what her ancestors could not compose.

Clifton often writes in first person, but her "I" is the huge "I" of the collective "we." Her words are painfully palpable, for example, as she intones, "I feel the Dahomey women gathering in my bones."

Then, the family edict: "Get what you want, you from Dahomey women" (*Generations: A Memoir* 1). This line makes a powerful declaration. Clifton tells us that she is not alone, that she is possessed by and imbued with the powers of her female line. She becomes not only a lone woman in the twentieth century but from an ancient city in Africa. Here Clifton borrows from an African archetype and creates an African American mythos, one that gives her momentum to move forward in a country that has truncated her lineage. With this conjuring of the Dahomey, she ministers to the broken links from Africa to America. She creates a powerful image, a warrior woman that fights against the pathos slavery has imposed.

The Dahomey is a pre-colonial African Kingdom made up of fierce fighting women. Clifton becomes one of these battling women, linking her ceremonially to a tribe of women. The edict to "get what you want" not only issues a command to act in a bold manner; it also offers vital information regarding place. That is unusual in itself as most African Americans at the time *Generations* was written were not privy to their African origins. Given this knowledge, Clifton secures a psychological foothold, which she then uses in her poetic grappling—a frequent theme in *Generations*. At first glance, the entry that begins the book might be dismissed as an unadorned obituary:

> They called her Caroline Donald Sales
> Born free in Afrika in 1822
> Died free in America in 1910 [*Generations: A Memoir* 1].

But Clifton, a master of compression, is doing a great deal of work as she employs her skillful craft in three lines. The power is in what she chooses to tell and what she chooses to omit. With the first phrase, "they called her," she implies that these other (white) onlookers are not privy to the interior of her grandmother's world. Being born free was a rarity and, of course, a point of pride that carried down through the Sayles family lore. Caroline, also known as Caline to those that knew her and loved her, was not only born free; she lived her whole life free. Others in the Sales family were slaves, but this matriarch was never chained. Thus her life takes on mythical dimensions. She becomes the vital link to the Motherland and sets a mentality of freedom in the mind of a great granddaughter-poet, whom identifies with her Dahomian legacy.

Clifton often uses repetition, especially with genealogical information—who begat whom and how they survived. She does so to engage and charge the reader with the past. In *Generations* Clifton creates her rendition of her familial Genesis. As she's tending to the blighted places of her family tree, we do much more than find out who begat whom. The book *Generations* becomes a document that she creates that holds not only dates and facts, but also substantial stories that act as tools of empowerment. In effect, Clifton hands us this book of her family's record saying: History did not leave me much to go on, no written documents, but I have taken this nothing and made something. She creates her own miracle, her own water-into-wine and multiplying-the-fishes-and-loaves creative act. In this window looking at the Sayles family, Clifton gives the reader a glimpse of the matriarch's psychology: "They called her Ca'line," Daddy would tell us. "What her African name was, I never heard her say. I asked her one time to tell she and me just shook her head. But it'll be forgot, I hollered at her. It'll be forgot. She just smiled at me and said 'Don't you worry, mister, don't you worry.'" (*Generations: A Memoir* 7)

Yet, Clifton does not forget. Clifton listens to her father's lore; she becomes a carrier of wisdom and knowledge. Only through the oral tradition Clifton becomes a benefactor of her father's wisdom. She takes her rightful place as a griot, a storyteller, educator, and historian responsible for passing on this information to the following generations. She, however, is the familial game changer: She is the griot not only with the spoken word but also—a first in her family—with the written word.

Clifton acknowledges the whole: her family's deficiencies and downfalls and their strengths. She does not flinch as she traverses the arterial byways of her family's suffering, demonstrating that their lack does not define her or them.

Clifton's poems and prose record her family's survival story, ironically written on paper, cut from literal and metaphorical trees. She charts a trail of leaf and bone, leaving a path that does not waver, no matter how far she has to descend to tend to the roots or how high she must ascend to stand on treetops to gain a useful artistic perspective.

In *The Book of Light,* published in 1994, we find Clifton doing similar work on a more individual note, yet no less mythologizing. In "won't you celebrate with me," one of Clifton's most highly quoted and most anthologized poems, she charges it with the immediacy and urgency of the Dahomey women and speaks with the authority of these archetypes.

In the early '90's I watched Lucille Clifton read "won't you celebrate with me" on Bill Moyer's "Language of Life" on PBS. The moment was monumental. I memorized the poem and carried it everywhere. How the words worked on me psychologically, poetically, and spiritually—turned my gaze to my own familial and personal tapestry. While I embodied the poem at first, I realized many years later that the poem was also speaking to me craft-wise. This fourteen-line untitled poem is a sparse and intentional missive in which every syllable and word resonates as she describes being born "in babylon" without a model but making herself up and succeeding triumphantly (*The Book of Light* 25). The poem is deceptively simple, because of its plain speech. Yet this choice of diction offers accessibility, giving the reader permission to feel both at ease and engaged. However, after thorough examination, it is discernible that the poem contains layers. The poem begins with what appears to be an informal invitation: "won't you celebrate with me."

This casual gesture of "you" and "me" appears to be a gentle solicitation to join and participate in a pleasurable uplifting act, a dance or a ditty. Yet the amiable tone of the poem shifts subtly, going from one line to the next without punctuation.

The second line of the poem continues the offering, but the "I" in the poem is asking for more than a party or a time to frolic. It's asking the reader, the listener, to come bear witness, to assess "what I have shaped into a kind of life." To peer into another's life and take stock and inventory is no small act; a life review is deeply personal and profound.

The deliberate line breaks slow the pacing of the poem, leaving room for realization—not room to cavort, but to plunge deeper and to witness the speaker's "kind of life." This heartbreaking not whole life, but "kind of life." The speaker refers to her patched up and resourceful manifestation. The capital "I" connotes a creator status. But the necessity to invent or re-create out of a void is implicit in the use of the lowercase "i." This "i" standing alone gives a sense of smallness, a lone person against the world. The flat four-word declaration "I had no model" feels slight and lonely too, but offers clarity rooted in firm ground. Pity could be the mood of the poem, but instead the pacing suggests otherwise: it suggests dignity. In the fourth line of the poem we find breath that offers strength with the bombastic use of "bs." The alliteration allows the words to reverberate like a drum beating out: "born in babylon." Naming this city is purposeful. Babylon is an ancient city and a biblical reference. Yet, Clifton's usage appears to be a more recent reference linking to the Rastafarian use of the term where Babylon is used to connote an oppressive and undermining regime. The speaker's outcry is that she has been born underneath this dome fraught with chaos and discord. The speaker's ancestry is rooted to slavery, linked like chattel possessions to a master. By using a locator such as Babylon, Clifton weights and sets the historical clock. She gives the unflattering timeline: how long humanity has been dealing with slavery and gigantic class divides.

Clifton is fearless as she raises her sword and strikes not only for racial equality but also for women's rights. On the one line in which she addresses issues of race and gender, she adroitly creates a seamless rhythm by once again using alliteration: *nonwhite and woman*. The music of the "Ws" in this line, different from the previous line's drumbeat, offers a reed-like energy. In one breath this line's three words make a statement that racial and gender discrimination are on the same uneven ground. Yet in this line race precedes gender: "born in babylon both nonwhite and woman"

In the sixth line of the poem, the narrator calls out again to the void: "What could I see to be, but myself?" as she is devoid of role models and lack of positive mirrors that reflected by her race. She is faced with whether to assimilate or to create models. The speaker chooses to mythologize herself.

Clifton is myth-making the Creation story as she points to her precarious lifespan beneath sky and on the earth. In the vastness she takes her own hand. This is a grand resourceful act, a gesture that symbolizes self-acceptance, self-love, self-determination, and re-creation. The journey of the poem continues, the walk deepens, encompassing a cosmic relationship, a spiral, and a circle within a circle. She becomes her archetype fully embodied and empowered on a bridge "between / starshine and clay," one hand tightly clasping the other.

The semicolon following this allows the reader to pause. Then another invitation offers a more personal and familiar beckoning. The tension previously built alerts the reader that this poem is about more than celebration; even though starshine has been presented there is also the clay, the toil. This is not just a dance under the moon and stars, but a full-bodied surrendering to all of life's struggles. The offer is extended once again more urgently: "come celebrate."

Though the speaker refers to the aforementioned ills that have hounded her—racism and sexism—she insists this life is not only about struggle. There is a hard-earned right to have a good time as well. Yet, before one can fully embrace this idea of a party, the last line is delivered with three words and a final declaration, resonating like hammered nails: every day, something has tried to kill her but failed.

The assonance in this "everyday" line gives wings. Yet ending with the "f" and "d" in "failed," the line introduces an exclamatory finality, an answer to the supposed annihilating blows. Clifton's poem is a cleverly concealed deceptive package: a bomb wrapped in the cellophane gift-wrap of celebration. It is a highly cerebral missive entering the territory of the heart, lighting a path for those in search of their own tools for survival. I myself was sick with fibromyalgia when I first encountered this poem. My doctors had said: You will not die, but you will sure wish that you would. But on hearing the poem's metaphorical invitation, I responded metaphorically and literally. It acted as a lightning rod. The sheer electricity of sound and deep meaning got me up off my fibromyalgic-ridden sick bed and I began to celebrate with Lucille Clifton.

I began writing poems again—celebrating my own life by writing. I found I had much in common with Clifton, being non-white and woman and also born into a Babylonian existence. Clifton became my model in a world where I had no poetic models growing up in the harsh racial climate of Piedmont, South Carolina. I began surveying my familial ground. Primarily I was taken with the strong women of my maternal line too. I wrote poems for mama and grandma: attempts to tell my familial plight.

It was as if Clifton were handing me a metaphorical torch. I caught hold. Though I actually had been writing poems since age twelve I picked the pen up again when Clifton reminded me of my own flame. My early adolescent poems were praise poems, in what I later learned was a West African poetic form meant to honor self, community, and God. But in those early years I did not know that I was writing in this particular form. Yet, I did not pursue poetry in college, however, poetry was gathering in my bones.

Eventually I took a DNA test through africanancestry.com to find where in Africa my family descended. The test indicated that my mother's side came from what is now Cameroon and my father's side came from what is now Nigeria, specifically the Yoruba tribe. As I continued my poetic familial research, I read Judith Gleason's book, *Leaf & Bone: African Praise Poems*. Here I discovered that the Yoruba are the chief praise poets of West Africa.

Though I did not have family lore handed down, like Lucille Clifton, from a father endowing me with place and a spirit of a people like the Dahomey, my lineage too began to take shape. In conjunction with the DNA test and this locator, my historical roots were rising up to meet me. As I had been writing a version of praise poems since I was twelve, it seems that my roots were always with me and that I was gaining awareness.

Clifton's work has acted as light force like the derivation of her name Lucille—more like a lightning bolt waking me from my own dark world. The light that she brought illuminated a deep place within history and myself. From her I learned to pick up the pen and utilize my vast store of imagination in order to make poetic sense of the devastation of my lineage. In a poem "Dear Mrs. Cunningham," for example, I am making a vital connection through which to continue this autobiographical poetic journey where I locate my maternal grandmother's existence on a slave plantation. Without Clifton's *Generations*, I do not know if I would be on this journey making these integral connections.

Clifton creates a new genre with *Generations*. It is poetic memoir, a creative genre that holds myth, facts, and stories, and a familial reference that resonates as a vital document. More importantly, it sets a precedent. It represents a keepsake for African Americans that begin to address closing the apertures of our torn legacies. Consciously and subconsciously, I have been following Clifton's path. The archetypes and myths she created have been life and soul sustaining to this poet, genealogist, and mythmaker.

WORKS CITED

Clifton, Lucille. *The Book of Light*. Port Townsend, Wash.: Copper Canyon Press, 1993.

———. *Generations: A Memoir*. New York: Random House, 1978.

Gleason, Judith. *Leaf and Bone: African Praise Poems*. London: Penguin, 1994.

Penelope at the Loom
Mythology and the Modern Workplace in the Poetry of 21st Century Women

KRISTIN BERKEY-ABBOTT

In most literature classes, students learn about the use of allusion in literary works. Literary scholars and cultural critics alike have worried that as the canon widens and the Internet offers more to read, we will lose the common currency that literature once provided. A writer today can no longer assume that the readers will all have been exposed to the same literary sources.

Happily, most of today's readers still have at least a glancing familiarity with Greek mythology. Even if readers haven't all read the same myths, most of them still understand the basic prototypes and plot lines of the form. Women writers have had a love-hate relationship with patriarchal mythology, and it's interesting to trace the influence of Greek and Roman myth in the feminist writings of the second half of the twentieth century. Whole books have been written on that subject.

Less has been written on the use of myth used by female poets as they analyze the workplace, especially the non-childcare/teaching workplaces into which women have moved in the last few decades. In so many ways, the lives of women have changed radically since the middle of the twentieth century—has the use of mythology changed too?

As women gained more control over their fertility in the twentieth century and as more career doors opened to women, many women left what they perceived to be the tedious labor of childcare to work in offices and other environments. My poem, "I Stand Here Shredding Documents" notes that many of us think of housework as menial and never-ending, with the baskets of clothes that need washing and ironing and all the other ongoing tasks of housework.

But much to many a woman's surprise, the office environment can include as much or more menial labor as a life spent at home rearing children.

During the last several decades, we've heard much talk and seen much planning about becoming a paperless society. So far, that still hasn't happened. In fact, despite all the talk of storing documents electronically either offsite or in local computers, we still see no signs of file cabinets full of paper going anywhere anytime soon.

All this paper needs care: files must be stored, monitored, and then shredded when no longer needed. I once inherited a file cabinet when I moved into a new office. That file cabinet was full of sensitive material. I spent weeks shredding it, because I worried about entrusting anyone else, like administrative assistants, with such sensitive documents.

As I stood over the shredder, I thought about the Tillie Olson story, "I Stand Here Ironing." I thought of my own desire to escape what I thought would be the mindless drudgery of housework only to find myself expected to engage in mindless drudgery of office work. If I had gone into clerical work, I might not have been so surprised; however, I had been promoted into administrative work as the Chair of a department.

I thought of all the different baskets we have: all the items that baskets can contain, like documents or laundry. I thought of inboxes that never seem to be completely sorted. I thought of the traditional worlds of women's work and men's work. My poem, "I Stand Here Shredding Documents" ends with the knowledge that no one can escape drudgery :

> Now I have become my father,
> a woman of file cabinets
> and endless meetings of infinite boredom.
> I stand at the shredder,
> my daily friend, and think of work
> that is never finished.

The thoughts of work never finished led me to Penelope, wife of Odysseus, who was presumed dead, since he never arrived back from his sea voyage. To stave off having to give her suitors a final answer as to whom she would marry next, she vowed that she would make a decision once she finished weaving a tapestry. For years, she managed to avoid a final decision as she wove by day and picked apart her work by night. More than once I have thought of Penelope's work as the most potent metaphor from Greek mythology for our modern cultures of work.

How many times do we send and resend the same e-mail? How many times do we work and rework the spreadsheets and charts? How often do we rewrite reports, round and round? I've always been afraid to compare initial drafts with final drafts, for fear that I'll find that I've worked my way back to the original. My poem "Penelope in the Office Cubicle" explores this very dilemma:

> Part of her team rewrites
> all the departmental objectives.
> When the missing members return
> from vacation and illness, the team changes
> the objectives again. As she synthesizes
> the various versions, she realizes
> that they've written and revised
> their way back to the original objectives.

The speaker in the poem also makes and remakes coffee and makes and remakes charts, all work that I've done, no matter what my station in the workplace hierarchy, a hierarchy that becomes more and more fluid as computer programs do more of the work that humans used to do. My poem "Cassandra Considers the Dust" makes mention of the fact that computers so often do the work that humans used to do, much of it the work of monitoring. Once this keeping watch would have required a much larger staff, and now, technology has solved that personnel problem.

"Cassandra Considers the Dust" presents a speaker cognizant of the fact that technology cannot solve all of our problems. Even human interaction cannot solve the most basic problem of how to restore health and maintain it.

We all know the statistics. We know that the doctor in this poem is a modern day Cassandra, telling the truth to people who don't want to hear it and won't follow her advice.

This poem ends with allusions to other modern day Cassandras, those who warn us of climate change and the irreparable harm we're doing to our planet. She arrives home and considers how long it has been since the house enjoyed a deep cleaning. But in the end, she gives a metaphorical shrug and leaves the dirt alone.

Kathleen Flenniken presents a similar exploration by juxtaposing women's work and larger social issues in her suite of poems, "Augean Suite." She uses the myth of Hercules cleaning out the Augean stables to explore the world of work in nuclear factories and the work of cleaning up toxins, work which can have a devastating impact to our bodies, particularly if we're women with larger fat stores, which will absorb more toxins and store them longer than if we had more muscular bodies, like many male bodies.

"The Fifth Labor of Hercules," the first poem in "Augean Suite," makes the most specific reference to Hercules by reminding us of the task and the killing of the king and the diverting of the rivers, the Alpheus and the Peneus. It ends with the connection to modern degradations of water pollution and people downstream exposing themselves to contamination as they wash clothes or bathe.

The remaining poems in the suite explore more modern nuclear pollution and make wonderful use of the wording found in actual documents generated by the government to explore the concept of acceptable risk at the Hanford site and others.

This work of environmental destruction and the circular nature of its clean up and repair takes me back to Penelope and the world of modern work that is so often a making and remaking only to destroy again. My poem "Penelope in the Office Cubicle" ends with an allusion to Penelope:

> Every day, she wakes up wondering
> what work she'll unweave today,
> only to reweave tomorrow.
> Every night, she dreams of voyages.

The more speakers I create who yearn for voyages, the more I'm reminded of captivity narratives.

When we think of captivity narratives, we likely think back to works of the nineteenth century and earlier, especially those stories of people captured by Native Americans of North America. But the workplace holds us captive in so many similar ways. For example, we're thrust into an environment that's not of our making, with people with whom we didn't choose to associate for 40–80 hours a week. We must make the best of it.

One of the aspects of the modern office that I find most exhausting is the noise. My poem "Sharing the Sea of Surround Sound" references the noises of the modern workplace: people shouting into cell phones and speaker phones, file cabinets opening and closing, multiple conversations going on within one person's earshot. It ends with the main character yearning for quiet.

Soon after I wrote this poem, I wrote "Eurydice in Miami." Eurydice may not be the first person who comes to mind when we think about captivity narratives, but she is held captive in a profound way. In my poem, Eurydice, too, suffers from noise pollution during her life with Orpheus and his need to be surrounded by music.

We might think of hell as the ultimate captivity of Eurydice. But in my poem, it's not so bad. She turns to a career of Scuba diving. The main benefit to this career choice is the quiet.

When we make career choices, we tend not to think about the daily minutiae involved, like noise issues. I often think back to my girlhood dreams of having a career, even when I wasn't sure of what that career would be. It was the 1970s, and all sorts of career paths seemed possible. Perhaps I would be an astronaut. Maybe I would be the first woman president. Or perhaps, I'd be happy creating my own business or becoming a writer. It was a time when girls were promised that we'd be judged by our brains and talents, not our looks.

Margaret Atwood's poem "Helen of Troy Does Counter Dancing" shows the dangers of being prized for one's looks. Atwood shows that even the most extreme beauty can't necessarily protect us from the drudgery of work. Even the most beautiful woman in the world might find herself descending to the underworld of the sex trade.

The culture of my childhood told a new generation of little girls that we could do anything, regardless of our beauty. I often look back on those cultural messages of that time when Title IX had just been signed into law, and I see the culture as Hades, tempting me with these beautiful flowers, and snatching me into the underworld of office work. A quick look through my poems about work show that I frequently mention the office in terms of the underworld, which is a different place in the world of my poems than Hell. My poem, "Pomegranate Office Treats" paints the picture this way:

> So, this then is hell.
> She thinks of her career
> in its early days,
> handsome stranger, beautiful flower,
> and now she's rooted in the underworld
> of work, the all-American office.

We might ask why so many people stay in the workplace if it's so unsatisfying, and there are all sorts of reasons. Many of us end up in jobs that are somewhat far afield of our training, with no clear path to make our way back to work we'd rather be doing. My poem "Nine Pomegranate Seeds" presents such an American worker:

> Her early training prepared her to teach
> Fairy Tales and Mythology. She looks, tiring,
> for a path of bread crumbs, a way to reach
> a way out of this haunted forest of budget cuts and firing.

Even when we have to do work that we wish would not be necessary, we must do it for a variety of reasons. Perhaps the most primary reason is the need to pay our bills and support our dependents. My poem "Nine Pomegranate Seeds" ends with by reminding us of this important fact:

> She knows it is too late. She has bitten
> the fruit and gone to the banquet to dine.
> She has sold her principles because she is so smitten
> with her health insurance, her salary, and fine wine.

Of course, not all work is drudgery done only for money. And even work that contains elements of drudgery has satisfaction that can be found. In my poem "Penelope Plans a Playdate," I created a speaker who was trained as a scientist: "Before motherhood, she had a more inspired brain. / It contemplated fractals and the tiny quark." This speaker earned a Ph.D., which she saw as "a shield / to keep her safe from hearth and home." Now the speaker must plan play dates and associate with women of lesser intellects:

> Now she maps out schedules of each play date.
> She associates with mothers dull and mean.
> She tries to accept it as her fate
> to talk about ways to keep house and laundry clean.

The poem seems on a crash course for an unhappy ending, abandonment of the child or the juggling of motherhood with a return to a career in a STEM field. But the poem ends somewhat happily with this couplet: "But when she thinks of returning to her career, / she reads to her child, determined to find happiness right here." In my circle of women friends, I've met many women who have sacrificed intellectual paths to give more time to their families, and they often find unexpected benefits in that sacrifice. I wanted my poem to give voice to that experience.

Endings are not always this happy; life in the heart of family can't always bring this kind of satisfaction. When I worked at an aftercare center which took care of elementary school children until their parents got off work, I was reminded of Penelope and Odysseus from a different angle. In my poem "Children of Ulysses," I painted the parents as explorers always ready to sail away again.

In this poem, the workplace is the adventure, home life the drudgery. Similarly, in her poem "Frontier Literature," Shefali Shah Choksi uses Greek myth to show that grown up life contains adventures, but perils as well; she references Circe, the Sirens, and the Gorgon.

I've done a somewhat exhaustive study of my own work and the work of others to discover very few poems that use Greek myth that see the workplace as a happy place. Why? Perhaps this is because the world of Greek mythology is a landscape fraught with peril, and thus, it makes sense that a poem referencing Greek myth depicts a workplace fraught with peril too.

I've been surprised by how few female writers are using Greek myth to explore the world of work. Is it because we're satisfied with our work lives? Or is it because so far, so few poets have been working in traditional, non-academic settings? Even the most lowly faculty job has benefits and protections from some of the more demeaning drudgeries of other modern workplaces. The reason may be more basic. So many of these Greek myths are rooted in emotional relationships that still resonate with modern readers, but characters in Greek myth work in settings that are completely unfamiliar to us. It makes sense that using Greek myth to explore personal relationships seems so much more compelling than using those myths to explore other aspects of modern life.

But I predict that as new generations of female poets occupy work places both foreign and familiar, we will see more references to Greek mythology in their work. Plus, as our world becomes more global, we'll likely see more poets exploring the mythology of other cultures too. Indeed, this process has begun. For example, Shefali Shah Choksi uses ancient mythology from India in her work, while Jeannine Hall Gailey explores the mythology of Japan throughout her second collection *She Returns to the Floating World*. Earlier, Denise Duhamel utilized Inuit mythology in her collection *The Woman with Two Vaginas*. At some point in the future, it will be interesting to do a comparative study to see how those myths are used across cultures.

We can be sure that mythology of all types will continue to be used since mythology connects us in a way that few other poetic tools can. After all, Greek mythology has continued to speak to us through the centuries in a potent way. Mythology weaves us to our collective past and helps us find our way into the future by offering a timeless appeal and a way to connect to the emotional landscape of humans long gone but not so different from ourselves.

Works Cited

Atwood, Margaret. "Helen of Troy Does Counter Dancing." *Morning in the Burned House*. New York: Houghton Mifflin, 1995. 33–36.

Berkey-Abbott, Kristin. "Cassandra Considers the Dust." *Southern Women's Review*. Volume 8. 43. http://swr.themodernbrandonline.com/wp-content/uploads/2015/03/FinalSewthernIssue.pdf

———. "Children of Ulysses." *Slant*. Summer 2012. 6.

———. "Eurydice in Miami." *Slant*. Summer 2008. 9.

———. "I Stand Here Shredding Documents." *I Stand Here Shredding Documents*. Georgetown, KY: Finishing Line Press, 2011. 26.

———. "Nine Pomegranate Seeds." *I Stand Here Shredding Documents*. Georgetown, KY: Finishing Line Press, 2011. 22.

———. "Penelope in the Office Cubicle." *I Stand Here Shredding Documents*. Georgetown, KY: Finishing Line Press, 2011. 19.

———. "Penelope Plans a Play Date." *I Stand Here Shredding Documents*. Georgetown, KY: Finishing Line Press, 2011. 10.

———. "Pomegranate Office Treats." Unpublished.

———. "Sharing the Sea of Surround Sound." *qaartsiluni*. November 2010. http://qarrtsiluni.com/2010/11/22/sharing-the-sea-of-surround-sound/

Choksi, Shefali Shah. "Frontier Literature." *Frontier Literature*. Allahabad, India: Cybernet, 2010. 18–19.

Duhamel, Denise. *The Woman with Two Vaginas*. Anchorage, AK: Salmon Run Press, 1995.

Flenniken, Kathleen. "Augean Suite." *Plume*. Seattle: University of Washington Press: 2012.

Gailey, Jeannine Hall. *She Returns to the Floating World*. Crawfordville, FL: Kitsune Books, 2011.

In My Own Image
Crafting Poetry
About the Sacred Feminine

PAULA J. VAUGHAN

Prefatory Note

The original poetry included within this essay has not been published elsewhere. These poems were meant to be here, shared in communion among women in a context that supports the meaning and relevance of the work. These poems are guideposts, markers leading toward an engagement of women's poetry about the sacred feminine as authentic means of speaking about ourselves.

For cultures who embrace the sacred feminine, goddesses are not mythical metaphor or abstract archetype: they are real. Goddesses are tenderly, often desperately, invoked through oblation and prayer, miraculously appearing to the devoted as apparitions, visions, or animals; the emphasis on appearing, on coming when called. Goddesses are at the ready to deliver women from the pain of childbirth, to comfort the grieving, to inspire creative works, to ferry humanity into death, and to protect the lost and forgotten. Goddesses are liminal beings straddling the otherworld and our own, embodying nature as the singular power that both destroys and creates. Inspiring communal ritual, supernatural belief, relationships to the landscape, and the interplay of gender roles, goddesses are extensions of the invisibles that guide and protect: conduits of the sentient, cosmic intelligence pulsing through creation made manifest within humanity's mythologies and women.

Goddesses reveal themselves through the myriad complexities of womanhood, the day-to-day struggle with tumultuous emotions driven by hormonal shifts that tend the moon. Within each woman, an entire pantheon of divinities exists at once specific to her culture and universal to womankind.

Each of these sacred beings signifies the immense capacity of the female to endure, to somehow withstand a monthly spiraling of increase and release, of bleeding without dying. Inside the female mind and body, a web of innate power and intuitive knowing is continuously spun to strands of experience, survival, and capability that bind families, cultures, and time. Goddesses serve as representations of this intricate, female, blood-and-bones connection with the eternal, making the sacred feminine in myth a personal revelation.

Mary

Human woman
you are the Great Goddess
who lived through the fears of mothers,
vulnerable,
alone,
undone,
yet, nurtured in the open heart of nature
by the soft
lowing,
bleating
gentility.

The voluptuous love
of baby to breast
carries mothers beyond
the gnawing tedium of domesticity
connecting us to you,
to one another,
in the flowing milk
that becomes
the blue covering of night,
    your robes
the stars,
    your eyes
the heavens,
    your outstretched arms
enveloping our bodies into yours.

As a mythologist, I nurture a tangible, felt relationship to the sacred feminine through writing poetry about goddesses in world mythology, an artistic path that joins me to women worldwide through its accessibility and healing potential. Following a creative trajectory beginning with intellectual research about the foundations of a goddess myth, I ascertain how a people's belief systems are played out within the story. I get acquainted with the culture, investigating the value it places upon women and the feminine. Within those societies where patriarchy and patrilineal kinship lines are followed, I attempt to unwrap layers of masculine influence covering the original meaning of a myth that may diminish or demonize the feminine. I consult feminist mythological and folkloric texts to uncover possible evidence of authentic first translations and authorship. In this way, I glean the essence of a goddess myth and the women whose lives are impacted by her tale. I grow to understand how the sacred feminine becomes either a reflection of a culture's reverence for women or their mistrust and misunderstanding of the female. My creative process moves me from the cerebral to the soulful, enabling me to write poems about goddesses as living women, as reflections of myself.

Many of the poems I craft utilize the sacred feminine or goddesses in mythology—the terms are interchangeable—to convey the largess of my thoughts, feelings, and physiological changes. Years researching goddesses within global mythologies from mythological, anthropological, feminist, psychological, and historical perspectives has placed the sacred feminine on the tip of my tongue, weaving the female divine throughout my consciousness. Studying the scholarship of Marija Gimbutas, Clarissa Pinkola Estés, Jean Shinoda Bolen, Anne Baring, Jules Cashford, and Charlene Spretnak has made the sacred feminine intimate for me. Likewise, a decade reading children's picture books to my daughter overflowing with gorgeous goddess images including the illustrations of Jackie Morris, Deborah Nourse Lattimore, Helen Cann, Christina Balit, and Kinuko Y. Craft in addition to studying the paintings of Susan Seddon Boulet, has made me *see*: women create goddesses in their own image—*mine*.

Performing research and pouring over goddess paintings have brought the sacred feminine into focus for me. Yet, it is the inward contemplation when writing poetry about a goddess, considering who she is and what her motivations are as a woman, which allow me to know the sacred feminine as an internalization of my own experiences and happenings. Contemplating the sacred feminine as a divine force made flesh through women illumines the immanence of womanhood and poetry transforms these imaginings into words. The metaphorical language bridging poetry and mythology is beautiful, a befitting means of communicating how a woman's body—*my body*—perpetually changes, dying to one stage to be reborn into another: a constant that is both merciless and sublime. When women write poetry envisioning themselves as the sacred feminine corporeal, we make the agony of our earthly metamorphoses holy and give voice to initiatory events that are otherwise left untold.

Demeter Wails

Her moans heard across time, caught
in the cosmic reaches,
moistest corners,
deepest, most pliant crevasses
of my body.
flesh of my flesh ...

*Her roiling rage, desperate despair, and
unchecked grief
are now mine,
churning my stomach, knotting reason.
Tempest-tossed mind,
I am consumed, devastated, exhausted
by the aftershocks
of ceaseless transformations through motherhood receiving no honor.*

flesh of my flesh ...

*Where is my daughter?
Where is my daughter!
Secreted away
by the hungry, needful ravages of time,
she disappeared.
Birthday parties failed,
doing no justice
to the finality of change.*

flesh of my flesh ...

*My daughter
transformed
into a maiden-woman.
Wandering, wailing, I scour my consciousness,
searching for an impossible substance
to fill the unmarked graves
bearing the outgrown skins
of my metamorphosis through motherhood.*

flesh of my flesh—sand through a sieve ...

Through crafting poetry about the sacred feminine, I am able to know women of varied ethnicities, religions, and locales as sisters within a global arena of womanhood. Because we are linked as human females sharing the same physiology and emotions, regardless of differing shapes, states, and degrees of intensity, writing poetry about the sacred feminine allows me to celebrate the triumphs and grieve the losses of all women, as a daughter, mother, or friend. When I write poetry about goddesses as mirrors of the lives I have lived within a single lifetime, I liberate ancient rage and despair, a curative act that reaches backward and forward through generations of women including my own mother, aunts, and grandmothers. The muscular use of poetic language I employ to state my truths and feelings plainly, without guilt or concern for propriety or offense, explodes in catharsis, a benediction and marker for people, transformations, and happenings lost and past.

In cultures where a woman's words of anger or grief are ignored or even worse, used against her as weapons to dismiss or deny her feelings as overly emotional, irrelevant, dangerous, or unworthy of attention, goddesses in poetry command notice of innate female wisdom and fortitude. Goddesses in women's poetry are evocative because they are familiar, shaking awake the reader or listener, committing them to hearing a woman's story being told. Placed within the lines of an honest poem, the sacred feminine works her magic by imprinting the minds of teller and reader with understanding, vaporizing illusory societal barriers keeping people apart based on their gender, age, ethnicity, or geography. When a woman writes poetry, speaking what's in her heart through the visage of a goddess, her audience comes to know her lived circumstance unashamed, and in turn, they are able to contend bravely with their own.

Medea

My mother is Medea,
but I lived.

Damaged,
her wraith-thin body
and ever-wide eyes stare
into a world only she sees.
Sharing her witch-wisdom shrouded in madness
over telephone lines
crackling with the impossibility of our situation,
I listen.

Walking through days of
confusion, anger,
wide-eyed pain,
I raise my own daughter.

Alone
in the peace of early mornings
I consider—
how will I mother my daughter
knowing I was left for dead?

You can't imagine,
(neither can I)
how excruciating this question is.

In addition to using candid, courageous words that affect both poet and reader, the manner in which a poem about the sacred feminine is written influences the ways in which it is told and heard: the use of form is a persuasive tool embodying voice. I learned about the impact of form in graduate school when assigned to write twenty poems using varied global forms (excluding haiku) within a course on ethnic poetry. Along with my classmates, none of us having anticipated we would be writing our own poetry as part of the course, I was able to joyfully craft poetic forms from around the globe thanks to our text, Robin Skelton's *The Shapes of Our Singing: A Comprehensive Guide to Verse Forms and Metres from Around the World*. Skelton's text is an excellent, accessible resource for anyone who wishes to experiment with poetic forms as play. The author clearly and concisely outlines the information needed to engage poetry as an exercise of freedom through limitation, arousing the desire to go beyond blank verse by equipping the poet with straightforward explanations and examples. Through my graduate course, I became aware that using set poetic parameters intensifies the subject matter and artistic experience, and that it is thrilling to select the right words for the right places to convey what is most dearly known but unsaid.

In this spirit of play, when writing poetry about the sacred feminine, a poet may correlate a goddess's country of origin to its indigenous poetic forms, allowing the narrative of her people to thrive. It is also compelling to first randomly choose a poetic form, and then feel through selecting a goddess about whom to write. For me personally, I come to poetry with goddesses in mind, already knowing their mythologies and my affinity for them. Following my intuition, I choose a form that will support the poetic story I wish to tell, envisioning specific details and employing certain punctuation to best emphasize my meaning. The Japanese poetic forms Katuata, Sedoka, and Waka portray my voice in a way that complements my writing style, despite the fact my ancestry is Scotch-Irish, Pennsylvania Dutch, Swedish, and Italian. Getting to know various poetic forms through experimentation is a fun way for any woman to uncover and emancipate her poetic self. Rather than binding a woman's creativity, myriad poetic forms can make our work most real. The use of variation in poetry lends itself to creating a body of work that is a map inward to the self; a series of choices, steps, and diversions that reflect who we are. Poetic experimentation lays a welcoming, worn, and traveled path for other women who too are searching for richness of meaning and boldness of expression.

Ishtar

Will wisdom harm me?
Stripped, tortured, and flayed, Ishtar
endured plagues to be reborn.
[Katauta Form—Japan].

Amaterasu

Rage-filled retreating
goddess rejects the maelstrom,
blackening light that sustains.

Your escape is the
fantasy of all mothers,
harried, exhausted and worn.
[Sedoka Form—Japan].

Women's Work

Vasilisa weaves
the Seal Maiden's wet, soft skin,

> *Alone, Demeter*
> *weeps for Medusa's lost eyes.*
> *Grief and change are women's work.*
> [Waka Form—Japan].

Another potent aspect of women's poetry about the sacred feminine is the intrinsic wholeness of this work. In my experience, poems about goddesses do not seem meant to stand alone, cast individually into the world. There is an element of shock when readers come upon a goddess poem that is not part of a collective work that keeps a bridge of understanding from being built between poet and audience. Perhaps because a woman's collection of poetry about the sacred feminine is a living agent for her female voice, spirit, and body, goddess poems find their greatest strength in a cohesiveness that attends the poet and reader as a vehicle of transformation. Fashioning a chapbook of twenty to thirty poems about the sacred feminine is a profound practice for producing a single repository of a woman's poetic voice. Chapbooks are albums of self, identifying who a woman is, what she has overcome, and who she wants to be. These small but substantial poetic pieces are the stones, the markers, showing the steps a woman has taken on her journey.

The poems and poetic methodology shared within this essay beckon the reader to create her own poetry about the sacred feminine. My poems are an offering, given with the intention of showing that each woman, be she aspiring poet or not, is imbued with the ability to craft poetry about the sacred feminine as a restorative, cathartic homage to the self. Whether you craft poems as part of your daily work, write poetic pieces when inspired, or prefer reading rather than writing poetry, there is tremendous spiritual and personal value in contemplating poems about the sacred feminine. Realizing goddess poems are essentially about women themselves makes their content meaningful and relevant, providing encouragement and reconnection with the mythic feminine. The revitalizing benefits of communing with the sacred feminine through poetry offer women words and imaginings that are precious, that are gifts wrapped in longing, empathy, deliverance, observance, and love.

A woman and mythologist both, writing poetry about the sacred feminine is a joining for me, a unification of intellect and spirit that satisfies and honors me as a whole person. When researching, examining, and simply being with goddesses through poetry, I am reminded of my own worth as a woman, as she who is the sacred feminine incarnate washing dishes, making beds, planting gardens, and raising a family. As a poem unfolds within my heart and mind, the separation between myself and a goddess such as Ishtar, Amaterasu, or Artemis disappears. I remember her story as my own. When I write her poem, I reclaim my own vitality, embracing my authentic self. For each goddess I study, there is a matching emotion, experience, or passage in my life. For each poem I write about her, there is healing and closure within myself, a testament to my own growth and rekindled bond with women worldwide. My goddess poems awaken the divine within me because *I am the sacred feminine—as are you.*

Woman Calls

Baba Yaga,
can you hear me?
I need you!
The human bones
leading to the door of your spinning hut
ply the darkness where I find myself,
waiting,
secure in the knowing
you will guide me through
to myself.

Ishtar,
where are you?
I need you!
Your veils, each one,
a skin I also shed
traveling the planetary spheres
inside myself
having hung on the rusty hook
my mother and stepmother, prepared;
dying,
I long to be reborn.

Artemis,
are you here?
I need you!
Pounding through the forest,
driving howling hounds and heady moonlight,
I long for you
to run naked in the wilds,
hot breath misting the cold night air,
unafraid
relentless
pure.

Mary,
do you see me?
I need you!
The blue cloak of stars
you wrap around my shoulders
heals my aching soul;
respite,
so elusive,
becomes real and I sleep
knowing you protect and care for my heart
as a tender mother her own child.

I call you Women—Mothers, all!

> The anorexic's exposed ribs,
> borderline's hidden cuts,
> addict's diseased sex,
> and homeless mother's prayers
> are
> woman calls
> begging you
> home!
>
> Despite
> the unyielding asphalt-covered earth
> no longer marking the paths
> to your temples, caves, and grottos,
> we still listen for you.
> In the crunch-crackle of fallen leaves,
> ticks and trills of nighttime sounds,
> yips and cackles of coyotes,
> and the quiet centers of our souls,
> we listen for your
> woman calls.
>
> You are here,
> aren't you?
>
> I feel your stirring ...

Telling a Truth versus Telling the Truth
On Writing from Personal History

JENNY SADRE-ORAFAI

"It would further be a lie to say that they weren't about me, because they are just as much about me as my other poetry."
—Anne Sexton on *Transformations*

Anne Sexton began writing because her therapist, Dr. Martin Orne, suggested it as part of her therapy. Perhaps not even Orne could have predicted how her writing would change both Sexton and her readers. Sexton was to be reckoned with primarily because of her honesty in dealing with the truth. The personal history in her work is both endearing and heartbreaking and she demonstrated quite a lot of bravery for sharing her realities. It should be no surprise then that just as she was starting to write that poet John Holmes, her creative writing professor, suggested she avoid the personal. She addresses his concerns about her work in her first collection *To Bedlam and Part Way Back* in the poem "For John, Who Begs Me Not to Inquire Further." In perhaps one of her best poems, Sexton defends her poetry. It should be noted that this is a defense that she felt needed to be expressed already so early in her career, as if it is her statement on poetry and her allegiance to the truth.

While Sexton, along with Sylvia Plath, John Berryman, and W.D. Snodgrass, led the confessional movement, she did briefly depart from this school of poetry. In her fifth collection, *Transformations*, Sexton adapted seventeen Grimm fairy tales. First published in 1971, the collection was written in just eight months. Sexton acknowledged in her letter to Paul Brooks, her editor at Houghton Mifflin, that the collection was, "a departure from my usual style. I would say that they lack the intensity and perhaps some of the confessional force of my previous work. I would like my readers to see this side of me, and it is not in every case the lighter side" (362).

Transformations allowed Sexton to move away from the truth, the personal confession of her earlier collections while still maintaining the qualities we identify with her poetry. For the most part, critics had positive reactions. Christopher Lehmann-Haupt of *The New York Times* posited that in previous collections Sexton had a "tendency to record raw disasters without curing them with her art. Her tortured confessions seemed to be personal yelps rather than universal cries" (33). He suggests that since she used the "artificial as the raw material of *Transformations* and working her way backwards to the immediacy of her personal vision, she draws her readers in more willingly." Of course after *Transformations*, Sexton returned to the confession and the personal in *The Book of Folly, The Death Notebooks*, and collections published posthumously.

The Speaker and the Poet

After graduating with my MFA, I half-heartedly sent the poetry manuscript and thesis I titled *Mistress of Restraint* to publishers. The truth is that I was the mistress. My restraint came in how I handled my marriage, my divorce, and all of the condolences afterwards. However, my fear of being associated with the speaker in the poems, in some cases with the person I was, for any longer than I had been was too much. I never went to pick up the three bound and hardback copies of the thesis I ordered from the university. I didn't want to live with those poems anymore. I didn't want to read them aloud ever again. And, so, I didn't.

I had gone back to school to earn my MFA the same year I got married. In fact, in the space of two months I adopted two new identities, wife and graduate student. I was in the creative writing program for two semesters before my first chapbook, *Weed Over Flower,* was accepted for publication. It was the first time I had compiled a chapbook manuscript, and the first publisher I sent it to published it. I was thrilled. Most of the sixteen poems are personal poems, true even. And, although I had a background hosting an open mic at a local bookstore and participating in slams, when I submitted the chapbook I didn't anticipate what it would be like when I would read these poems aloud to people who didn't know me. I didn't consider what it would feel like to know that someone had bought the chapbook, had read the poems, and wanted to know more.

It was after the chapbook was published that I received my first real introduction to the confessional poets. I admired them for baring it all and not apologizing for what they felt or for how they expressed these feelings. I was mesmerized by their work, but especially with Sexton. I was rapt with how she documented her experiences with the feminine, with the housewife, with the mother, with the madness. Perhaps I found a sort of confidante in her poetry at a time when I was struggling with who I was and who I was becoming.

Two years after my wedding, I filed for a divorce. The divorce was quietly finalized during a hot familiar Southern summer. In fact, much had grown quiet. I didn't know if I had anything to say and so I wasn't writing much. I knew that I would have to write eventually since I had a poetry manuscript thesis requirement. After a year of near silence, I began again. However, I found that most of the poems from *Weed Over Flower* (which I would include in the thesis) were about domesticity and being married. I let my Type A personality and my love for cohesion dictate how the rest of the thesis would be written. I decided that the book would be about the marriage and about the dissolution of the marriage. While I had some idea of what the manuscript would be about, the poems were written organically for the most part. But, to get back to that place, to get back to who I was just one year and two years before was difficult.

I began to imagine what a woman who wasn't me might feel about her divorce. Then, I wrote those poems through this persona I invented. I wrote poems like "Full Circle," in which the speaker says in the final stanza—"I await your unsafe return. Without/breakfast, I imagine you hungry and weak. I know you'll eat my desperate message." Writing the poem wasn't difficult. Reading the poem was. Actually, it was *the reaction* to my reading that was difficult. When I read the poem, I mostly looked up to pity and some horror. Typically the audience assumed the speaker was the poet. I also wrote poems like "Wreck," that involved a little more personal history. In the poem, I hoped to document how people respond to women who have gone through a divorce—"They know it's coming already. They want / to put both hands on it. Stand witness. / Measure her before and after. Place bets." I also wrote "The Former Wife Does Penance"—"Talks it into swallowing its shameful tongue. Makes it promise to never say his name again." While on some levels these poems were personal, they never really felt like me. They were a truth but not the truth.

Mapping Poems

I didn't know how I would write new poems. I didn't know what I would write about. I was mute and anxious. Then, I went to speak with a good friend and fellow poet's very smart students at another university. When I spoke with him about my work, I told him that I was tired of talking about myself in my poems. After he left the room, I turned to my friend and said, "I think I'm going to write a chapbook from Priscilla Presley's perspective." He told me that I should. Then, I thought of Sexton. Did her exhaustion with herself as poet, speaker, and subject lead her to *Transformations*? Was she tired of telling the truth?

Driving home that day, I considered different approaches I could take in writing a new chapbook. Since my first chapbook was written organically, I felt like having structure going into the composition of the manuscript would push me and give me the stability I needed. After brainstorming for themes or topics to bind the twenty-four or so poems together, I decided to write about my mother as a wife, a sewer, and a pregnant mother. Writing from my mother's perspective, my mother as the "she" in the poem, afforded me the space that I wanted so badly. It also created this myth of my mother since I made assumptions about how she must have felt. To give the chapbook some structure and direction, I researched sewing patterns from the years she was pregnant with me. I crafted each poem after one pattern from 1976–1977. And, in some ways, my third chapbook, *Dressing the Throat Plate*, was a success in that I was able to not write about myself so explicitly. I was slightly invisible.

Shortly after writing the third chapbook, I began writing the fourth chapbook, *Avoid Disaster*. Since I wasn't too eager to revisit my personal history, I sought out another theme and another framework. I didn't have to dig too deep again to find something that was of interest to me and something that would I could explore in a shorter manuscript like a chapbook. Being an extremely superstitious person and being half Iranian (which may or may not be related), I began researching superstitions from around the world. Like myths, superstitions are one way we make sense of the world. I only chose the lesser-known superstitions to write about and I wrote one poem per superstition. Again, I was allowing other people to populate the poems. I was no longer the speaker and the subject. I was the poet only.

Sexton argues that *Transformations* were "just about me as much as my other poetry" (362). When I think about my last two "planned" chapbooks, I do think they are still about me. As much as any poet at any time wants to escape herself, perhaps there is only so much she truly can. The chapbooks still have me in them. Even though I invoked myths to write them, there are still faint outlines of me here and there. And while *Dressing the Throat Plate* and *Avoid Disaster* were successful in keeping me from me, they also kept me from my reader and my listener. I rarely read the poems from these chapbooks. When I have, it seems that there is less interest and less investment from the reader and listener. This is not to say that a poet must write for an audience; however, I don't think that one should *only* write for herself either.

Telling the Truth

During my 2011 spring break, I devised a schedule for writing a full-length collection. I would write eight poems a day for seven days. Each poem would be about a real or imagined dream and to allow the poems to be even more surreal, they would all be prose poems. I was taking what I learned from my chapbooks and applying it to a longer, not-yet-written manuscript. I succeeded in writing all fifty-six poems in one week. I thought the manuscript was somewhat strong and began editing it. I sent it out to some publishers, but it wasn't accepted for publication. I didn't know if what I had done with the chapbooks could sustain itself in a full-length manuscript.

A year after writing it, revising it, and sending it out, I decided to apply to the Tin House Writer's Workshop. There, I worked with Matthew Zapruder. I learned that while the dream poems were surreal and weird, I was cutting the poems off. I was getting anxious about how to end the poems and would just stop. A funny thing happened, though, after I applied to the workshop and before I actually went that summer, I began writing poems spontaneously again. I wrote poems without any real plan of how they would fit into a chapbook or a collection. And, the poems were about me, about men I kissed or men I thought loved or about a teenage prank that involved a piano in an ocean that I saw on the news. I was visible in the poem again, and there was no plan to get me out just like there was no plan where these poems would go after they were written. I was telling the truth.

While some of these newer poems have been published in literary journals, I'm just now starting to look at how they will live together in one collection. Honestly, the collection is an afterthought. The poems came first. The manuscript comes next. I've let go of the idea that I have to have structure in order to write. I've let go of the idea that I have to write about someone or something that isn't me in order to write. I've let so much go.

And, when I read these poems, I'm present completely. I'm reading about my grandmother and the fortunes she told from people's coffee dregs. I'm reading about a friend who told me he was crowned king of the bears when he went to Yosemite. These poems belong to me just as much as all of my other poems. And, there are people at the readings who want to talk about fortune telling or Yosemite and bears. There are conversations that I really missed having.

I understand that every poet approaches her poetry differently. I might write another chapbook from a perspective that doesn't belong to me. And, I might never write that way again. Regardless, I'm glad I wrote and even if those poems didn't correspond accurately and explicitly with my personal history, they are a truth. In fact, Anne Sexton's curiosity and bravery in writing *Transformations* is what allowed me to let go of me and trust that what I said could still tell a truth and it could still matter. Poet and essayist Diana Hume George points out: "While *Transformations* marks a shift in style and approach, it is important to recognize that Sexton is still dealing with the subjects that have concerned her from start." And, absolutely, a Sexton poem is a Sexton poem regardless of how it's told, and it is always true.

Works Cited

George, Diana Hume. "An Overview of Sexton's Canon." *Sexton: Selected Criticism.* Ed. Diana George Hume. Urbana: University of Illinois Press, 1988. Print.

Lehmann-Haupt, Christopher. "Grimms' Fairy Tales Retold." *The New York Times* 27 Sept. 1971: 33. Web. 15 Dec. 2012.

Sexton, Linda Gray and Lois Ames, eds. *Anne Sexton: A Self-Portrait in Letters.* Boston: Houghton Mifflin, 1977. Print.

They're Not Mermaids, Really
Shame and Re-visioning the Mermaid Mythos

JENNIFER JEAN

The worst thing a millennial poet can be called is sentimental; and, you can bet, sentimental academics get no respect. Still, I found myself, both poet and academic, persisting for over a dozen years with my passion project: a sequence of poems which re-visioned the mermaid mythos. In creating the "Fishwife," an elegant oceanic shape shifter charged with restoring her maternal lineage, I felt so much shame! It was as if the specter of Ariel, the gumptious Disney mermaid, hung like a swoony damsel or albatross around my neck. In these years this sequence grew to a fifty-six page manuscript; over forty pages of the manuscript were either published in individual literary journals, as a multi-media chapbook, or sung as art songs in a collaborative CD. Despite this success with the work, the shame persists. Why?

First of all my idea for the Fishwife did not come from *The Little Mermaid* Disney's 1989 animated movie, or even from the Hans Christian Anderson story. I was exposed to the former on a bad blind date and to the latter as a Japanese anime film ending on an image of the "Den lille havfrue" (literally: "the little sea woman") statue in Holland. They were part of my consciousness but their relative sentimentality did not inspire me to dedicate hours and hours to writing and collaborative efforts. Oscar Wilde, in *De Profundis*, said: "A sentimentalist is simply one who wants to have the luxury of an emotion without paying for it" (56). I know I've "paid for" the emotion, the substance, of my manuscript Fishwife Tales with the intensive parsing and lyricizing of my journey through marriage and motherhood. As well, I've paid with careful research and connectivity to ancient literature and traditions.

This is clear when looking at the genesis of the series. I wrote the first poem during grad school, after my wedding. I was a happy bride in many ways but I was also wary of leaving so many females behind. With some ladies from church I'd formed what we called "Sisters Meetings" where we shared the emotional content of our lives one at a time and then ended those afternoons in a crescendo of mirth, chiding, wisdom, and support. Marriage seemed to mean the end, or at least the serious curtailing, of these meetings and our satisfying, seemingly chaotic way of communicating with each other. We were all lithe—not yet bossomy, waddly, squawkers like the elder women of the congregation. This was the first time I needed my poetry to help me unknot a set of conundrums and feelings. I needed a way—specifically: a metaphor—to talk about this transition into marriage, about my close encounter with the realm of men.

Speaking of "close encounters," I briefly considered using an alien life-form metaphor because this was the heyday of *Men Are from Mars, Women Are from Venus*. But the transition into the heavy-bosomed squawkers didn't lend itself so readily to scenes in outer space. Then I remembered my grandmother, who'd made her last trip west, her last trip ever, to attend my wedding. Her second husband was a cook on fishing boats leaving Providence Rhode Island area ports. She was a classic fishwife type—with her island heritage (Azorean and Cape Verdean), gradient voice booming, wide-solid girth, hands worn from all kinds of repetitious work, eyes worn from the perils of sons' antics. I might become her. She might have been me. I needed, then, the sea.

I started with the language of the sea to catch at what I'd most miss from my former female-centric life. I researched dolphin chatter, whale songs, and fishy utterances. These verbal snippets had the sound of surfacing bubbles but also the sound of a swift, emotive communication.

Swimming patterns of schools of fish seemed to match the social structures of my particular group of females—with their complex system of communication that leads them to move as one. I thought here of the seed of truth in the old joke about women always going to the bathroom together. As well, a fish's onomatopoeic sounds ("blp blp") reminded me of "Bli-Blip," an Ella Fitzgerald scat-song: "bli-blip, bobby, flam, flam, flam, hit the yaddle oddle bayou" (line 3). This is a jittery love song with the lines: "Your love to me I've sworn" (line 11). This sensibility, matched with the scat language and the image of a school of fish, resulted in these lines from "gifts from future Fishwife fish," the first poem in the Fishwife series: "we could pack sand catch crabs body bury/ dream of blp blp blue" ("gifts" 3–4). These creatures see a man fishing and respond collectively:

> …we flew and in transit discussed him
> should we bear gifts from our womb? shall we love him at all?
> come together and we'll demonstrate the doze to our friends
> then collect opinions!

> meals eluded us we blp
> blp became slim and slept
> dreamt of clam interiors [12–18].

The poem ends with a determination to go above water: "because our love makes him / a Man" (27–28). This perpetually unnamed Fisherman is automatically individuated by the article "a" but he is also generalized with a capitalized label. His being-hood is tied to these females. They don't see it occurring in reverse. They don't understand how entirely different he is, how differently complex. They don't see an exchange in this new relationship because sameness in relationships has always been assumed—hence, their later struggles on land, in marriage.

I wrote a few more poems about this pre-settlement era; remaining in the final manuscript is a transition poem, "The Air," which employs first person narration and capitalization but utilizes verbal disjunction to indicate the shock walking and breathing—the shock of a move to land, i.e., a male-shared, realm: "Now, as I speak—it / invades and soon balloons, / but does not buoy, / limbs" ("Air" 1–4). Another transitional piece called "Fishwife Cleaving, a Myth" is mostly made of the Fishwife's new land-learned-language except for a few stanzas comprised of the Fishwife's transitional/disjunctive language:

> She whispers, steeling herself. She nearly croons...
>
> *I was a vessel, meaning love while one follows*
> *an Other, all others—my mother! my mother!*
> *falling immobile before me from her life—*
> *torn from the hook by a fist, from the hook*
> *lifting me from my hazel harbor onto the chafe of cotton sheets.... Oh!*
> *We are lost...*
> The spell eases—her feet ache and awake.
> Odorless salt huddles, contained on the kitchen table ["Cleaving" 4, 9–14].

Here we see her life is quite serrated, so I drew on the biblical meaning of cleave: as in cleaving to, or uniting with, your husband; this definition was then juxtaposed against an image of the Fishwife holding a cleaver—a rather violent instrument of separation—over "her breathless sisters" (16). Which is to say, the catch-of-the-day. She "scoops thrashing kin / ...up from the bucket to the [chopping] block / ...matter-of fact" (15–16). These poems further signified the severed connection to the all-female—which was a sad turn during the time of composition because that's when I got pregnant and needed female company most. That's also when we moved east from San Francisco.

That is, we moved from my West to my husband's East. Gloucester, Massachusetts, was a way station before settling in nearby Salem. There we were housed with fishermen friends, near the ports and the rigging and the sails and gulls. I walked through town and to the beaches before the crowds lagged in and knew I'd continue the series. Fishwives of all ages abounded. They waddled to the corner market, shouted across pubs, scuffed children on Main Street. And, I felt more round, that is to say more feminine, than ever. While my husband looked for work, I used to walk to Niles Beach and let my growing belly buoy on the water. To quote "Distended," which began to brew then:

> ...the water allows
> me
> to be lithe again,
> lets me steer
> clear of ground, of being
> distended like a puffer,
> or ugly like the toxic
> liver of a blowfish [40–7].

It was a hot summer and I felt cooled and light, though unfamiliar to myself in this new form. Soon after, I wrote "Shore Sirens" about the immobilized, landlocked Fishwife souring while her husband earns money at sea. Her husband leaves her, however necessarily, in a strange land—which is to say: on land. For my part I was doing my best not to sour, but I missed my friends and the Pacific which crashes differently than the waters in and around Cape Ann. The Fishwife began to incorporate all my darkest parts—her marriage more of a mission than an adventure.

I grew in width and wrote "With Child," about the conflicting feelings surrounding motherhood:

> Oh, trout-school upstream!
> midwife coaxes...
> alight from the whale road
> safety into the miracle
> vessel of our family.
> Into my tepid hands [19–20, 23–7].

As a character the Fishwife had more trouble resolving this relationship—she needed to bequeath traditions of her special maternal lineage as seen in "The Legend of Liban the Merrow":

> *Know me*, said the Mother
> God. And Liban heard. Then
> the Father said, *You are wanting.*
> *Love and grow as Woman,*
> *save and be saved*
> *by Man.* And she believed,
> like I believe [42–8].

I've been suspicious of people's motives for insisting on matrilineality in my own life—insisting I am Jewish because my mother was born so, regardless of my being baptized and brought up Catholic. But I've been fascinated by the concept as well—what of history can be passed on through the female line! It is a kind of empowerment. In "The Water," a sister-poem to "With Child" that alludes to pregnancy and lineage—I reference the Jewish holy book, the Torah, in depicting lovemaking between a female deity of the sea, and the male deity of the land: "darkness was on the face of the deep, and the spirit of God was hovering over the face of the water" (Bereishit). Mythologist Joseph Campbell, in his book *The Masks of God*, says "water is the vehicle of the power of the goddess" and that the goddess "personifies the mystery of the waters of birth and dissolution" (64). He goes on to say the union of a god and goddess is a common trope in creation stories around the world. I was glad to see how much of the Fishwife's story unintentionally fell in line with historical tropes—it was a sort of validation.

I first studied the Torah and Campbell's teachings over a decade ago when prepping to teach my first World Literature class. This is where I first taught epics like *Beowulf*, where warriors introduced themselves by introducing their lineage: "We belong by birth to the Great people / and owe allegiance to Lord Hygelac. / In his day, my father was a famous man, / a noble warrior-lord named Ecgtheow" (Heaney 260-4). What about me would my child inherit and acknowledge, I wondered. And what of their children, and their children, and so on?

I think that being pregnant when I arrived at that University, for only my second appointment as an adjunct lecturer, left such an impression that if I now gain a few pounds, which invariably appear as a tire around my waist first, co-workers ask if I'm pregnant. They also seemed to think me unambitious because of the pregnancy. Well, I'm sure my next pregnancy, two years later, was a contributing factor. "You're still here?" said one tenured fellow quite baldly. He was also a fellow teacher/writer so I tried to respond congenially—though I could only stammer a return. I'd like to think it was that old female chitter made unintelligible by exposure to air. But I think it was just the sound of despair—I began to believe that pregnancy, and therefore I, had no place in academia.

Still, I continued to write. I wrote "Wheel and Treadle" about the Fishwife finding work, specifically creative work, to supplement the family coffers. A group of my poems was accepted for publication; among the works was "gifts for future Fishwife fish." An editor had validated my work and I think I took this newest external validation to heart. That driving force began to work on me more than my original drive to create a landscape, or in my case a seascape, for hashing out my conundrums.

I saw that this seascape could eventually be an epic in the style of Milton's *Paradise Lost*. I considered making everything over into form so that it would seem like "serious" work. But there seemed to be an unforgiving rigidity to meter and rhyme. Fluidity would be lost. Fluidity of language, mood and setting. No—my epic had to be in free verse. It had been presenting itself to me as free verse which happens to mirror the always-irregular pattern of waves on a shore.

With this new resolve, I began to show the newest pieces to a writers group I co-founded with some colleagues. The group was open to the community, so with each new attendee I needed to explain the backstory of the Fishwife character. I realized quickly I didn't know what to say! Sometimes I said she was "selkie-like," sometimes I said "shape-shifter," and sometimes I tried to invent the language for what she was, but that never worked and used up my workshopping time. Eventually, I'd say "mermaid" and people said, "Ah!" and bent their heads to their copy of my poem. She was me in fact and her journey unfolded as mine unfolded. But folks there were consistent—they wanted to tell the story for me. It was always based on their understanding of what a mermaid was: invariably, a one-dimensional creature with one-dimensional goals and attendant images. They were newer writers, not necessarily young, just new to their commitment; they'd encourage me towards the ease of sentiment: "Why don't you put in something about how she brushes her long hair!" If they were seasoned writers their advice was the same, though it was given dismissively—as if that's all the story could be: "Yeah. Put in something about how she brushes her long hair."

Around this time, I became aware of myself as a publishing academic and that any work, especially book length epic style work, would need a source other than myself, a purpose other than personal metaphor. I began to research mermaids. I found mermaid mentionings in "The Book of the Dun Cow" which is the oldest surviving Irish text. This work claimed that Liban was royalty turned into first a salmon by "The Mother of All Gods," who then turned herself into classic mermaid form—upper body of a female and lower body of a fish—before she was sanctified as a saint. This was exciting to read because the ancient tale coincided with my further separation of Fishwife and Fisherman by their separate, though ultimately compatible, deities.

This text also gave me an origin story for the Fishwife. I knew she needed to share it with her husband, specifically. In my own life, I needed to feel heard by my husband, and he needed me not to crab so much about being gone to work when he was sincerely doing his best to address our near-poverty. Though I initially wondered what he'd be listening to if I wasn't crabbing—I found that things generally began to improve after we both began to regularly see a therapist and had attended several helpful marriage retreats which focused specifically on communication skills. This life experience was a catalyst for me to give the Fishwife a long monologue—she'd lived in his world for so long, now he had a chance to understand her world.

Of course that Fisherman was a willing, albeit tentative and rusty, listener.

He learned about the Fishwife's maternal lineage and how all her mothers' mothers and she herself are charged with finding a way to successfully reconcile the two worlds. This section ends with the Fishwife becoming fully scaled but in full human female form and guiding her husband's boat to safety as he navigates a deadly storm. Their subsequent lovemaking was difficult to write. I couldn't conceive of any other appropriate metaphor for unity but the pull towards sentiment was hard to avoid. I rewrote the scene almost a dozen times. I kept thinking that none of the epics in the canon depict such scenes. Again the idea of what was "serious" and what was not intruded on my creative process. Even now, I'm not sure if that poem is finished:

> This man is her
> natural enemy,
> they are intimates—
> yet, in truth, in full, this is the first
> they touch.

By this time I'd been an adjunct nearly six years and I knew then as I know now that a full length published book was what could help get a much-needed full time job—the cost of two children and a husband in grad school was difficult to bear. I'd heard about a "poetry doctor" in Boston who'd mid-wived many manuscripts into the world—so, I scraped some cash together and went to her basement writing domain—it was grand! One cozy room with a conference table, one for private meetings and her writing desk with inspiring prints on all the walls and framed letters of grateful clients. She was elegant, had unmistakable taste and carried herself with authority and wisdom. I gratefully handed over my manuscript. She flipped through it, said, "You need to write from the viewpoint of Fisherman. You need a man's point of view or you won't get this published." This stunned me. She further frightened me with, very likely true, stories of co-judging contests with male poets who had all pre-picked their choice for winner among their male protégés.

As I drove off, I was struck that she'd never said that the work was badly written, or needed a global overhaul because of craft issues, and she didn't do any line edits as promised. All she did was make me understand what would make it publishable, i.e., viable in the world of serious Poetry. "They won't have anything to relate to," she said. "Men know about transformation—they transform too," I remember choking out, "Not like this." She was telling me that they wouldn't listen to a stranger from a strange land. As much as I don't like to admit it—her advice affected me. Every time I got a rejection letter from a publisher or a contest—I'd sent the full manuscript out about one hundred times—I chalked it up to the thing's inherent unpublishabilty due to its female-centric content.

I began to get depressed when applying for full time professorships, wishing I had some other, better ornament to hock; I felt like a snake oil salesman—sure of my lie, never mind my toothy smile and energetic sales pitch. And yes, I was still energetically sending out and developing the work. More and more individual poems were published. Two separate painters created a series of works based on the poems and each had showings of their work. A shorter version of the manuscript received a finalist nod in a chapbook contest. A different shorter version was turned into a multi-media chapbook. Reader's responses were fantastic—many, many women told me personally that they related to the Fishwife, were deeply moved by her, and wanted more of her story.

I began to work on art song and accompanied recitation versions with a talented female composer—we even began to perform our collaborative effort at area festivals and venues. Soon we released our CD. But even after this, I kept changing things on her—changing the "elevator speech" that was to explain the Fishwife's story, because it always sounded wrong. It sounded so wrong I even began to attempt to take the poetry-doctor's advice. However, it made me nauseous to force out drafts from the Fisherman's perspective. I just couldn't do it; I trashed those papers. I was mad! His point of view was already shared through the omniscient narrator I'd used in several poems. And his viewpoint wasn't the point. His viewpoint had been shared, in fact, by many men throughout history. It was her turn, I realized. Her turn to talk about her sort of transformation.

I think the nausea when drafting came from a feeling of shame—which is itself a form of anger:

> Guilt and shame are forms of anger that arise when your boundary has been broken from the inside by something you have done wrong or have been convinced is wrong. ...we're often coerced into embodying other people's idea of right and wrong. "Good girls don't cry...." In this onslaught, we become overwhelmed by untruths, foreign messages, damaging contracts and inauthentic shame [McLaren 52].

So, it was actually "inauthentic shame" I was experiencing. Am experiencing. Since promoting the *Fishwife Tales* CD last year, I've put away the manuscript and moved on to other projects. I couldn't force certain perspectives but I finally became cowed enough to drop my passion project. In composing this essay, in analyzing what happened to the *Fishwife Tales,* I see that I let something important slip away.

I've gotten more universally positive responses to my current project which is a series of poems addressing issues surrounding human trafficking in America. I didn't choose this new project because it seemed more "serious." It developed organically and its poems are being generated in much the same way as the Fishwife poems: through intense inspiration, through research, and linked to my personal story in ways that don't need to be entirely obvious to a reader.

These unseen links are what I need to own. One of the things a mature artist realizes is one must own one's work even if the world hasn't. I should say "if the world hasn't yet." I guess I'm letting my pessimism show here. I guess I'm still overly concerned about the world. But at least now, I know I need to say, "Yeah, I wrote this and I like it." Because I did, and I do. I know I need to be my authentic self working with the writing that is coming to me, coming through me. Otherwise this art becomes all about second-guessing and career building. It becomes soulless. And certain stories, necessary and beautiful stories, will be smaller, muddled. Or worse yet—silenced.

WORKS CITED

"Bereishit." Genesis 1:2. Web. 30 Jan. 2013. http://www.chabad.org/library/bible_cdo/aid/8165/jewish/Chapter-1.htm
"Bli-Blip Lyrics." *MetroLyrics*. Web. 30 Jan. 2013. http://www.metrolyrics.com/bli-blip-lyrics-ella-fitzgerald.html
Campbell, Joseph. *The Masks of God*. New York: Viking, 1959. Print.
Heaney, Seamus. *Beowulf*. London: Faber, 1999. Print.
Jean, Jennifer. "The Air." *Lyre Lyre*. Apr. 2012. Web. http://lyrelyre.com/archives/issue-3/issue-three-audio-poetry/.
_____. "Fishwife Cleaving, a Myth." *North Dakota Quarterly* (2005): 111–12. Print.
_____. "Gifts for Future Fishwife Fish." *North Dakota Quarterly* (2005): 109–10. Print.
McLaren, Karla. *The Language of Emotions: What Your Feelings Are Trying to Tell You*. Boulder, CO: Sounds True, 2010. Print.
Wilde, Oscar. *De PRofundis: The Ballad of Reading Gaol and Other Writings*. USA: Wordsworth Editions, 2002. Print.

Calling the Goddess

JANINE CANAN

> What are the lives of poets
> but offerings to the goddess they adore?
> —Erica Jong, *Love Comes First* (73)

Myths are lights that shine upon our human journey. They are the big stories that show us where we have been and where we are going. Myths carry key moral teachings, and provide us with guidance, consolation, entertainment and sheer delight. And always, they overflow into the songs of the poets.

Indeed, poets are often the mythmakers themselves. In the third millennium BCE, the first recorded poet, Sumerian moon priestess Enheduanna offered her hymns invoking the mighty Goddess Inanna. Many centuries later, the ancient seer poets of India—the *rishis*—channeled the spiritual treasure of the *Upanishads*. In the first millennium BCE, a Greek bard called Homer recited heroic war epics, and a few hundred years later the sublime singer of Lesbos, Sappho, praised with her lyre Aphrodite, Goddess of Love. In the past millennium, European titans Shakespeare and Goethe made myths for their time that still haunt us.

All peoples have poets who retell, embellish and transform the myths that contain their worldview, sensibility and deepest truths. In America, if we listen we can hear the sacred stories of its earliest inhabitants being remade in the art of Joy Harjo, Linda Hogan and others. No modern poet remains unaffected by the mega-myth of Science, constantly pelting the Cosmos with theories. And sooner or later, the poets themselves become myths. Sappho's *oeuvre* was eradicated by patriarchy, but her own myth runs rampant. Shakespeare, Dickinson and Plath are similar examples of iconic poets whose celebrity is as powerful as their work. Poetry and Myth go hand in hand—mythology inspiring poetry and poetry creating mythology in an endless cycle. And so the question naturally arises, what myths are inspiring poetry today? And what new myths are the poets creating?

In the past century the world has undergone massive changes, and changes keep coming at an ever-increasing speed. How can the Big Story keep up? An explosive human population with more and more technology, travel and war, is devastating the Earth, reducing plant and animal species—one every few seconds—and human cultures as well. Ways of life transform and disappear at an alarming rate, as cultures and civilizations converge, collide and combine. People are relentlessly bombarded by alien stories, tastes, mores and values with the potential to enrich or destroy. More than ever, we need stories to orient, guide, comfort and enlighten us. Many of the old stories seem passé, irrelevant, even harmful. How can we preserve precious old traditions and keep them alive? How can we adapt old myths to make them current? How can we find fresh new stories that really speak to us and help us live? These are some of the challenges of the moment.

But don't worry, mythology's worker bees, the poets, are busy at work, already gathering pollen for the next big Story, diligently collecting, sorting and salvaging old myths to glean what is most relevant, beautiful and true. Masters of synthesis, distillation and concision, they are reworking old gold into contemporary concerns and themes. And the most visionary among them are already getting glimpses of a Story of the Future that will hopefully have the power to guide humanity through the massive physical and spiritual changes now unfolding and affecting every corner of the Earth. This amazing process can be seen in the work of well-known American poets like Maya Angelou, Diane di Prima, Judy Grahn, Susan Griffin, Joy Harjo, Erica Jong, Carolyn Kizer, Mary Oliver, lesser known spiritual poets like Gael Belden, Leslene della Madre, Tamara Rasmussen, Mary Saracino, Elizabeth Welles, and countless others around the world.

What light can my own journey as a poet shed on this Work-in-Progress? Born in the City of the Queen of Angels—*La Ciudad de la Reina de los Angeles*—brutally called *L.A.* today—I grew up in a mid-twentieth century Catholic neighborhood where families still prayed to Mary, Mother of God. On Sunday in our family Presbyterian church, I listened to Mid-Eastern tales of a renegade Jewish savior; while at home I often read in a comfortable chair in the glow of a golden bronze Quan Yin lamp, rescued from China's recent revolution. The cultural atmosphere of European, Japanese, African and Jewish schoolmates pervaded my consciousness. And from across town came the influence of an Indian yogi named Yogananda, who was importing the god and goddess-laden culture of India, with its concept of Self-realization.

Thanks to my mother there were plenty of books in our house, among them volumes of poetry. Mother sang lullabies and read us stories, as mothers used to do. At school we learned Longfellow's "The Children's Hour" by heart, and at night I started jotting thoughts on scraps of paper, tucking them into the drawer by my bed. A first short love poem occurred at thirteen. In summer school I eagerly began studying American Literature, and in the cool dark downtown library as I pored over books way over my head, "The Love Song of J. Alfred Prufrock" made T. S. Eliot my "first poet."

And so it all began. How could I know I was on a path to becoming the Goddess's personal poet (not the only one, of course, for She has legions). With my spontaneous affinity for all things feminine—dolls, girlfriends, book heroines, all the arts of beauty—how could I ever dream that beyond my world, men everywhere imagined they owned the planet and had women hoodwinked into believing them (or terrorized into pretending). I took early morning creative writing class in high school, majored in French literature at Stanford (temporarily abandoning pre-med) and tried to study German literature at the University of California in Berkeley amid the exuberance of the Sixties. In private, I wrote exploratory poems, later taking classes with Peter Scott and Carolyn Kizer, and joining a group of San Francisco women poets. And I began a translation of German Jewish poet Else Lasker-Schüler which would be published much later (*Star in My Forehead*).

By the Seventies, while attending medical school in New York City on my way to becoming a psychiatrist, poetry had to bear with the demands of medicine. I came home to my studio late and tired but stimulated, poured a glass of wine, sat down at a desk of scavenged fruit crates and tapped away on my old Royal typewriter, or I read Levertov and Auden. By the end of medical school—I was 33—I had gathered a collection of poetic sketches called *Of Your Seed* for Robert Hawley, whose Oyez Press published early di Prima, Duncan, Everson, Levertov, Miles, Olson, and the Swedish poets Södergran and Transtrømer.

My next books were self-published—following the example of Blake, Barrett Browning, Whitman, Jammes, Stein, Sandburg, Wilde, Lawrence, Pound, Eliot, Cummings, Ginsberg and many others—by my own Emily Dickinson Press: *Daughter, Who Buried the Breast of Dreams*, and *Shapes of Self*. Already She was putting in appearances, as in my 1975 prayer to "Beautiful Mother of Words." Maybe She was pleased, because the words have been flowing ever since. At the same time I discovered, in *Up Haste*, a Berkeley women's bookstore, *Gods & Goddesses of Old Europe* by archeologist Marija Gimbutas, and was delivered a stimulating shock of recognition: somehow, I had always known She was there.

After completing psychiatric training, I flew to Athens, ferrying south to the island of Lesbos and as I gazed over the Aegean in the timeless presence of "Sappho of Eressos," Aphrodite appeared. Next came the Sumerian Goddess Inanna, Queen of the Above and Below, discovered in Jungian analyst Sylvia Perera's *Descent to the Goddess*. I attempted a new version of her myth in

"Inanna's Descent," and both poems appeared in my next book, *Her Magnificent Body: New & Selected Poems*, which had a cover photograph of an Egyptian-derived pink Goddess sculpted by Washington artist Elaine Hanowell. The Goddess was clearly in the air!

I was in the midst, now, of a mid-life search for meaning and direction, for a path that would lead me through the remainder of my life. I was searching for my Self, in a world that seemed to be one gigantic Male Myth—"millenniums old, endowing males with a sense of entitlement, of being the preferred sex, of having been promised at birth opportunities for dominance, aggression, and patronage," as Carolyn Heilbrun finely put it in her final memoir, *The Last Gift of Time* (175). After my fifteen-year meditation on the male viewpoint at Stanford, University of California, New York University and five teaching hospitals, no wonder I felt isolated, depressed. And since all the major religions of the world were patriarchal—to Whom could I turn?

I started working on an all-encompassing prayer to Her, trying to assemble what *Her* might mean, and at the same time posing the fundamental question of all faith regarding the existence of evil. "Lady, how can I speak?" I stuttered...

>...my mouth mute
>as the hills, dumb with fear and desire.
>Lady of a myriad Names, your beauty and destruction
>freeze my heart. How can I approach You
>
>from the city paved with bone? Highways roar
>with trucks of nerve gas, rivers carry poisoned fish
>and human heads. Villages are wrecked, people starving,
>war missiles planted throughout the earth
>["Our Lady," *Her Magnificent Body*].

With this urgent prayer, I was reaching for a new Creation myth that included a feminine Creator and a message affirming Life. Stuffing my poem with my favorite things—skies, flowers, animals, poets—I offered Whoever-She-Was my heart and beseeched Her to come!

And then in June of 1987, at a Perinatal Psychology Conference in San Francisco, at a numinous exhibit of Mother Goddess art, in all her glory, She was there. Was something analogous going on in contemporary poetry as well, I suddenly needed to know. And the anthology which I rapidly compiled, *She Rises like the Sun: Invocations of the Goddess by Contemporary American Women Poets*, was the answer: twenty-nine diverse voices calling Her in a vibrant female chorus that included Angelou, di Prima, Grahn, Griffin, Harjo, Hogan, Kizer, Le Sueur, Levertov, Lorde, Mackey, Morgan, Piercy, Sarton, Shange, Villanueva, Wakoski and Waldman. A deeply held longing for the divine feminine was, indeed, flowering across women's arts.

With *She Rises* I had wanted to sing back the Goddess and introduce

Her to an immature nation whose ignorance was imperiling the world, a nation where "not masculine" qualities like natural beauty, cultured creativity, integrative intelligence, selfless service, maternal compassion, and reverence for Life were missing, denied, even scorned. And, above all, I wanted to encourage and empower women, just beginning to thaw after millennia of bondage as men's slaves, toys and scapegoats, with the positive image of woman that automatically accompanies the Goddess.

The next year, Lithuanian-born archeologist Marija Gimbutas who had narrowly escaped patriarchy's latest nightmare, the power dreams of Hitler and Stalin, gave an awakening presentation of her life work on Goddess culture at the California Institute for Integral Studies. Her next book, *The Language of the Goddess*, was already in press, and her culminating work, *The Civilization of the Goddess*, would appear just/only a few years later. Richly illustrated and brilliantly analyzed, these beautiful tomes were the fruit of one woman's heroic digs of Neolithic Europe, explorations revealing a peaceful, egalitarian, woman-centered, Goddess-worshipping society lasting thousands of years, with magnificent temples, comfortable homes, orderly villages, and sophisticated arts delighting in Nature. Gimbutas' expanded vision of human history transformed my own idea of what it is—what it can be—to be human, brightening my heart and bringing new mythic content to my work, as in my narrative poem "Oh Century, my Century," which addresses our current world crisis in the light of past history:

> O Century, my Century, whence have you come?
> Sheep and cows once blissfully grazed on Mother's
> millennial mounds...
> [*Changing Woman*].

Travels to Europe and Asia, as in America, in the years surrounding the millennium expanded my knowledge, as I encountered Paleolithic, Neolithic, Celtic, Greek, Roman and Christian forms of feminine deity, whether as Our Lady in Europe, Guadalupe in Mexico, Changing Woman in the Navajo Nation, Devi Sri in Bali, Tara in Nepal, Quan Yin in China, or The Goddess of a Thousand Names in ancient India, where Durga the Great Goddess and her divine daughters—Saraswati, Lakshmi, Kali and their sisters—are still worshipped by a huge population. For the Goddess is everywhere—if you have eyes. In the foothills of the Pyrenees, where the most ancient human face known as "Lady of Brassempouy," carved in mastodon ivory 24,000 years ago, was found at the entrance to a cave, I understood that the story of the Goddess is as ancient as any story can be.

And yet, my search was not ended. It became even more full-bodied as I sought out living souls said to incarnate the divine feminine. The most astounding of these was the phenomenal Mata Amritanandamayi, called

Amma or "Mother," who had arrived in San Francisco during the same summer days that blasted me with visions of the Divine Mother inspiring *She Rises like the Sun*. A small dark woman from south India in a billowing white sari, Amma sang thrilling songs, embraced strangers by the hundreds, and brought a teaching of *universal motherhood:* loving compassion for all people, not just one's own children, and all of Nature too. Born in matriarchal Kerala on the southwestern coast of Dravidian India—a modern state where women still go home to their mothers for the first year of their baby's life—she embodied the eternal Way of the Mother. Transgressing many taboos, she hugged, consoled and assisted people regardless of gender, class or religion, demonstrating matriarchal values of love, equality, responsibility, and respect for Life. "Men and women *both* need to feel and express the deep nurturing of a mother," she taught (*Love Is My Religion*).

A formidable humanitarian, Amma's Embracing the World volunteer network provides food, houses, medicine, financial aid, education of all kinds, sanitation, reforestation, research, and disaster relief, in an atmosphere of loving celebration. To date, Amma has embraced over thirty million people, touring twenty countries annually for twenty-five years, and ETW has given free medical care to over a million people and planted over a million trees. Her self-sacrifice, achievement and wisdom moved me to edit three collections of her teachings: *Messages from Amma: In the Language of the Heart* ("Best Spiritual Book 2004"), *Garland of Love*, and *Love Is My Religion*. Another door to understanding was opened by a film documenting the matriarchal Mosuo of western China, *Im Matriarchat der Mosuo*, shown at an Archaeomythology conference in Greece in 1998. Until this time, I had carried in my mind a picture of how human beings *might* be, but as a patriarchal *woman* ("man's wife" in Anglo Saxon) I had mainly experienced men who tended toward aggression, domination, lust and violence, and women damaged as a consequence. Now, through the lens of Heide Goettner-Abendroth's camera, I saw my inner vision come to life in men without power issues who were gentle, respectful and constructive, and women who were healthy, loving and productive.

Goettner-Abendroth's book *Matriarchal Societies*, based on decades of research on living matriarchies on every continent, summarizes matriarchy as a sacred, consensus-based, egalitarian, sustainable society created by women and founded on core values of maternal care. Women live with their Mother clan, have few children (less than one each among the Mosuo), raise them with their sisters, accept lovers, marry or divorce as they wish. Marriage is irrelevant to the overall shape of a woman's life, which follows the natural stages of young beauty, mature motherhood, and elderly wisdom. Nor are children needed for love and value. The Mosuo Matriarch, for example, is *chosen* among sisters for her ability to care for others. The clan lives in attunement with Nature, without delusion of ownership, never burdening or assaulting the Earth, and female abuse is unimaginable—as shown in this poetic vignette from Heide's film:

> Patriarchal man (with bullying laughter):
> "You do what your women want."
> Matriarchal man (with incredulous scorn):
> "And you *abuse* your women"
> ["Encounter," *Ardor*].

We erroneously imagine there is no other way to live than with the horrors of patriarchy. But it is not so. "Men don't have to be like this," I insist in "No Reason" (*Ardor*). "They are capable of knowing their place / and living happily in it."

The first episode of *Tribal Wives*, a 2008 British documentary directed by Joseph Maxwell, featuring an Englishwoman's stay with the matriarchal Kuna of Panama, confirms Goettner-Abendroth's research. With tears streaming, after thirty years of trying, as a psychiatrist, to help heal unnurtured, unappreciated women, I watched this typical modern daughter of patriarchy—tense, insecure, unloved by her own mother—flower in only a few weeks as her deepest psychic wounds were lanced and treated by the wise and loving hands of a Kuna matriarch and her spouse. If only we could adopt some of the ways of mother-centered societies, wouldn't most of our problems vanish?

In my latest book, *Ardor: Poems of Life*, I cry with love and grief to women young and old:

> Woman, you have no idea
> of your beauty—only glimpses.
> Every mirror shows you
> the domineering body of a man.
>
> How can you know
> how beautiful you are?
> How can you be
> as beautiful as you are?
>
> How can you be you?
> Oh beautiful glorious
> indestructible Women—
> turn off his music.
>
> Look in your own inner mirror
> where beauty never ceases,
> and you are that beautiful Woman
> in her infinite forms,
>
> soaring flesh and spirit
> superior and subtle,
> refined and strong,
> brilliant and forever blessed.
> ["Woman"].

What is woman beyond man's chattel? What is she in the greater reality beyond the patriarchal story of the last several thousand years? What is she to Nature, to God, to the Goddess, to her Self? Why does she do most of the work, get paid less than men, receive rare acknowledgment, own less than 1 percent of the land, and sustain endless abuse and murder in every nation on Earth? In the United States alone, CNN reported on August 20, 2012, a woman is raped every six seconds. As long as children are raised in the patriarchal mode, there is little hope for improvement. Death-worshipping patriarchy will continue to write its living manual on *How Not to Live*, how to devise ever uglier hells on Earth, and leave a moral cemetery as its legacy. And so, I exhort the mothers of the world:

> Women, teach your sons
> to know their place,
> to love and serve
> Creation.
> ["No Reason," *Ardor*].

For woman brings not only human life, she bring beauty, wisdom, the highest level of skill and accomplishment, and most importantly, she brings compassion, caring and love. Women are the road to the future, any future that humanity might hope for. And the new/old myth of the Goddess is one that teaches her value and sanctity. Nothing is more important than what women now bring to the consciousness of all humanity. And so I implore all artists to record with gusto the rising myth of our time, the myth of the New Woman who has regained her sacred strength and power.

As for me, the Goddess is ever more present. She walks at my side, and today She is quite talkative! When I wrote my first little love poem at thirteen, She didn't tell me I was her poet, but with the patience of a mother waited for me to call Her. Kali! Mary! Madrona Mother! Bird Mother! Goddess of Flowers! Changing Woman! Our Dark Lady! Tara! Vesta! Ma! I cried for years.

> You laid the golden egg.
> You rolled the silver disk.
> You flew the emerald world.
> You made all this and made us, too.
> Goddess, come back and tell us why!
> ["Goddess," *Ardor*].

My work is full of her in *Changing Woman*, *In the Palace of Creation: Selected Works 1969–1999*, *Journeys with Justine*, *Goddesses Goddesses: Essays by Janine Canan*, and *Walk Now in Beauty: The Legend of Changing Woman*. But in my newest books, written in my sixties and seventies—*Ardor: Poems of Life*, *Mystic Bliss*, and *My Millennium: Culture, Spirituality, the Divine Feminine*—She is omnipresent. She pervades everything. And I pray to Her incessantly. For She came back. She told us why. And now, it is for us to listen.

Today, I continue to meditate on the Divine Mother, that supreme energy of the Universe, and She continues to power my work as I record new poetry and compile further collections of women's visionary poetry and Amma's transformative teachings. We are entering a new era. Some expect an all-male world of super-duper machinery; others, storytelling round the fire and hunts for roots and water. I hope it will be one that rediscovers the worth of motherly wisdom. Not long ago, while meditating with Amma, I felt this:

> And the heavens are turning
> over a new creation.
> And the breezes are soft
> with compassion.
> And she breathes...
> ["The Saint," *Ardor*].

The "myth" of the Goddess is, for people like me, no myth at all. It represents the simple truth of the beauty, wisdom and holiness of the eternal Feminine. The Goddess is alive. She always has been. It is we who have been moribund. She is in us. *She is us.* May my own work help us become aware of this. The mythology fundamental to my work honors and worships the feminine, the beauty and goodness of life, the reality of love and compassion. The Divine Mother, the Goddess in her countless forms, is nothing but the concretized, humanized embodiment of those ideals and that power.

Life is infinitely complex. And Love is its greatest mystery. Thank Goodness for the poets and other artists who try put it all together for us. What they do is yet another mystery—do not bother trying to understand how it comes about. Of my muse I recently wrote:

> But now! Like a river jumping banks
> she floods and crashes, washing away everything.
>
> And I am her slave, washed in her irresistible
> roiling passion, this absolute Energy
> that seizes me like a limp brittle puppet.
>
> Oh I know she commands me *Speak*
> in flames that crackle, roar and bleed,
> laugh and sing out what we *have* to hear
>
> and *long* to hear—what alone makes us weep,
> unashamed, with naked shattering joy:
> her answer of undeniable, mysterious Love
> ["Conquering Muse," *Ardor*].

The poet is sent on some beam of Light and speaks for humanity in the voice of her soul. It is her only instrument. And the responsibility—as for all of us here—is enormous—a *responsibility* to grow into.

In the end, we are all humbled by Life's mystery and our place in it. All I know is She is the very breath I breathe, the breath with which I speak and sing. How can I not dedicate my poetry to Her?

> You are the living Goddess
> and I bow to You.
> All the crickets chant *Om*
> and the moon glows.
>
> Time lies down
> in the corpse pose.
> And the night births
> hundreds of thousands of galaxies.
>
> You are the Mystery
> without question or answer.
> And we are the inevitable
> explosion of Awe
> ["Mystery," *Mystic Bliss*].

WORKS CITED

Amritanandamayi, Mata. *Garland of Love*. Ed Janine Canan. San Ramon, CA: M. A. Center, 2013.
_____. *Love Is My Religion*. Ed Janine Canan. UK: Mantra/John Hunt, 2016.
_____. *Messages from Amma: In the Language of the Heart*. Ed. Janine Canan. Berkeley: Celestial Arts/Random House, 2004.
Canan, Janine. *Ardor: Poems of Life*. Varanasi: Pilgrims, 2012.
_____. *Goddesses, Goddesses: Essays by Janine Canan*. Berkeley: Regent, 2007.
_____. "Goddesses, Goddesses: From Archeology to Poetry of the Feminine." *From the Realm of the Ancestors: An Anthology in Honor of Marija Gimbutas*. Ed. Joan Marler. Manchester, CT: Knowledge Ideas & Trends, 1997. 552.
_____. *Her Magnificent Body: New & Selected Poems*. San Francisco: Manroot, 1986.
_____. *In the Palace of Creation: Selected Works 1969–1999*. Illustrated by Meagan Shapiro. Chicago: Scars, 2002.
_____. *Journeys with Justine*. Illustrated by Cristina Biaggi. Berkeley: Regent, 2007.
_____. *My Millennium: Culture, Spirituality, the Divine Feminine*. Illustrated by Cristina Biaggi. Berkeley: Regent, 2015.
_____. *Mystic Bliss*. Sonoma: Emily Dickinson Press, 2015.
_____. *Walk Now in Beauty: The Legend of Changing Woman*. Trilingual in English, Spanish & Japanese. Illustrated by Ernest Posey. Berkeley: Regent, 2007.
_____, ed. *She Rises Like the Sun: Invocations of the Goddess by Contemporary American Women Poets*. Freedom, CA: The Crossing Press, 1989.
_____, trans. *Star in My Forehead: Selected Poems by Else Lasker-Schüler*. Duluth: Holy Cow!, 2000.
Cornell, Judith. *Amma: Healing the Heart of the World*. New York: William Morrow/Harper Collins, 2004.
Gimbutas, Marija. *The Civilization of the Goddess*. New York: HarperCollins, 1991.
_____. *The Gods and Goddesses of Old Europe*. Berkeley: University of California, 1982.
_____. *The Language of the Goddess*. San Francisco: Harper & Row, 1989; London/New York: Thames & Hudson, 2001.

Goettner-Abendroth, Heide. *Im Matriarchat der Mosuo*. Documentary film. Munich: Akademie HAGIA, 1995.
_____. *Matriarchal Societies*. New York: Peter Lang, 2012.
Harjo, Joy. *How We Became Human: New & Selected Poems*. New York: W. W. Norton, 2004.
Heilbrun, Carolyn. *The Last Gift of Time: Life Beyond Sixty*. New York: Ballantine, 1998.
Jong, Erica. *Love Comes First*. New York: Tarcher/Penguin, 2009.
Perera, Sylvia. *Descent to the Goddess*. Toronto: Inner City, 1981.
Tribal Wives: Episode 1: The Kuna. Television Documentary. Dir. Joseph Maxwell. London: Diverse Productions, 2008.

About the Contributors

Kristin **Berkey-Abbott** earned a Ph.D. from the University of South Carolina and oversees the general education department at the Art Institute of Ft. Lauderdale. She is the author of three chapbooks, *Whistling Past the Graveyard* (2004), *I Stand Here Shredding Documents* (2011), and *Life in the Holocene Extinction* (2016). Her website is Kristinberkey-abbott.com.

Charlotte **Beyer** is a senior lecturer in English studies at the University of Gloucestershire. She has published widely on contemporary literature, including a number of articles and book chapters on crime and spy fiction. She is editing the 2017 special issue on contemporary crime fiction for the journal *American, British and Canadian Studies*. She is also on the Steering Committee for the Crime Studies Network and on the editorial board for *American, British and Canadian Studies*.

Janine **Canan**, M.D., poet, and psychiatrist, has authored more than 20 books, including the anthologies *Messages from Amma* and *She Rises Like the Sun*; translations of poets Francis Jammes and Else Lasker-Schüler; essay collections *Goddesses, Goddesses* and *My Millennium: Culture, Spirituality & the Divine Feminine*; and original poetry including *Of Your Seed, Ardor: Poems of Life* and *Mystic Bliss*. She graduated from Stanford and NYU School of Medicine. Visit JanineCanan.com.

Phil **Fitzsimmons** is the assistant dean of research and associate professor of education in the Faculty of Education, Business and Science at Avondale College of Higher Education, Cooranbong, Australia. Prior to taking up this appointment he was director of research at the San Roque Research Institute, Santa Barbara, California. His research interests lie in the areas of writing and spirituality.

Valerie Estelle **Frankel** is the author of many books on pop culture, including on *Doctor Who*, *Outlander*, and *Game of Thrones*. Other books focus on the roles of women in life and fiction, from her heroine's journey guides *From Girl to Goddess* and *Buffy and the Heroine's Journey* to books like *Women in Game of Thrones* and *The Many Faces of Katniss Everdeen*. Once a lecturer at San Jose State University, she now enjoys speaking at conferences. Visit her website VEFrankel.com.

Tami **Haaland** is the author of two books of poetry: *When We Wake in the Night*, and *Breath in Every Room*. Her poems have appeared in many journals and anthologies and have been featured on *The Writer's Almanac*, *Verse Daily*, and *American Life in Poetry*. She teaches creative writing at Montana State University Billings.

Janine **Harrison**, M.A., M.F.A., poet, writer of fiction and nonfiction, teaches creative writing at Purdue University Calumet. Her work has appeared in *Veils, Halos, and Shackles: International Poetry on the Oppression and Empowerment of Women* and other publications. Indiana Poet Laureate George Kalamaras included her in his "Six Indiana Women Poets" feature in *The Wabash Watershed*. Her first poetry collection is entitled *Weight of Silence*.

Kate **Hovey** is the author of three award-winning books of poetry for young readers: *Arachne Speaks, Ancient Voices* and *Voices of the Trojan War*. A mask maker and metalsmith, she performs and conducts workshops at schools across the country. Her poetry has appeared most recently in *PoemMemoirStory, subTerrain, Switched-on Gutenberg, The Bookwoman, The River Styx* and *The Lyric Moment*, an anthology. For more information visit KateHovey.com.

Jennifer **Jean**'s debut poetry collection is *The Fool* (2013). Her chapbooks include *In the War* (2010) and *The Archivist* (2011), and she recently released *Fishwife Tales*, a collaborative CD. Her work has been published in *Rattle, Waxwing, Drunken Boat, Tidal Basin, Denver Quarterly,* and *Solstice*. She is the poetry editor of *The Mom Egg Review*, teaches Free2Write poetry workshops to sex-trafficking survivors, and is on the advisory board of the Massachusetts Poetry Festival.

Leigh C. **Johnson** is an assistant professor at Marymount University, where she teaches multicultural literature, gender studies, American literature, and composition. Her recent publications focus on Chicana writers' use of double-voiced discourse and violence. She is working on a project about competing versions of history from Anglo, Chicana, and Latina perspectives.

Elizabeth **Johnston** teaches writing, literature, and gender studies at Monroe Community College in Rochester, NY. Her scholarly work centers on female sexuality in literature, television, and film. She has an essay about female rivalry among eighteenth-century women writers forthcoming in *Studies in the Literary Imagination* (2016). Her writing has been nominated for Pushcart awards and published widely in academic and literary journals and books.

Rachel **McCoppin**, Ph.D., is a professor of literature at the University of Minnesota Crookston. She has published articles and book chapters on the topics of mythology and comparative literature. She is the author of *The Lessons of Nature in Mythology* (2015) and her work has appeared in many journals, including *Symbiosis, Studies in American Humor, Studies in the Novel,* and *World Literary Review*.

Coco **Owen** has published poems in the *Antioch Review, 1913: A Journal of Forms, CutBank, The Journal, Rio Grande Review* and *The Feminist Wire*. She was a finalist in several book contests, including the May Swenson Poetry Award, and has chapbooks forthcoming from *Tammy* and dancing girl press. She serves on the board of Les Figues Press. Her work is online at Cocoowenphd.com.

Glenis **Redmond** is a native of Greenville, South Carolina, where she is the poet in residence at the Peace Center for the Performing Arts. She graduated from Erskine College and completed an MFA in Poetry at Warren Wilson College. She is a North Carolina Literary Fellowship Recipient from the North Carolina Arts Council and a Kennedy Center Teaching Artist. Her latest book of poetry is titled *Under the Sun*.

About the Contributors

Jenny **Sadre-Orafai** is the author of *Paper, Cotton, Leather* (Press 53) and four chapbooks. Recent poetry has appeared in *Tammy, Linebreak, Redivider, Eleven Eleven, Thrush Poetry Journal, PANK*, and *Rhino*. Recent prose has appeared in *The Rumpus, The Toast, and South Loop Review*. She is co-founding editor of *Josephine Quarterly* and an associate professor of English at Kennesaw State University.

Lisa D. **Simon** is an independent humanities scholar, a poetry activist, and an art gallery owner in Missoula, Montana, with a Ph.D. in literary modernism from the University of Washington, Seattle. She is co-editor of and contributor to *These Living Songs: Reading Montana Poetry* (2014), and is also the creator and producer of a weekly public radio program entitled "Reflections West."

Paula J. **Vaughan** is a mythologist and educator. She holds a master's degree in humanities and and also studied world mythologies and cultural anthropology. She teaches online mythology and humanities courses for Foothill College and Harrisburg Area Community College. Her poetry has appeared in *Red Silk: A Red Tent Anthology*.

Pramila **Venkateswaran**, poet laureate of Suffolk County, Long Island (2013–15), and author of *Thirtha* (2002), *Behind Dark Waters* (2008), *Draw Me Inmost* (2009), *Trace* (2011), and *Thirteen Days to Let Go* (2015) teaches English and women's studies at Nassau Community College, New York. Recently, she won the Local Gems Chapbook contest for her volume *Slow Ripening*. For more information, visit Pramilav.com.

Sarah R. **Wakefield** is an associate professor of English at Prairie View A&M University in Texas, where she teaches composition, literature, and the occasional course in mythology. Her research interests in women, gender, and the fantastic led her to write *Folklore in British Literature: Naming and Narrating in Women's Fiction, 1750 to 1880*. Her recent projects involve the work of Sandra Cisneros and Stephenie Meyer.

Wendy **Whelan-Stewart** is an assistant professor of English at McNeese State University where she teaches American literature. She has published articles on Sylvia Plath and Gwendolyn Brooks and is a sub-field editor for *The Eighteenth-Century: A Current Bibliography*.

Kate **Williams** is interested in the ways that women writers communicate their experiences of motherhood through literature including novels, poetry, and memoirs. She has a Ph.D. in English language and literature from the University of Tulsa, and her research interests include American literature, digital media studies (specifically blogging), women's and gender studies, Native American studies, and African American studies.

Laura Madeline **Wiseman** is the author of 20 books and chapbooks and the editor of *Women Write Resistance: Poets Resist Gender Violence*. Her book *Intimates and Fools* was an Honor Book for the 2015 Nebraska Book Award. Her critical reviews have appeared in *Prairie Schooner, Ploughshares, Calyx*, and *The Iowa Review*. She teaches poetry in the Writing for the Schools Program and in the women's and gender studies department at the University of Nebraska–Lincoln.

About the Contributors

James A. **Wren** holds a Ph.D. in comparative literature from the University of Washington. He pursued a career in medicine in Japan before moving into literature at Rhodes College and the University of Hawai'i and has widely published on modern Japanese and Indonesian literature, medical history and narrative theory. He retired as professor of modern Japanese and comparative literature and languages at San José State University.

Index

Abignyana Sakuntala 98
abortion, 61
abuse 8, 31, 69, 70, 142, 161
Achilles 5–9
adolescent 46, 185
adultery 7
Aeneid 29, 32, 65, 152
African 73, 75, 79, 125, 179, 180–182, 185–186, 219
agency 1, 28, 31, 90, 140, 141, 143–146
Agha-Jaffar, Tamara 162, 163, 165
Alcosser, Sandra 2, 91–92, 95
Amaterasu 199–200
Amma's Embracing the World 223
ancestors 81, 84, 86, 89, 141, 179, 181
angel 60, 142
Angelou, Maya 219, 221
anger 19, 36, 40, 41, 44, 67, 70, 87, 88, 99, 118, 119, 197, 198, 216
anthropoetics 26
anthropology 26, 28, 32, 84
Anzaldúa, Gloria 2, 68, 69, 70, 72
Aphrodite 7, 29, 115, 218, 220
Apollo 9, 14, 34, 35, 46, 152
archeology 2, 27–29, 31–32
archetypes 1, 3, 9, 15, 19–21, 45, 47, 48, 85–89, 91, 140, 141, 143, 146, 183, 186
Arjuna 99–100
art 15, 18, 27–29, 46, 52, 61, 64, 78, 86–88, 90, 126–129, 148, 150, 152, 179, 204, 209, 216–218, 221; *see also* paintings
Artemis 7, 152, 200, 201
Asian 73, 75, 100, 104
assimilation 141, 145
Atwood, Margaret 1, 3, 5, 7–10, 12, 50, 54, 57, 153, 191
Aunt Jemima 127
Australian 2, 106, 107–112
autonomy 21, 55, 59, 63, 92
Aztec 1, 2, 67–72, 146

Baba Yaga 201
Babylon 114, 183–185

Barbie 121, 126, 127, 132, 134
Baring, Anne 196
Barthes, Roland 130, 131
beauty shops 78
Beowulf 213
Bhavani 103
Bible 17, 59, 61, 62, 181, 183, 211, 213
bird 6, 102, 180
blood 90, 111, 143, 148, 195
bodies 1, 5–11, 18, 19, 26, 30, 39, 46, 51–54, 56, 59–63, 68, 71, 75, 77, 79, 89, 92, 93, 109, 111, 115, 122, 179, 189, 195–200, 210, 214, 224
Bogan, Louise 3, 126
Bolen, Jean Shinoda 196
borders 108, 111
Brave New Voices 144
breast 8, 99, 115, 195
British Museum 27–32
Buddhism 2, 75

Campbell, Joseph 45, 91, 95, 136, 213
Candelaria, Cordelia 141–142
Carlson, Kathie 163–165
Carroll, Lewis 130
Carter, Angela 122, 128
Cashford, Jules 196
Cassandra 25, 32, 189
Castillo, Ana 69, 71
castrate 144
catharsis 197
Catholicism 124, 213
Celtic *see* Irish
Cervantes, Lorna Dee 2, 69–72
Chakrabarthi, Nirendranath 99
Changing Woman 18, 222, 225
chapbook 200, 204, 206, 207, 209
Chicana 67, 69, 71, 140–146
child 5, 11, 17, 45, 46, 48, 54, 69–71, 77–79, 102, 145, 164, 174, 176, 192, 201, 213
childbirth 17, 30, 34, 35, 38, 44, 48, 55, 63, 68–72, 84, 109, 111, 117–120, 141, 150, 194, 213, 221
childcare 187

233

234 Index

children 2, 28, 60, 68, 74, 78, 131, 141–145, 149, 188, 192, 196, 212–215, 223, 225
China 219, 222, 223
Chinese 75
Choksi, Shefali Shah 3, 192, 193
Christian 2, 14, 62, 89, 93, 102, 142, 222; see also Bible
Cillapatikaram 99
Circe 5, 8, 9, 12, 32, 192
Cisneros, Sandra 126, 140
Civil War 174
civilization 28, 84, 89, 92, 107
Clash of the Titans 122, 126, 136
class 9, 14, 77, 122, 123, 125, 128–132, 140, 142, 153, 160, 184, 198, 213, 223
Clifton, Lucille 3, 179–186
clothing 28, 62, 117, 151, 179
Coatlicue 2, 67–72
collective unconscious 98
college 32, 121, 122, 129, 160, 213
colonialism 70, 83, 87, 110, 111, 143, 145, 161, 181
colors 70, 153, 165
comics 67
composition 129, 206, 211
confessional poems 59, 61, 203, 204
cooking 28, 78, 79
costumes 149
Coyolxauhqui 67–69
creation 21, 44, 46, 55, 64, 86, 89, 93, 102, 111, 126, 152, 184, 194, 213, 226
creative writing 3, 79, 203, 204, 220
creativity 1, 51, 52, 56, 61, 88, 149, 158, 199, 222
crone 46, 118, 163
cyclical 34–41, 46, 89

Daedalus 8
Dahomey 3, 181, 183, 185
dance 39, 86, 87, 93, 98, 183, 184
Dante 65, 162
Daphne 1, 5, 7–11, 160
darkness 37, 38, 45, 77, 86, 110, 114, 117, 118, 201, 213
daughter 10, 19, 36, 44–47, 54, 56, 67–71, 74, 127, 145, 151, 161–164, 196–198, 222, 224
de Alba, Alicia Garcia 141–143
death 2, 5–7, 16–18, 22, 30, 31, 34–41, 45–48, 59, 61, 63, 64, 67–71, 91–95, 99, 102, 108, 111, 114–120, 124, 163, 194
deer 98
de Hoyos, Angela 141, 146
Demeter 25, 34–38, 41–48, 161–166, 196, 200
demons 67
depth psychology 15
desert 106, 108, 110, 143, 169, 170
Devi Sri 222
dharma 103
Diana 124
Dickinson, Emily 60, 218, 220

Dido 44–45
Dionysus 34–35, 38–39, 44
di Prima, Diane 17, 21, 219- 221
dismemberment 35, 39
divorce 204, 205, 223
dog 102, 103, 111, 170
domesticity 64, 195, 205
dominant cultural narratives 15, 51
Donovan, Katie 1, 50, 52–56
Doolittle, Hilda see H.D.
Dove, Rita 1, 2, 35–36, 164
Draupadi 103
Duhamel, Denise 3, 193
Durga 222

earth 36–39, 43–45, 47, 68, 70, 74, 84, 89, 93, 115–117, 161, 165, 166, 184, 202, 221
educated 14, 27, 97
Egyptian 1, 6, 7, 12, 28, 30, 69, 221
elementary school 149, 192
Eleusinian Mysteries 34, 38, 48, 161
Ellis, Kelly Norman 2, 73–81
Emplumada 2, 69–72
endure 40, 195
environment 142, 190
epithet 30, 114, 117
equality 146, 184, 223
Ereshkigal 34, 116–120
Estés, Clarissa Pinkola 196
Euripides 29–32
Eurydice 1, 3, 25, 26, 34–41, 190
Eve 2, 121, 126, 136

Fainlight, Ruth 1, 50–55
fairy tales 54, 127, 146, 203, 209
family legends 3, 174
family tree 175, 182
fantasy 10, 109, 199
female experience 17, 18, 54, 60, 63
femininity 47, 50, 51, 121, 124, 125
feminism 17, 25, 26, 31, 51–56, 68, 83, 97, 100, 103, 123, 125–129, 132, 134, 141, 144, 145, 164, 165, 187, 195, 196
fertility 34–36, 68, 109, 114, 117, 187
Finney, Nikky 2, 73–81
fish 98, 102, 210, 213, 214, 221
fishing 77, 210
Fitzgerald, Ella 210
Flenniken, Kathleen 189
food 10, 44, 70, 78, 116, 179, 223
Foucault, Michel 130, 136
Freud 15–19, 22, 126

Gaia 36
Gailey, Jeannine Hall 3, 193
gaze 28, 29, 63, 109, 111, 142, 180
genocide 83
Gimbutas, Marija 136, 196, 220, 222
Glück, Louise 1–3, 5, 9–11, 14–21, 43–48, 100, 164–166

God 62, 65, 71, 77, 81, 103, 185, 212, 213, 219, 225
Goettner-Abendroth, Heide 223–224
grandmother 74, 76, 77, 80, 170, 174, 182, 186, 197, 207
Great Mother 77
Greek 2, 3, 5, 7, 9, 14, 21, 27, 28, 31, 34–44, 67, 68, 70–120, 125, 142, 148–152, 161, 187, 188, 192, 193, 218, 222
Grimm 143
Guadalupe 222

Hadas, Pamela White 1, 2, 35, 40, 41
Hades 16, 19, 20, 35–38, 41, 43–48, 161–166, 191
hair 62, 74, 78, 79, 92, 149, 158, 214
Harlequin 129
hatred 29, 31, 89
Hawaiian 2, 83–90
H.D. 1–22, 25–32, 35, 40, 41, 60, 153
healing 7, 9, 10, 75, 93, 180, 195, 200
Helen Dentritis 7
Helen in Egypt 1, 5, 11, 30 -32
Helen of Troy 1–9, 12, 25–31, 191
Hercules 189
Hermes 44, 161
heroin 144
heroine's journey 43, 45, 47
heroism 45, 59, 79, 99, 100, 106, 108, 112, 117, 150, 163
Hesiod 28, 30
Hi'iaka 86
Hillman, James 15, 19–21
Hindu 12, 100, 103
Homer 2, 5, 11, 27–32, 43–48, 125, 150, 153, 161–164, 218
homophobic 145
Huitzilopochtli 67–71
human experience 10, 148
humanities 121, 129
Hurricane Beulah 76
Hurricane Katrina 75, 80
Hymn to Demeter 161

Icarus 8
icons 121–135
identity 6, 7, 20, 32, 41, 43, 45, 46, 51, 52, 56, 65, 68, 70, 74, 83, 87, 92, 93, 106–112, 143
Iliad 6, 7, 29, 32, 125, 152
imagery 2, 7–10, 16, 55, 60, 85, 125
Inanna 2, 34, 114–120, 218, 220, 221
India 1, 2, 3, 28, 98–100, 103, 193, 218–223
infanticide 102, 141
innocent 36, 37, 44–48
interdisciplinary 121, 123, 129, 162
Inuit 3, 193
Irish 1, 52–55, 199, 214, 222
Ishtar 34, 114, 116, 119, 199- 201
Isis 6, 7, 69
Iyengar, Srinivasa 98–99
Izanami 34

Jackson, Helen Hunt 60
Japan 3, 34, 85, 193, 199, 200, 209, 219
Jerusalem 102
Jesus 61, 62, 75, 93
Jewish 212, 213, 219, 220
Job 181
Jones, Alice 1, 2, 35–37
Joyce, James 90
Jung, Carl 15, 16, 39, 45, 68, 220; see also archetypes

Kali 98, 222, 225
Kandasamy, Meena 103, 104
Kannagi 2, 99
kitchen 64, 78, 170, 211
Krishna 99, 101, 104
Kwan Yin 2, 3, 75, 76, 219, 222

Lady Lazarus 2, 59, 61–65
Leda and the Swan 160
Le Guin, Ursula K. 126
Levertov, Denise 1, 2, 14, 35, 38–40, 220, 221
liminal 107, 108, 110, 115, 194
lion 74, 92, 93
Little Red Riding Hood 121, 122, 128, 132–136
Llorona 2, 140–147
Lofton, Ramona 75
Lorde, Audre 180
Lowell, Amy 59, 60
Lowell, Robert 61
Loy, Mina 60
Lucifer 62

Macha 1, 55
madness 35, 76, 198, 205
Madonna 121, 124
Madrona 225
maenads 39, 40
Mahabharata 99, 103, 104
maiden 45–47, 116, 118, 160, 197
male lover/partner 8, 10, 19
Malinche 2, 140–147
Mammy Water 73–74
Mansell, Chris 107–112
Marlowe, Christopher 28
marriage 10, 142, 176, 177, 204, 205, 209–214
Mary *see* Virgin Mary
mask-making 2, 150, 153
masks 17, 22, 25, 148–154
maternal 1, 51–57, 74, 77, 78, 185, 186, 212, 215, 222, 223
matriarch 73–77, 81, 163–165, 223
matriarchal culture 69, 166, 223–224
matricide 69
Medb 1, 52, 53
Medea 198
Medusa 3, 121, 122, 125, 126, 131, 132, 136, 160, 192, 200
mermaid 3, 74, 209, 214
Metamorphosis 29, 125

236 Index

Mexico 67, 69–74, 140, 143, 222
milk 75, 195
miracle 62, 93, 182, 212
mirror 56, 214, 224
misogynists 1, 43, 145
Modernism 15, 25, 32, 35, 60
monkey 98
monologues 25, 149, 214
Monroe, Marilyn 3, 121, 124, 131, 133
moon 44, 47, 68, 69, 74, 152, 184, 194, 218, 227
Moore, Marianne 60
Moreno, Victoria 141, 144
motherhood 6, 7, 11, 12, 15, 18, 19, 36, 37, 43–47, 53–56, 60, 61, 64, 67–71, 74, 77, 80, 99, 115–118, 144–146, 161–166, 185, 192, 197, 198, 201, 202, 205, 206, 209–212, 219, 223–225
Motown 78–79
muses 3, 14, 61
music 22, 38, 39, 78, 79, 84, 86, 126, 129, 150, 184, 190, 224
Muslim 103
mythotropism 14, 17, 18, 21

Narcissus 161, 164
narrator 97, 184, 216
Native American 2, 125, 190
nature 2, 15, 21, 34–46, 61, 67, 71, 73, 76, 78, 81, 83, 86, 88, 89, 92, 95, 109–112, 114, 119, 141, 149, 164, 190, 194, 195, 222–225
Nekhbet 6
Neolithic 222
New Orleans 2, 3, 74, 77, 80
Nicaragua 102
Nigeria 2, 73
Niobe 18
nostalgia 70, 83, 107, 173
nuclear waste 189, 190

Odysseus 5, 8, 9, 10, 11, 20, 44, 100, 188, 192
Odyssey 9, 29, 32, 152, 153
Olson, Tillie 188
Olympus 31
oral tradition 150, 179–182
Orestes 29
Orpheus 17, 18, 34, 35–41, 150, 152, 190
Oshun 74–75
Ovid 5, 8–12, 28, 29, 44, 125, 150, 153, 161–163
Oya 74–75

pagan 142
painting 26, 30, 121, 122, 125, 127, 130, 162, 196; *see also* art
pantheon 67, 71, 194
Paradise Lost 126, 213
parents 78, 79, 142, 144, 151, 192
Paris 6, 7, 12, 27–29
Parks, Rosa 79, 80, 121, 125
Parthasarathy 99
patriarchy 3, 12, 14–18, 46, 51, 55, 56, 60, 61, 69–71, 99, 100, 103, 118, 123, 125, 144, 145, 161–166, 187, 195, 218, 221–225
Paz, Octavio 144
Pele 2, 83–89
Penelope 1, 5, 10, 11, 187–193
Percy Jackson 126
Persephone 1–3, 16, 19, 34–49, 160–166
personal relationships 192
Philomela 160
phoenix 7, 61, 63, 65
photographs 121, 172, 175
Plath, Sylvia 2, 18, 59–65, 122, 126, 203, 218
Pocahontas 3, 121, 125, 127, 146
poetry slams 204
poiesis 16, 17, 21
point of view 8, 41, 44, 79, 80, 97, 99, 215, 216
pollution 3, 9, 12, 189, 190
pomegranate 161, 163, 191
post-modernism 97
power 1, 8, 14, 16, 18–21, 36, 40, 41, 46, 53, 55, 59–72, 75, 80, 81, 84–86, 93, 99, 109, 115, 117, 121, 124, 130, 131, 141–146, 150, 161–165, 180, 181, 194, 195, 213, 222–226
praise poems 185
pregnancy 55, 61, 63, 67, 69, 119, 206, 211, 213
psychological 14–21, 85, 108, 181
psychologist 15
punish 10, 44, 119, 142

queen 37, 43, 46, 48, 52, 53, 74, 115, 118–121, 124, 132, 133, 160–163, 166, 220
Queen Elizabeth 121, 124, 132
Quetzalcoatl 68

race 16, 55, 69, 71, 76, 80, 90, 123–125, 127, 144, 145, 184
racism 28, 75, 83, 109, 141, 145, 184
Radha 101
Ramayana 99, 101, 104
rape 8, 10, 16, 43, 45, 63, 67, 70, 74, 131, 160–165, 225
Readers Theater 149, 150, 152
rebirth 6, 7, 34, 35, 38, 59, 74, 77, 109, 111, 112
The Red Shoes 1, 54
Reese, Lizette Woodworth 60
rewriting myth 17, 25
Rich, Adrienne 51, 57, 100, 121, 135
rite of passage 78–79
ritual 26, 28, 30, 31, 48, 78, 79, 81, 86–89, 95, 108, 110, 194
Rogers, Pattiann 2, 91–95
Roman 9, 27–29, 67, 69, 73, 125, 148, 160–161, 166, 187, 222
rose 64, 99, 102, 116
Rukeyser, Muriel 1, 14–22
runner 75, 76, 169

sacrifice 70, 71, 78, 114, 192, 223
sadness 36, 102
Sankara 100–101

Index 237

Sappho 17, 18, 25, 218, 220
Saturnalia 19
The Scarlet Letter 45
Schliemann, Heinrich 27
scrapbook 170–177
sculpture 30, 98, 125, 128, 162
Sea Garden 27
segregation 75
semiotic 123, 128–132
Seneca Falls 134, 171
sex 2, 12, 35, 47, 55, 60, 63, 70, 75, 86, 109, 114, 125, 160–166, 191, 202, 213, 215, 221
sexism 184
Sexton, Anne 3, 59, 203–208
shadow 38, 40, 46, 47, 69, 118
Shakespeare, William 218
Shelly, Percy 125
sibyl 1, 52, 54, 55
silence 40, 172, 180, 205
Sirens 153, 192, 212
sister 2, 34, 54, 68, 74, 86, 114–120, 201, 213
Sita 2, 99–104
slave narrative 80
slavery 75, 81, 179–181, 184
Smith, Patricia 2, 73, 77–81, 126
snake 36, 37, 67–72, 97, 216
solitude 10
song 22, 30, 38–40, 55, 79, 86, 87, 122, 125, 128, 133, 179, 210, 216
sons 67, 70, 151, 210, 225
soul 6, 7, 10, 19–22, 39, 63, 67, 90, 102, 109, 145, 148, 151, 186, 201, 226
South Africa 3
spiritual 19, 35–38, 44, 85, 88, 95, 101, 115, 117, 200, 218, 219
Spretnak, Charlene 196
Stein, Gertrude 32, 60
stereotypes 53, 121, 127
storyteller 97, 182
students 32, 54, 67, 70, 74, 121–136, 140, 141, 143, 146–152, 160–166, 187, 205
subordinate 36, 107
suicide 59–65, 83, 102
Sumerian 2, 34, 126, 218, 220
superhero 67, 74, 79
symbols 71, 78, 95, 108, 112, 115, 129, 146, 149–152, 158, 184

taboo 34, 38, 40, 223
Tafolla, Carmen 141, 145
Telemachus 11
temples 29, 98, 115, 202, 222
therapy 203
Theseus 7
Thetis 7, 32

Tin House Writer's Workshop 207
Tlazolteotl 70
transformation 5, 7–12, 15, 18, 21, 34, 95, 97, 108, 112, 150, 196, 200, 216
Trask, Haunani-Kay 2, 83, 84, 85, 89
trauma 6, 83, 85, 88
tree 7–11, 38, 39, 40, 77, 93, 98, 99, 117, 130, 160, 171
trickster 111

unconscious 15–19, 35, 41, 50, 83, 85, 89, 107, 116
underworld 2, 15, 19, 21, 34–41, 43, 47, 48, 114–119, 161, 165, 166, 191

Valente, Catherynne M. 2, 114–120
Vasilisa 199
Vazirani, Reetika 100–104
Venus 162–163
victim 37, 45, 69, 70, 81, 145, 166
violence 6, 19, 69, 83, 91, 103, 104, 141, 142, 160, 161, 166, 179, 223
Virgil 28–30, 32
virgin birth 68
Virgin Mary 3, 121, 124, 131, 201, 219, 225
virginity 162; *see also* maiden
Vishnu 103–104
voice 1–5, 8, 35, 40, 41, 47, 51, 53, 54, 59, 64, 65, 71, 79–85, 92, 99, 100, 103, 109, 117, 119, 142–145, 148, 180, 181, 192, 196, 198–200, 210, 221, 226
voiceless 99
vulnerability 6, 8, 63, 131

war 6, 27, 29, 30, 46, 64, 68–71, 86, 87, 103–106, 109, 218–221
warrior 53, 65, 67–71, 116, 181, 213
water 48, 74, 76, 93, 111, 118, 119, 141, 182, 189, 211–213, 226
Wilde, Oscar 209, 220
wilderness 8, 107
witchcraft 126
wives 5, 34, 40, 60, 63, 74, 101, 104, 107, 116, 143, 151, 176, 188, 204, 206, 213, 223
womb 68, 110, 119, 210
Women's Studies 134
Wonder Woman 67, 121, 136
World War I 27, 35, 106

Yemonja 3, 74–75
Yoruba 74–75, 185
Yuddhisthira 102

Zeus 44, 46, 68, 152, 160–165
Zucker, Rachel 165

www.ingramcontent.com/pod-product-compliance
Ingram Content Group UK Ltd.
Pitfield, Milton Keynes, MK11 3LW, UK
UKHW041941140426
5217IPUK00014B/608